THE PASSION OF
PIER PAOLO PASOLINI

PERSPECTIVES

Series Editors: Colin MacCabe and Paul Willemen

THE PASSION OF
PIER PAOLO PASOLINI

Sam Rohdie

INDIANA UNIVERSITY PRESS
Bloomington and Indianapolis

BFI PUBLISHING

First published in 1995 by the
British Film Institute
21 Stephen Street, London W1P 2LN
and the
Indiana University Press
601 North Morton Street, Bloomington, Indiana 47404

The British Film Institute exists to promote appreciation, protection and
development of moving image culture in and throughout the whole of the
United Kingdom. Its activities include the National Film and Television Archive;
the National Film Theatre; the London Film Festival; the Museum of the Moving
Image; the production and distribution of film and video; funding and support for
regional activities; Library and Information Services; Stills, Posters and Designs;
Research; Publishing and Education; and the monthly *Sight and Sound* magazine.

British Library Cataloguing in Publication Data
A catalogue record for this book is available from the British Library

ISBN   0-85170-517-0 hbk
       0-85170-518-9 pbk

US Cataloguing data available from the Library of Congress
A CIP catalog record for this book is available from the Library of Congress

ISBN   0-253-32951-5 (clothbound)
       0-253-21010-0 (paperbound)

Cover design: Romas Foord
Front cover: *Salò o le 120 giornate di Sodoma* (1975)
Back cover: Pasolini filming *Appunti per un' Orestiade africana* (1970)

Typeset by
D R Bungay Associates, Burghfield, Berks

Printed in Great Britain by
St Edmundsbury Press Ltd, Bury St Edmunds, Suffolk

per il mio caro amico Giorgio

Contents

Acknowledgments

I want to thank above all my editor Paul Willemen for his help, encouragement and care. I want to thank particularly Geoffrey Nowell-Smith for his help, comments and affection. I also want to thank Zygmunt Baranski, Ross Gibson, Colin MacCabe and Bill Routt for reading the book in manuscript and their always stimulating remarks. I am especially grateful for the help and responses I received from Maria Barbieri, Virginia Handley, Ann Langusch and Sally Semmens. Rosemund Howe did a splendid job of copy-editing the manuscript.

Laura Betti, Rosa Maria Facciolo, Marina Falanga, Giuseppe Iafrate and Rita Marcucci were extremely generous to me at the Fondo Pasolini in Rome. I want to thank them for their help and their friendship. I am most grateful to Julie Marshall and the research staff at the library at La Trobe University. And I am also grateful for the kind help of Cheng Ka Man, Yu Ka Wai and Beverley Purnell. In unmeasurable ways I was helped by Emanuele De Vincenti, Marta De Vincenti and Lam Shuk Foon. I want to thank also Lino Miccichè and Chris Wagstaff. I am grateful to La Trobe University and Hong Kong Baptist University for their generosity in granting me leave time, funding and facilities.

Preface

There is more than a single voice in this essay. One voice is critical. It is attentive to Pasolini's writings in the broadest sense of writing – his novels, his poetry, his films, his paintings. It seeks to engage with them as language and as form rather than, strictly speaking, to explain them. It is an attempt to see how Pasolini's writings work, not what they mean, or what they say, or what they reveal of him. It is about their productivity, hence their structure.

Pasolini romanticised a primitivism that was less actual than it was mythical. He seized on certain realities and transformed them into myth, that is into poetry: the poor, the rural, the Third World, the prehistoric. He mythicised not by representing these others in his terms, within his language, but by imitating them on their terms, within their language. His poetry was a mimetic poetry ('Divine mimesis'). His writings were simultaneously the writing of the 'other' and his own writing by the fact of imitation/invention. His dialect poems and Roman slang novels were an example. The Poet spoke in dialect, but dialect made literary. And when the Poet spoke directly in the novel as narrator, his literary speech approached the dialect speech it cited. His writing was a contaminated, mixed speech, plurilinguistic at its heart. This is also true of his films.

To celebrate, and also to make present and understand the other, whether real or imagined, was not, for Pasolini, primarily an analytic activity, but a mimetic one. It was to speak like the other and at the same time to remain oneself. His imitations were open imitations, like the wearing of a mask, or the donning of fancy dress. It was an activity of duplication and mirroring. Pasolini's entry into the language of the other was simultaneously the citation of it and creation of it by a second-order language which was its analogy. Pasolini always wrote in metalanguages which mirrored an object-language, the other, and also contained it.

Pasolini's intentions may have been cognitive, but his means were poetic, and, as he said, irrational. What he knew of the other was not stated, but rather linguistically performed. It was as if his works were linguistic/critical dramas where language was acted out by metalinguistic masquerades. It was in these masquerades that his language engaged with the language of the other. The engagement of languages which brushed past one another and sometimes grated constituted the sound, hence the sense of his works.

A writer in fancy dress, who wears a mask, who creates linguistic mirrors to infinity, who masquerades as the other in order to be himself, is not a writer easily found. Perhaps, the poet can only be found poetically. Just as Pasolini created languages analogous to the languages he loved, a similar operation is required to comprehend Pasolini. One needs to find appropriate forms to identify with his forms, in short, one needs to find equivalences.

No critic, as Barthes has pointed out, has an extra-territorial right to know the language of the artist. The critic ought not to assume, in relation to the work, positions of superiority and possession. My own language is different from Pasolini's. It has been an academic and positivist language even as it decried positivism. Writing about Pasolini has placed my own language in crisis. Much as I would have liked to have taken hold of him as an object for biography, ideology, meaning, history, including a history of forms, Pasolini escaped my attempt to do so. Every time I thought I had him, he was gone. Even a formalist analysis proved inadequate.

In order for the crisis in my own speech to be made manifest, it needs to be given voice. In order to find other voices, I need to begin with the one I have, even, and especially, because Pasolini has made me doubt it. This study, consequently, is a mixed bag.

Chapter 1

Pasolini Fragments

Borders

In Rossellini's *Stromboli* (1949), the tuna fishing sequence is shot as it occurs. It is not a staged event for the camera, but an event in reality which the camera catches, then frames. The sequence signifies itself: the fishermen of Stromboli are catching the tuna. But it also signifies within the fiction Karin's distress at nature and the power of it which works upon her. That power is reiterated when she tries to escape from Stromboli only to be overcome once again by its sublimity. The real, at the fringes of the fictional film, is absorbed by the fiction. From a real event, it becomes a fictional sign, motivated within the actions of the film.

Nevertheless, the sequence also tears the texture of the fiction. Its reality is too much for the fiction to absorb completely. Rather than serving the context in which it is inserted, it also disrupts that context by moving away from the fiction towards the reality whence it came. The film complicates the edge between the text and what lies beyond its fringes, what is classed as real.

Italian neo-realism, particularly in the films of De Sica and Rossellini, deployed strategies for rendering reality 'in' film. In Rossellini's use of the sequence shot – as in *Stromboli* – time and space were rendered whole. Reality was not disrupted, and the distance between pro-filmic event and filmic representation was reduced as much as possible, almost to the point where the difference between them disappeared. It was precisely the wholeness of reality and the strength it attained in the film that overwhelmed Karin with its strangeness and power. It also overwhelms the audience. Both audience and character experience the miracle of the real. This miracle 'in' and 'of' reality disrupts the fiction.

Rossellini's films hover on a line between reality and text. 'Reality' is united to the structures of the film, but the union is temporary and unstable. The alterity of reality is not suppressed by the fiction (as it is in classic film narratives). On the one hand, reality is fictionalised by the film;

1

on the other hand, it is cited by it. Reality is in the film and outside the film, a fragment of an exterior continuity brought into the fiction, but whose force, nevertheless, exceeds the film's constructed continuity of a fictional illusory real.

Pasolini's Rome novels are structured, like Rossellini's films, along a boundary, on one side of which is Roman dialect-slang, and on the other literary language. The one language, as structured by Pasolini, is real and popular, the other artificial and bourgeois (albeit spoken by millions of Italians!). The real is textualised by Pasolini and made literary (characters speak, not persons), while the artificial, because marked as such, assumes the full presence of its artificiality.

> With *Ragazzi di vita* and *Una vita violenta* – which a lot of fools think is the result of a superficial documentarism – I placed myself in a line with Verga, Joyce and Gadda: and this was at the price of a tremendous literary effort: anything but documentary immediacy! To refashion, to mimic the 'interior language' of a character is terribly difficult, added to the fact that in my case – as was often the case with Gadda – my character spoke and thought in dialect. It was necessary to descend to the linguistic level of the character, using dialect in direct speech, and using a difficult linguistic contamination in indirect speech: that is, in the entire narrational part, since the world is the world 'as seen by the character'. The sounding of a false note is always a risk in the writing: it is enough to go a bit too far towards 'language' or towards dialect and the difficult amalgam is destroyed, and goodbye style.[1]

One language in the novels is cited by another. In part this is because speech becomes writing. This is not a representational gesture, but an act of quotation, like an actor speaking lines. It is language performed. Whether trying to speak like Proust or trying to speak like a Roman pimp, Pasolini's language nevertheless can be felt within the other language. The narrator may *write* like Proust, but it is only a likeness. The characters may *speak* like Rome slum kids, but it is a speech corrupted by literature. Such imitation presupposed, as Pasolini said, 'a frightening literary effort'.[2]

For Pasolini neo-realist writing was different from this. Neo-realist writers, for him, sought to represent the speech of ordinary Italians by naturalising it, as if, in their novels, ordinary Italians were speaking. Pasolini's slum kids only spoke like slum kids; that is, rather than attempting to naturalise their speech, he sought to artificialise. The analogy is marked, not masked. Pasolini framed reality in mimetic analogies of it, pointing to the analogy, rather than creating a make-believe illusion of reality. His reality included the object imitated (the object-language) and the linguistic act of imitation (the metalanguage which cited the object-language).

André Bazin categorised film history as a history of two cinemas: a 'cinema of reality' and a 'cinema of the image'.³ He preferred the former. Pasolini belonged with the latter, more with Soviet silent cinema, with Vertov and Eisenstein, than with Italian neo-realist cinema. 'Reality is there, why manipulate it?' Rossellini had said.⁴

Even in the densely edited sequences of classical cinema – shot-reverse-shot dialogue scenes – the spectator is caught in a fictional web, from which it is difficult to be free. Each shot and every change of shot have motives within the fiction. It is within that logic that the spectator is caught. At every point in Pasolini's fictions, written or filmed, Pasolini used various means, principally mimetic – citation, quotation, pastiche, parody, analogy, repetition, rhyme – to pull the spectator out of a fictional logic, beyond the edge of fiction, to its other side, to the 'writing' which produced it. Writing is always present in the Pasolinian fiction, not to destroy the fictionality of the fiction, but on the contrary to emphasise it by starring it.

To watch Pasolini's films is to watch a parable, a type of non-fictional fiction, evidently made up and false, yet whose falsity is there to express a truth. It is also like a fairy tale. There is a similar sense to Kafka, or in Pasolini's posthumous novel, *Petrolio*; certainly it is present in Pasolini's plays. It has great force in his films like *Teorema* (1968) and *Porcile* (1969). It might be argued that this is true of all literature, certainly of most interpretations of literature, but Pasolini's writing is overmarked; hence the artificiality of the fiction as only an effect of writing marked. The fact that his language cites itself as well as the other languages it contains makes his writing something different.

Pasolini's novels are a meeting place of languages. The writing does not represent. It cites. It repeats. It forms analogies. Literary language and dialect scrape at the edges of one another. At the same time, because the languages are mimed, the mimed languages touch the borders of the originals. It is this touch which reveals reality.⁵

I am reminded of Dziga Vertov and *The Man with a Movie Camera* (1929) where the film being watched is an imitation of the film being made in the film being watched. The interconnection of mirrors and citations is vertiginous, especially at the level of time. The film the spectators are watching in the film is the film which is being made which includes them and which is the film that we watch as second-order spectators; the imitation by Vertov, but an imitation at one remove, is a metalanguage, which knows. Primarily, it knows the cinema. It knows it not by explanation, but by exemplification. The Vertov film, like Pasolini's films, is part parable of cinema, part illustration of it.

In Pasolini's work (and also Vertov's), reality is twofold and a paradox. It is the reality of the language cited and the reality of its citation, that is, the reality of its artistic deformation. The drama of Pasolini's writing is at the neuralgic points of the paradox. At these points his writing becomes beautiful.

In *Accattone* (1961), squalid scenes are accompanied by the sacred music of Bach's *St Matthew's Passion*: the brutal beating of Maddalena by the Neapolitans; Accattone's theft of the necklace from his son; his fight with his brother-in-law. Accattone, a pimp and a thief, is framed and lit like a Mannerist saint. The scenes are stylistic imitations of contrary styles. Reality is mimed by a realist-naturalist language, contaminated by a high-art framing of the realism by imitations of the style of epic religious paintings: 'a technique of sacrality', Pasolini called it; 'In *Accattone*, I walk above an abyss, one side formed by the religious epic, the other by realist "naturalism"'.

> With *Accattone*, inexpert as I was in cinema, I simplified to the maximum the objective simplicity of the cinema. And the result ought to have been – and in part was – a sacredness: a *technique of sacredness* that profoundly affected settings and characters. There is nothing more technically sacred than a slow pan. Especially when this is discovered by a dilettante, and used for the first time. ... Sacredness, frontality. Hence, religion. Many have spoken of the religiosity of Accattone; of the fatality of his psychology, etc. Even the lenses were kept at 50mm and 75mm; lenses which weigh on things, emphasise their fullness, their chiaroscuro, give them density, often unpleasantly, like wood eaten by termites or soft stone. ... Especially if it is used with 'dirty' lighting – backlighting ... which hollows out the eye sockets, produces shadows under the nose and around the mouth, dilates the image and gives it a grainy effect, almost like a photographic negative, etc. ... And by the fact of this – this technical, or if you like stylistic, procedure – you can speak, I would say, of 'religiosity' with regard to *Accattone* ... because only by means of these technical procedures and these stilemes is it possible to recognise the real value of this religiosity ... religiosity is not so much the need of the character for personal salvation (who goes from pimp to thief?) or, externally ... the sign of the cross at the scene of the fatal accident, which determines and concludes everything, but rather it is 'in the way of seeing the world'; in the technique of sacredness by which he is seen. ... My vision of the world is in essence epico-religious; thus also and above all they are in squalid characters, characters outside of historical consciousness and thus outside bourgeois consciousness; these elements, at play in the psychology of a poor, poverty-stricken wretch, a lumpenproletarian, are always in a certain measure 'pure' because they are without consciousness and thus 'essential'.[6]

What do a contemporary Roman pimp and a sixteenth-century Mannerist Christ have in common? The pimp was made sacred by Pasolini because the pimp was regarded by him as a prelapsarian primitive. Though existing in modern society, he was outside it, or at the edge of it, an archaism, an ancient shard, left-over in the present. Pasolini said he entered the *borgate* like an anthropologist-archaeologist, notebook in hand, to dig out language.

The pimp simply acted, simply was. For Pasolini, he acted unconsciously, instinctively, beyond the social, hence beyond the law, above all beyond the law of the symbolic and of language and meaning.

The purity of the pimp was the purity of someone in an unsullied state of being; appropriately, he was made to speak a language that was beautiful rather than meaningful. He performed language. His language was a language of grunts, roars, shouts, bursts of laughter, giggles, farts, imprecations, curses. His language sounded more than it signified. It was language before Language. It was language before history.

The pimp did not use language. His language was no more useful than he was. His language was the expression of language, its joy, not its use to represent. He did not speak in functional signs. He spoke expressively, phatically. And he spoke innocently (unlike the poet). His speech communicated nothing, and because of that it was beautiful and living: ' ... the people of the *borgate*: they were alive, their speech was alive. Words, phrases were a continuous, joyous inventiveness, everything that came out of their mouths was a pearl.'[7]

The pimp was like the poet, but he was a poet without consciousness. The poet began with the meaningfulness of symbolic language, which he then compromised with sound, with rhyme, with beat and metre. The poet had to seek, by great effort, the absolute beauty which the pimp naturally already possessed. Poetry was a metalinguistic imitation of an original innocence, a lost innocence, which poetry restored in action, in the poem, but also retained as a conscious memory of what had been lost.

Poetry was the knowledge of innocence and the frame of it.

The uselessness of the pimp guaranteed, for Pasolini, the pimp's sacredness. Because the pimp was outside the social – who could be less productive than the pimp? – Pasolini could think of him as outside the symbolic. With a language which was direct and meaningless, beautiful and nonfunctional, he invented the pimp who lived a life that was equally so: pure expression, pure poetry, utter uselessness. It was this pure poetry which the poet toiled to refind. The pimp was not only the analogue of the poet, he was at the heart of poetry. On the other hand, the pimp was a poetic creation. He was Pasolini's sign of the poetic.

The pimp was innocence in action, yet falsely so. He was a product of artifice, raised by art to a position whereby he could speak the truth of a reality which did not exist, which was ideal and absent, a potential reality, one that could be supposed to be still innocent of the world, and thought to have, impossibly, predated History. This 'reality' was in a critical, essentially linguistic relation to reality.

At the moment in the film that Accattone understands and appreciates the innocence he has lived unconsciously, he dies, thus losing reality at the precise instant that he gains the consciousness of it. This is a parable of the Fall. And it is also a parable about writing and poetry. This loss of innocence and gain of consciousness – a tale about the entry into the symbolic – does not occur once and for all, but it occurs, necessarily, again and again. It needs to be repeated as the precondition for creating anything at all. Poetry is that repetition. Pasolini mourned, in his funereal parables, a loss he not only engendered, but celebrated. After all, wasn't it he who told the tale? 'This way of finding oneself in the other, this objectification, is always more or less a form of alienation, *at once a loss of oneself and a recovery of oneself.*'[8]

The sacred language in which Accattone is framed – by the camera, by the painterly *mise en scène*, by the lighting, by the music – is the equivalent of a literary language, of a Gaddian language. It is also simultaneously the formalisation and imitation of the pure expressive primitive language of the pimp. The artifice cites that language, and also duplicates it, though of course at another level. The citation brings out, performs sacredness.

Reality is and is not the subject of Pasolini's work. He points to it, but by using it. Reality is not what he represents in his work, but rather the element that 'acts' within it. Reality is essentially linguistic and formal. It is a predicate and the work is the predication of reality, the enactment of it in language, not the representation of reality by language. Pasolini theorised the cinema as the 'written language of reality'; the cinema, he said, 'writes reality with reality'. This theory is a theory of mimesis, hence it is a theory of language and the activity of language.

By the sign one usually means a match of signifier and signified, writing and object, in a recto-verso relation, as if signifier and signified were the two sides of a coin. It is this relation that is posited in representational aesthetics. Strictly speaking, there is no signified to Pasolini's writing, or at least not 'exactly'. The signified of his writing is only another writing which he sometimes called 'reality'. The cinema of Pasolini is the metalanguage of reality, its anamorphosis. There is not reality, then the image as its sign, but only languages whose edges touch, and ignite.

Abjure

Pasolini went from one unsatisfactory situation to another only to find, when he arrived at the new, that he was structurally and ideologically in the same place. He tried to resolve a paradox of the opposition, which language contaminated, between 'reality' and the 'symbolic'. At the point of their resolution – the renunciation of the symbolic and the entry into reality – he discovered that he had arrived exactly where he had first set out from: within the paradox. It was a structure his films forever reiterated. Pasolini, the writer/film-maker, necessarily was condemned to language, no matter how intense was his longing for a reality lost and outside it. Reality could only be linguistically expressed. This was a necessary condition of his writing and, perhaps, as well, a necessary condition of fiction.

When, in the films of John Ford, you weep for a world lost, the tears are sweet. Ford refound, in the activity of making fiction, what the fictions he made evoked as lost. To make a film, for him, was at once a liberation from loss (the writing) and a confirmation of it (the written). Characters in Ford films mourned at gravesides, but as a spur to action, and thus, more importantly, a spur to the movement of the fiction. Death was a fictional motive.

The act of mourning, in Ford films, was performed by a celebratory 'writing'. The writing recorded a death, while giving life in an image. Typically, Ford's images evoked the photograph. They were images which looked 'like' still images, or were carefully posed *tableaux vivants*. The still image, more than the moving image, records an absence. It was also a place, far-fetched as this may seem, where Ford's fictions paused, as at a graveside. It is far-fetched because it reminds me of Yasujiro Ozu's work, those splendid places of silence where the film stops itself to gaze at an object or an empty room, investing them with all the emotions that had once been there.

The state of innocence which Pasolini called reality was a linguistic effect. By that fact it was also a fictional location. Every time Pasolini called out for reality in an unreal world, he was forced to return to fiction as the only place where reality could truly be possessed, that is within a form and a structure. Pasolinian reality was necessarily, and wonderfully, a myth, and Pasolini knew it.

For Pasolini, reality and writing presupposed each other, but also negated each other. The paradox was a productive instrument for the infinite generation of a writing which sought to resolve the paradox, but which always reproduced it, motivating a further writing to escape it. The paradox was a writing-making, language-making machine.

At every turn Pasolini renounced his earlier place, but the machine made it impossible for him ever to stop writing, from ever escaping the symbolic, however much, as acts of denial/hope, he shifted between substances, languages and forms: dialect to Italian, poetry to prose, fiction to essays, writing to film, film to theatre. At each renunciation he avowed that he had discovered forms closer to reality: for example, the cinema (a language of transparent images, of reality), rather than poetry (a language of symbolic signs). Hence, Pasolini's enormous productivity. Hence too, the multiple languages and substances in which he wrote.

When, for the cinema, he declared he had found the language of reality, he cut it into bits, edited its fragments, and so destroyed the wholeness of a natural reproduction of time and space characteristic, for example, of moments in neo-realism. Pasolini violated reality in order to create a linguistic simulacrum of it. It enabled him to declare, linguistically, a reality beyond language. Thus, simultaneously, he insisted on his art and he insisted on reality.

The insistence was involved in his often vaunted 'sincerity'.

Pasolinian sincerity was the refusal of any naturalism (neo-realism), because all naturalism, to him, was false. It was false because it made believe that it was true. It was illusionism. It clung to the illusion of truth in seeking to hide the fact that truth was linguistically engineered. Truth (reality) required, for Pasolini, not only the paradox of its construction, but the consciousness of the paradox. He sought to restore the paradox against a naturalism which had tried to deny it.

Naturalism aimed at erasing the gap between the real and the written. Writing, in a naturalist aesthetic, was not the production of a simulacrum of the real, the likeness of reality, but rather the fact of reality, that is the disappearance of writing before an illusion of the real which is a ploy of representational art.

Pasolini's anti-naturalism produced instead a 'false-true'. The simulacrum, the analogical likeness, was his way to restore reality to art. The special effects, which occur in many of his films, are transparently false, as miraculous and untrue as the miracles of Christ.

Even if the cinema in theory may have seemed the perfect duplicate of reality, it remained nevertheless a language, albeit analogical and mimetic. Pasolini understood that. He carefully distinguished between a theoretical cinema of reality duplicated – the infinite shot-sequence – and actual films which were discursive and linguistic, films composed of framed reality fragments.

Thus, while Pasolini abjured the symbolic, he retained the poetic. Poetry, or art in general, transcended the symbolic by its irrationality and beauty; it had a sensuality which was of a different order from the symbolic. The poetic signifier, in whatever substance, in film or in poetry, though subject to symbolic language was also liberated from it in rhyme, repetition, sound, colour, movement, in short in forms. Poetry could be thought of as a liberation from the functional necessity to be meaningful or representational. Poetry was the means to issue from the paradox contained in the relation of reality to writing. It possessed the wonderful trick of restating the paradox, though at a different level. The liberation from necessity was possible only in the consciousness that necessity was, after all, indispensable. Perhaps it was the reason his films always turned a full circle, like a tautology.

Citation

In the making of *Accattone*, Pasolini used an Arriflex camera mounted on a tripod. He removed the up/down lever, thereby fixing the camera. The set-up was normal for shooting newsreel and documentaries; what was abnormal was the fixity. Because the camera was fixed, so too were the shots. 'In fact, it was a return to the origins of the cinema.' Bernardo Bertolucci, who worked on *Accattone* as its assistant director, recalled: 'Thus I watched the reinvention of the language of the cinema by Pier Paolo ...'[9]

But Pasolini was not reinventing the first gestures of the cinema, he was copying them. For a first film it was a declaration of sorts, not primarily as homage/appreciation, in the manner of the French New Wave, to cinematic fathers, but rather as a declaration against fathers altogether. The impulse was not representational (to reproduce a reality), but citational (to reproduce a language).

Accattone and *Mamma Roma* (1962) are unquestionably narrative films. But, because the languages which form them are marked as languages, the representational character of the films is not secure. By composing films in cited languages, some of which were archaic, Pasolini set his films in opposition to the history of cinema even as he cited that history. The history of the cinema is a history of representation. Pasolini returned to the early codes of cinema in order to cite those codes. The fact of citation made his archaisms modern. Citation broke with representation and, thus, with its history.

Pasolini has been celebrated (as a romantic) and criticised (as a reactionary) for his archaisms. These views, however, are essentially views of substances, as if Pasolini were recommending cannibals and grunts as an Edenic alternative to the modern world. Pasolini's archaisms are primarily linguistic/stylistic. His cannibals and pimps are forms, not substances; he used them to think with and to write with. He introduced into a structured contemporary language archaic 'words' from another, past language. In a single citational gesture, he thus disrupted the dominant language of the cinema and enriched it by causing a shift.

Pasolini's regressions were ways to go forward. He was not opposing the old to the new, but rather opposing the contemporary with the new; this new took the form of borrowed and invented or mythical languages. Pasolini was not celebrating the past, or the sweet smell of India against the stench of European capitalism, but rather was trying to disrupt representational forms with poetic ones. Now these representational forms were definitely connected to these odours.

Regression did serve Pasolini. He seemed to believe that the past, or at least a certain past, contained a sacredness and poetry which the contemporary rationalist Cartesian world had lost. This 'truth', for him, was primarily linguistic, and literary/poetic, not real. He was, after all, a 'modern' who used language in a new way to challenge the conventions in which it repetitively seemed to turn. The past was gone; Pasolini never thought to revive it. He wanted, instead, to revive a sense of sacredness. And that was a poetic idea. And the poetry, though it used the ancients, and collected shards from varied antiquities, was not itself ancient. How else could it quote? How else could it cite? How else could it turn the past into language?

Citation 2

In *La ricotta* (1963), a film is being made on the periphery of Rome, whose subject is Christ's Passion. The director of the film within the film is Orson Welles. During a break in shooting, the Welles character is interviewed by a reporter. He is asked his views about Italy, God, politics, Fellini. At the end of the interview he reads out a poem from the preface of the published script of *Mamma Roma*. The poem is Pasolini's poem; Welles is his impersonator. On the other hand, Welles's presence is so overwhelming in the film that there is never any pretence that it is any more than a masquerade. Welles does not hide. He also impersonates himself. The Pasolini poem, read out by Welles, insofar as Welles *is* Pasolini in the film, is a quotation by Pasolini of Pasolini. The poem mirrors itself and becomes thus self-parody.

The poem is *serious* only outside the boundaries of *La ricotta*; within its boundaries, the poem read by Welles in the film mocks the very same poem written by Pasolini outside the film, exactly as Pasolini derides himself by means of his duplicate, Orson Welles.

Pasolini's dialect poems were 'doubled' on the page by their translation into Italian poems; the translation served as the 'communication' in Italian of the pure 'expression' in dialect; the dialect poems, for most readers, were only sound and metre, but could not be 'read'. The consciousness provided by the Italian was not consciousness as comprehensibility, but a consciousness of language made evident in the contrasts; the force of these poems was at the boundaries where these two languages touched; the poems mirrored each other in sense, but not in sound. The mirror and the duplicate, rather than statements, were the means for understanding. It was metalanguage in poetic practice.

Equally, the film Welles is making within *La ricotta* of the Passion is a film which the larger, framing film, *La ricotta*, being made by Pasolini, ridicules. The film-within-a-film being made by Welles is the foretaste of the film Pasolini *would make* on the Passion, his *Il Vangelo secondo Matteo* (1964); it was ridicule in a future tense. There are multiple citations at boundary points between different levels of language and between different kinds of languages.

The citations are often travesties of what they cite, even when the originals cited are the works of the one who is laughing; it is the case with Pasolini's poem. Welles is not simply a parody of Pasolini, but a parody of himself. When, as often was the case, Pasolini had people play themselves 'in' films – whether they were poets or sub-proletarian pimps – the reality of their position outside the film was mocked by their artificiality within the film; they were always quoting themselves. The use of real persons to play themselves as fictitious persons was not a realistic strategy as it was in neo-realist films where boundaries were dissolved as actors were plucked from the streets, but rather was realistic by pointing to a reality beyond the film by artificial means within the film: by the quote and the mirror. Sometimes, as if to guarantee that the point was not lost, actors put on funny hats and made faces, making believe they were someone else.

La ricotta mimics itself in a series of reflecting mirrors; in the spiral of citations which are thus created, boundaries are crossed and contaminated. Welles is so infinitely duplicated (as is Pasolini) and what constitutes inside and outside so mixed (the diegetic and what lies beyond it), that categories and positions cannot be held down. Places, and identities, literally proliferate.

I am reminded of Benjamin's essay describing Naples in the 1920s: houses spill over into the streets and the streets invade the houses; the clarity of public and private dissolve, as does the line between life and spectacle; even night and day are mixed: unable to sleep at night in overcrowded rooms, people sleep in the day in doorways, in boxes. The poor of Naples confound bourgeois order, not by revolution, but by their existence. They deny that order; Naples teems. It propagates beyond all edges; Benjamin used the word that Pasolini always used: contamination. Naples corrupts order by mixing categories and by so doing, it creates 'life', and life so close to death that it confounds even existence. Pasolini's language has a similar structure. Like the city, he mingled life (as pure reality) with death (as its writing and consciousness); his writing, thus, was always at the edge of existence. Pasolini's 'writing', I think, was often so brave because it was so risky. Benjamin (1924):

> The language of gestures goes further here than anywhere else in Italy. The conversation is impenetrable to anyone from outside. Ears, nose, eyes, breast, and shoulders are signalling stations activated by the fingers. These configurations return to their fastidiously specialised eroticism. Helping gestures and impatient touches attract the stranger's attention through a regularity that excludes chance. Yes, here his cause would be hopelessly lost, but the Neapolitan benevolently sends him away, sends him a few kilometres farther on to Mori. '*Vedere Napoli e poi Mori*', he says, repeating an old pun. 'See Naples and die', says the foreigner after him.[10]

Linguistic contamination conflates categories, defies logic, exceeds order; it turns language inside-out, topsy-turvy; as dialect, from below, from a nether world beneath the bourgeois one, corrupts the official bourgeois language that dominates at the top; this dominant language defines what society is, and, more importantly, what it is not. Dialect belongs to this 'is not'; the fact that it is excluded from any official place, and that Pasolini re-places it within the very heart of bourgeois culture – in literature – causes it to contaminate, infecting an entire hierarchy of authority. In Pasolini's writing, contamination is not simply a linguistic-artistic strategy, but a political-ideological one; in Naples, contamination is a way of life.

The anti-naturalism of Pasolini's style is a way of turning language into a spectacle, of theatricalisation; his principal devices are the mirror, the duplicate, the citation. Naples, too, is essentially theatrical. In an essay on Stendhal, Barthes remarked that at La Scala there was not only opera on-stage, but opera off-stage: movement, colour, exhibitionism ... and *gelati*; the Italians by nature, he said, were plurilinguistic.[11]

Naturalism is a bourgeois aesthetic; it forms illusions of reality by making everything within the illusion cohere and thus creating a complete duplicate of the 'real' world that is exterior to the fiction, while erasing any trace of the duplication. Reality is never actually permitted to invade the fiction. If it did, it would undermine the fictional order which was created in the first instance to assert an ordered world against the disorderliness of the reality beyond it, and the threat of that reality to naturalism. Pasolini's aesthetic is anti-naturalist.

For Pasolini, reality was the reality of the poor, the unconscious, the 'other', the reality of unreason, of unmannerliness, of things which outraged social codes, the things the European bourgeoisie incarcerated, expelled beyond its borders, banished from sight; it did so not only by aesthetic forms and positivist language, but by institutions, by law, by prisons, schools, hospitals. Forms, however, like iron bars, also imprisoned. Prisons, as de Sade revealed, were structured like languages; they could also, from within, generate languages, like de Sade's, which undermined. Pasolini made reality erupt, against the linguistic forms which sought to hold it in place, by means of a language which was impolite.

Naples is a state of mind as much as a fact; that state of mind is widespread in Italy: it is the image of 'the south'; southernness is a quality outside the civility of northern Italian order, of what is bourgeois, and capitalist.

From the south, across what seemed to be a chasm, Mamma Roma looked out on a north only a few hundred metres away. In the film, she renounces her south to enter the north, using her earnings as a prostitute to finance a respectability – she sells fruit – and catapult her son, Ettore, from the rural south into a different class, hence into bourgeois History, into *the* world, into the 'North'. That world is a world longed for by the petit-bourgeois, longing to be other and ashamed of what one is. The dream of conformity destroys her completely, and it kills her son; Ettore, having absorbed the values of an alien world, literally dies of shame when he discovers his mother is a whore. At the end of the film, with the death of her son – he is laid out on a bed of penitence in the pose of Mantegna's *Cristo morto* – Mamma Roma tries to fling herself from the window that looked out to the north.

Pasolini cleaved to 'the south'. Except for his dialect poems in Friulian, and his two early novels of adolescence in the Friulian countryside, the north had little interest for him as subject or setting, any more than did the Italian bourgeoisie. Besides, by the fact of dialect, or by the fact of the nostalgic memory of a lost rural innocence, Pasolini's Friulian north was in the south. Though he was a bourgeois writer, and a northerner – he spoke the sounds of Bologna, mixed in accents of the Veneto and Friuli – the north in his films is bourgeois, fascist, dead, unreal and murderous: the Milanese industrialist family in *Teorema* (1969), the German industrialist family in *Porcile* (1969), the libertines on the banks of Lake Garda in *Salò* (1975). Though he did sometimes represent the bourgeoisie, he did so as unrepresentable; they were unspeakable.

For Pasolini, the south challenged, with 'life', the dead unreality of bourgeois northern culture. And especially, it challenged its anti-dialect, technicist, centrist, bureaucratic, functional language: the singular, dominant, technocratic-televisual, mass-communication Italian. But as the Italian south seemed to him to become increasingly absorbed by a capitalist north, he found reality, hence poetry, in a Third World, beyond the borders of Italy, at the peripheries of capitalism. For the poet, it was only on the other side of bourgeois order that languages were truly alive.

But, as the Third World equally became, for him, lost to a global capitalism, Pasolini's films turned to myth, to an archaic world that had been wiped out. Thus, he turned away from any reference to reality towards a purity of forms, like the models of medieval tales in *Trilogia della vita* (1971–4): Chaucer, Boccaccio, the Arabs. The sense of myth is already clear in his first films, in *Accattone*, *La ricotta*, but in the last ones there is no longer an actuality to hold on to; the *borgate* had gone; the south had been colonised; he saw genocide everywhere, cultures and peoples wiped out. This destruction (of 'reality') was the subject of his Third World films: the documentary/travel films on Palestine, South Yemen, India, Africa, and his fictionalisations of the Third World in the myths of *Edipo re* (1967), *Medea* (1969), and the fables of *Il fiore delle Mille e una notte* (1974).

The films were attempts to hold on to the few fragments left of a world being lost. The south had become solely a state of mind and a state of fiction. Pasolini's resistance to bourgeois order was in poetry: stories, dreams, language. His language refused to succumb; it stood firm as a point of resistance, or it fought back; it adulterated, defiled, desecrated, violated, besmirched, befouled, parodied, burst into laughter, became tumescent, buggered, proliferated. This was the scandal of his writing. And though it was writing at the highest literary and filmic levels, it imitated styles and perspectives which were base, which were in the muck, in a homage to baseness. The low had been defined by those who dominated at the top. Pasolini turned the world around in language. He decentred it. It was a way to renew language and assert the values of the Poetic. The shit eaten in *Salò* is food for thought; it is reality written with reality. The shit is lexical.

One needs to take care judging Pasolini's regressions. They are not simply reactionary; they are also disruptive. They profane and blaspheme.

> Io sono una forza del Passato.
> Solo nella tradizione è il mio amore.
> Vengo dai ruderi, dalle Chiese,
> dalle pale d'altare, dai borghi
> dimenticati sugli Appennini e sulle Prealpi,
> dove sono vissuti i fratelli.
> Giro per la Tuscolana come un pazzo,
> per l'Appia come un cane senza padrone.
> O guardo i crepuscoli, le mattine
> su Roma, sulla Ciociaria, sul mondo,
> come i primi atti della Dopostoria,
> cui io assisto per privilegio d'anagrafe,
> dall'orlo estremo di qualche età
> sepolta. Mostruoso è chi è nato
> dalle viscere di una donna morta.
> E io, feto adulto, mi aggiro
> più moderno di ogni moderno
> a cercare fratelli che non sono più.[12]

> I am a force from the Past.
> My love is in tradition alone.
> I come from the ruins, from the Churches,
> from the altar-pieces, from the villages
> forgotten on the Appennines and on the Pre-Alps,
> where the brothers lived.
> I wander on Tuscolana like a madman,
> on the Appia like a dog without a master.
> Oh look at the twilights, the dawns
> over Rome, over Ciociaria, over the world,
> like the first acts of Post-History,
> at which I am present thanks to the year of my birth,
> at the extreme edge of some buried
> age. Monstrous is he who is born
> from the womb of a dead woman.
> And I, adult foetus, wander about
> more modern than any modern
> in search of brothers who are no longer.

Citation 3

Let us assume that what Bertolucci said about *Accattone* is true: in *Accattone*, Pasolini reinvented the language of the cinema. *Accattone* has two subjects: the story and the forms which produced it. The reflection on linguistic-stylistic forms within the film necessarily is a general reflection on film language, and, given Pasolini's view of the regressive features of that language, on film history.

The language of the film is cited. It is used to construct the film and is also the subject of that film, as if at the interior of the film there was a mirror. The language is primitive, that is, minimal with respect to the linguistic elaboration of the cinema up to date.

A similar regressiveness is noticeable in Italian neo-realism. The apparent naturalism and objectivity of neo-realism, as opposed to Pasolini's realism and subjectivity, is not what is important. Rather what is important is the fact that the impulse in neo-realism to render reality unmanipulated resulted in a destylisation and simplification of the conventions of the cinema as they appeared just before the beginning of the Second World War. These conventions, according to Bazin, had reached a classical perfection; at the same time, they had become exhausted.

It was as if, to find reality, the cinema had to return to its origins, to enable it to contemplate the reality of its language. Hence, within neo-realism, and explicitly so in Pasolini, is the entry into films of the object cinema, the taking of cinema as the subject of films. Reality was not simply, as many argued it to be for neo-realism, objective recorded facts, but already text, since reality, necessarily, was implicated in the language which instituted it.

It could be argued, in the case of neo-realism, that the motive for the renewal of film language was extra-cinematic and primarily political-social: it was an attempt to render a new reality, that of the Resistance and the immediate post-war; but the rendition of it, whatever the motives, necessarily required an interrogation of the means for rendering it. No longer could the means of cinema be simply assumed; the importance of Italian neo-realism is precisely that it questioned the assumptions of the cinema to realise its passion in describing the world.

The politics of neo-realism joined with a politics of language: these two positions presupposed each other, and though French critics, like Bazin, tended to concentrate on the revolution in language in neo-realism, while Italian critics wrote about the content of social commitment, this aspect of social commitment was involved in the linguistic transformation of the cinema, while at the same time that linguistic transformation had been spurred by a social and political one: the Resistance, the end of fascism. The questioning of film language was the precondition for the discovery of reality. Thus, within the aesthetic of neo-realism, the cinema was not primarily a means for 'making artificial', no matter how fictional that cinema was, but rather a means for finding truth and reality, and, in this case, a reality which included the forms established to search for it. Fiction became a means, not an end.

It was a sad thing, perhaps, that while the language of neo-realism and its political intentions went hand in hand, they also divided it; the populist-political impulse to go out to the people and to represent them was compromised by a language too experimental and difficult to attract those to whom it was addressed. Neo-realism was not a popular cinema. A similar problem, within similar terms of political commitment and artistic commitment, remained equally unresolved in the work of Pasolini. And it produced a restlessness. His popular cinema was succeeded by a difficult, unpopular one, to be succeeded, in turn, by a popular one. It was at the heart too of his novels and poetry: the slang of the people, redesigned for the bourgeoisie.

Thus, reflected within neo-realism was not only the world, but the cinema. In a neo-realist landscape, you find the simultaneous presence of the landscape as objective fact, and the landscape as recorded image. The image does not disappear before reality, since reality has been instituted by the image: both image and reality become the subjects of the shot, as if, because it was made conscious, the image you are watching is duplicated as an instrument for a self-reflection. The cinematic was not, as it was in classical cinema, a window through which you gazed out on the world, even if the world was make-believe, but rather a mirror where you saw yourself as one of the components of the world; your look, hence your language, was included in the objects you regarded and those you sought to shape.

In the films of Rossellini, there is a sense that you are watching not a film, but a film being made and being made to discover its own motives in discovering the realities which fascinate it, making the film a diary, and a record, of its own production. On the whole, Pasolini, rather unthinkingly, condemned all of neo-realism as naturalist, that is as merely reproductive. His exception was Rossellini.

Though neo-realism minimalised the artificial spectacle of the cinema and simplified its language, in fact by making the relation of image to reality more complicated – and more questionable – its simplification of language made the language of cinema more dense and complex. It was comparable to what had occurred in painting and the novel: a stripping bare of language to the point of abstraction. Language became less subject to being functional for representation and thereby assumed a new, concrete presence, not as pure abstraction, but as the reality of language. True, cinema remains primarily figurative, and certainly that is true for neo-realism, but the experimentation with language that occurred within it had other ends than representational ones. This new cinema raised the problem of representation and to that extent it was a theoretical cinema, or, as Pasolini insisted, a 'metalinguistic' one.

Since the image of the neo-realist landscape included the subject of the shot of the landscape, the mimetic quality of neo-realist films is not that they imitate the real, but that they reproduce themselves through forms and language in their quest for reality. Hence, Rossellini's improvisation, his sketching with film, made the 'writing' of film an actual presence in his films, unlike a finished film, where 'writing' tended towards invisibility. The sketch, the gestural trace, are as much characteristic of the modernity of Rossellini as they are of the modernity of Jackson Pollock.

The film image was never the same after neo-realism. What the neo-realists revealed about it was not its stability but its subjectivity. By including the production of the image within the image, it broke a fictional lens which tried to exclude reality in order to guarantee the illusion of fiction. Neo-realism is not less linguistic than a Hollywood extravaganza, rather it is more real because, paradoxically, more subjective.

You can see this immediately in *the* Italian heir to neo-realism, Michelangelo Antonioni. When the photographer in *Blow-Up* (1966) looks at the enlarged shots of the couple in the park, the camera is simultaneously with the photographer looking at the shots, and not with him, looking at the shots on its own. There is a prior play in the scene between subjective and objective looks, but such as to confound their difference. When the camera looks on its own, it is outside the fiction; in that place it comes to regard and contemplate not simply the photographs and the photographer, but its own gaze, until it seems that the film you are watching is a documentary of itself. It is a film encountering itself and, thereby, encountering the cinema. What it documents is the uncertainty of reality because reality is linked to the uncertainty of the subject regarding reality; this regard includes the subject-camera and the film-maker; and it also includes the spectator, no longer secure in a seat in the theatre, no longer able to dominate fictional reality, any more than the spectator is able to dominate actual reality. One is always part of it, never, like God, above it.

Pasolini on *Accattone*:

> In *Accattone* there is never a shot, in close-up or not, where one sees someone from over the shoulder; there is never a character who enters and then exits from the frame; there is never the use of the dolly in its sinuous, impressionist movements; very rarely are there close-ups of profiles, or if there are, they are as a result of a movement. ... For me all these characteristics have to do with the fact that my cinematographic tastes are not essentially cinematographic, but figurative ... when the camera moves in my images, they are movements akin to a camera moving along a canvas; I always think of the background of shots like a ground of painting and for this reason I *always* shoot frontally. And figures are *always* moved against this background, as far as possible symmetrically: close-up against close-up, a forward pan against a backward pan, a regulated rhythm (thirds) of shots, etc., etc. There is almost never a coupling of close-ups and long shots. Figures in long shot are in the background, followed by a pan, which, I repeat, appears always symmetrically, as if I was looking at a painting – where figures can only be dimly seen. I would use the shot to see the details better.[13]

And on *Mamma Roma*:

> I look for plasticity, above all the plasticity of the image, along a path, which I can never forget, begun by Masaccio: his bold *chiaroscuro*, his black and white – or the path, if you like, of archaic painters, a strange mix of subtlety and crudeness. I can't be an impressionist. I like the background, not the landscape. One can't think of an altar-piece with figures in movement. I hate that fact that figures move. Therefore none of my shots can begin with a 'field', that is an empty landscape. There will always be, even if very small, a character. But very small for only a moment, because I tell the faithful Delli Colli to use a 75mm lens: and then I approach the figure: a face in detail. And, behind it, the background – the background, not the landscape.[14]

Why regress to the 'primitive' cinema as a way to reform the language of cinema? Probably because the language of early cinema, fascinated as it was by resemblance, and having a closer link to the magic lantern, found the reproduction of movement and the simulation of time so wondrous and magical. It was, as Bazin suggested, like the re-creation of the world.

The early language of the cinema was more mimetic than symbolic; for that reason the earliest cinema images sometimes required an actor/narrator on-stage to explain the action (this practice endured in Japan even after the introduction of sound); later, of course, there were printed titles. The mimetic is ambiguous. It is not representational, but reproductive. It does not signify reality, it imitates it.

At the centre of Bazin's aesthetic was a return to the mimetic. In effect, Bazin argued that classical cinema had written with the signs of reality; modern cinema needed to write with things themselves, to write, as Pasolini insisted, with reality. It was a call – in the name of modernism – to make the cinema once again primarily a mimetic art. Paradoxically, this permitted, more than had been the case previously, the introduction into the cinema, and in a direct fashion, of literature, the novel, paintings. These artefacts entered the cinema in two ways: as citations (Rosso Fiorentino's *Deposition of Christ* is directly quoted in *La ricotta*); or as duplicated style (Pasolini's 'la sacralità tecnica' as the imitation of the language of Renaissance painting). These artefacts did not enter the modern cinema or Pasolini's cinema as they had entered the classical cinema, as adaptations; they entered instead in their own right.

Pasolini's cinema, which is overwhelmingly citational (of literature and painting), is a cinema which reproduces texts literally, but does not adapt them. This is especially true of his most openly literary-based works: *Il Decameron* (1971) (Boccaccio); *I racconti di Canterbury* (1972) (Chaucer); *Il fiore delle Mille e una notte* (from *Alf Laylah wa-Laylah*); *Salò, o Le 120 giornate di Sodoma* (de Sade). The films are places where the languages of these texts are cited and encountered, a place where cinema and literature meet, not where literature ends and from which it takes its leave. The mimetic permitted the literary to enter cinema as language, rather than to be a mere pretext for a representation. The mimetic was curiously more linguistic than classical cinema, while at the same time being less semiotic.

Articulation

Representation in cinema is less a matter of individual shots than of the joins between shots. It is the joins that articulate, narrate, tell a tale, make significant. Montage substituted itself for the actor-narrator who pointed to the film from on-stage in primitive cinema, and for the titles in silent cinema. The ability to articulate, hence to narrate and represent, gave Griffith the immense importance he had, especially for those kings of montage, the Soviet film-makers, whose cinema Bazin did not particularly like.

The Soviet cinema was too semiotic for Bazin. The shot-sequence and depth-of-field of neo-realist cinema was the opposite of Soviet cinema. Because it seemed less manipulated, it also seemed to be more mimetic, more ambiguous, hence more realistic. Sense was present, but not specified. The shot-sequence, as Bazin understood it, refused centring, pointing, the hierarchy.

In Pasolini's film theory, the mimetic and the semiotic are distinguished as between ideal cinema and actual film; Pasolini extended the idea of the shot to an infinite time-space, the 'infinite shot-sequence'. It was cinema as absolute mimesis. The ideal cinema of the infinite shot-sequence was not an objective record of reality, or if it was, it contained the subjectivity behind the camera. Reality was unmanipulated, yet, also, selected.

Pasolini's mimetic, ideal cinema remained a trace in actual films, most particularly in the shot, which recalled the wholeness of cinema, the infinite shot-sequence, of which it was the fragment. Cinema was always in film, or, more exactly, the mimetic was always contained in the semiotic. This was what Pasolini meant by the 'irrational' core of films, their primitivism, no matter how much film was representational, narrational and signifying. Thus, the mimetic – Cinema – always threatened the stability of sense, just as sound might compromise significance in poetry. The mimetic was an essentially designifying element.

What needs to be stressed in Pasolini's theory is that the mimetic is an activity; thus, though the ideal cinema might reproduce reality, it nevertheless reproduced reality subjectively. The mimetic ideal cinema was a mirror of reality, but one which included the subjectivity of its formation; the cinema, precisely in its ideal as reproduction, nevertheless remained language: 'the written language of reality'. For most film-makers, including those like Rossellini or Antonioni whose cinema was experimental and had metalinguistic, self-reflective aspects, the shots and compositions of their films did not exclusively have these theoretical ends.

But Pasolini's films did. Every shot referred back to cinema's mimetic ideal, as a reality lost. The loss was twofold: the magic of the reality lost (a more primitive world) and the magic of the mimetic forgotten (a more primitive art). The purpose of his films was to mourn the loss of reality and reinstitute its presence in the only place it could be remembered: in language.

The problem was, in what language would that mourning-remembrance be expressed? Actual films were not mimetic but semiotic. For Pasolini, the neo-realist experiment in mimesis had degenerated into a naturalism, more illusory, and real-seeming, than even the most illusionist Hollywood film. Pasolini had to invent a new language which recalled the regressive, the mimetic and the cinematic, while being at the same time, in order that this lost reality would be remembered, wholly on the side of the linguistic.

For example, compared to Soviet cinema, or Hollywood classical cinema, Pasolini's films are extensively edited, certainly composed of more shots than the neo-realist film. But the purpose of those shots was to tell a story of a lost reality and lost primitivism (*all* his films), as well as to exemplify the loss in the shot itself. The loss was remembered threefold: in the story evoked of a lost wholeness; in the shot carved from that wholeness; and in the refusal of articulation, that is to say in the refusal of the semiotic.

This refusal of articulation requires some explanation.

There are, at least, three levels of disarticulation in Pasolini's films. Two of these occur within the fiction. Actors often act without fictional motivation. They may address no one. Or their actions seem to lack a sense. The non-motivated action occurs sometimes at the boundary between actor and character: a burst of laughter, a fart, a grimace, an erection, shitting, a cough, a yawn; that is to say, the eruption of the body of the actor within the casing of the character and in that sense, even if hypothetical and fictional, the eruption of reality into the fictional, or the body against language. In both cases reality compromises a semiotic significance within a narrative stream. It disrupts the narrative by the bursting forth of 'reality'.

The third level of disarticulation is formal, in the shot itself. Just as the actor may act without motivation, or the real body become tumescent within the fictional body, shots may often lack motivation in their conjunctions, as if, rather than shots relating to each other, they relate to the reality outside the shot which the shot has reproduced. That is, the shot serves a mimetic, not narrative, semiotic function. But it does so – it points to the mimesis – within a language which disarticulates motives and connectives. Pasolini's language exists to star reality, and at an essentially poetic, stylistic level different from reality itself. His language is not completely mimetic, in the sense that it does not reproduce reality whole, nor is it completely semiotic, since it subverts significance in the gesture of forming it; it breaks up the mimetic, but only to point to it, in fragments. These fragments, unlike the montage bits of Soviet cinema, are not fully articulated with each other.

It is a negation of reality in order to reassert reality in language; it is also a negation of language in order to celebrate it in reality.

It could be argued that poetry is mimetic at the point at which metre, rhyme, rhythm, sound cease to be functional for the production of sense and return to a magic of language which is pure and primitive and which Pasolini called the irrational. What is mimetic is that the language imitates a nature before there was sense, a reality before there was culture, however cultivated the means are in the production and formation of these linguistic sounds in the poem. Words are not primarily connected in the poem representationally, but rather connected sensually, that is, in Pasolini's terms, mimetically.

In this manner, the films, precisely for their extreme artificiality of means and worked-upon quality of style, are mimetic too. There *are* connectives between shots, but they are not narrative ones; the connectives are poetic in the way I have described them, that is they sound, they rhyme, they echo, and they do so not narratively, that is semiotically, but irrationally, that is mimetically. In effect, Pasolini, while dividing Cinema (mimesis) from Film (semiosis), rejoined these by finding a language in film analogous to the ideal language of cinema whose analogy he formed by an immense stylistic effort.

Citation 4

Pasolini's citations of paintings mostly came from the Renaissance: its early period (Giotto, Masaccio), through to Piero della Francesca, and including Mannerism (Michelangelo, Pontormo, Rosso Fiorentino). His citations were of two kinds though the boundary between them was not always clear: citations of particular paintings, often mocked (Mantegna's *Cristo morto*; Pontormo's *Deposizione*; Fiorentino's *Deposizione*; Buoninsegna's *Maestà*); and citations of a painter's style rather than of any one painting. Pasolini either mocked a Giotto painting, or he filmed like Giotto painted, or he impersonated Giotto.

Renaissance painting instituted time by means of perspective, that is it instituted time spatially. Everything in a Renaissance painting, even despite the 'distortions' and unnaturalness of the Mannerists, had a fixed place within a perspective order. That order was representational, illusionist and historical. Things were connected, through perspective, to all other things. Those connections were made to appear as perfectly logical, while the logic, in turn, was meant to signify a logic and rationality in the world which the painting then represented. This was its essential, and secular, meaning. Renaissance paintings may have had sacred subjects, but they were not in themselves sacred objects. The illusionism of Renaissance paintings depended on a geometric perspective with the spectator at its centre. It was an illusion of reason and order at the same time as it confirmed the possession of that order by the subject to whom it was addressed. Space and time were connected in this order; it was necessary for the subject to take a visual journey over time within the ordered space of the painting, and thus to take a journey into history.

Only when the cinema has to do with the composition of the shot is the matter of perspective a visual one. There is a temporal narrative perspective which concerns the connections between shots. In Renaissance painting, this narrative perspective was composed by a perspective in depth. Neo-realism loosened the connective logic between shots, favouring a logic within them; its cinema tended to be more spatial than it was temporal with a corresponding reduction of the narrational. Sometimes it was said that neo-realism presented facts, not a story.

Pasolini's strategy was different. By sometimes refusing to link shots narratively, and denying them a logical progression, he abrogated a narrative perspective. This disarticulation and loss of perspective did not always or necessarily link the shots to the reality which they reproduced: rather they cut them off from any reality whatsoever. It turned the shot into an analogue of painting. The lack of connectives in time helped to frame it as an individual image. It was like an altar-piece or the Giotto frescoes in Assisi and Padua. Pasolini's films often have that quality: of establishing connectives, but connectives of separately framed images.

Often Pasolini's images are not images for another image in a series, or images consequent on preceding images, but rather images cut loose from any (narrative) function or linear logic. These images, and they are frequently citations of painting, weaken representation. They not only cite images which are 'outside' the narrative fiction, but they cite these images in their quality as images. What is framed, therefore, is explicitly stylistic and linguistic, not representational. It is one language citing another.

In Renaissance painting, representational and dependent on perspective, painting is secular and non-sacred, independent of the subject it depicts. It is not a sacred object, but only a glass through which sacredness may be glimpsed. The spirit of Renaissance painting is more rationalist than religious. Pasolini reinstated the sacred by his dissolution of perspective. His art is not secular, as much of the Renaissance art he cites was. By cutting the image off from a representational chain and an illusory perspective order, he reinstated the image in its reality as an image, as pure language. It is that status, utterly non-functional, that he declared sacred. His films were like altar-pieces to the cinema, or perhaps more accurately to poetry. It is by the fact of citing the Renaissance that Pasolini distanced himself from it; the citational image which either copied or quoted Renaissance images was an exact contrast to them. It was a site of linguistic oppositions. His images, as sacred and religious, correspond more to Byzantine art. Byzantine art is a less realistic art than that of the

Renaissance. However, its paintings are more real as objects: it was the art of the icon. This regressive medievalism on the part of Pasolini, however, was a thoroughly modernist gesture.

Imitation

I am writing this in Hong Kong. It is just before Christmas. Decorations are going up on the face of buildings. 'Merry Christmas from National Mutual.' Hong Kong is a Chinese city; it is also a capitalist one. But the West seems to be here only on the surface. In Benjamin's *One Way Street*, one of the fragments is called 'Chinese Curios': 'These are days when no one should rely unduly on his "competence". Strength lies in improvisation. All the decisive blows are struck left-handed.'

A thought has been captured by writing it; it is not simply bringing an idea into form, but finding the idea as it is formed; there is no before to the writing. Nor is the writing 'finished'. Language and writing are completely experimental. The writing glances by the idea, rather than communicating it. Perhaps, because the idea is an effect of improvisation, it hardly stands as an idea 'thought'. Benjamin:

> The power of a country road is different when one is walking along it from when one is flying over it by airplane. In the same way, the power of a text is different when it is read from when it is copied out. The airplane passenger sees only how the road pushes through the landscape, how it unfolds according to the same laws as the terrain surrounding it. Only he who walks the road on foot learns of the power it commands, and of how, from the very scenery that for the flier is only the unfurled plain, it calls forth distances, belvederes, clearings, prospects at each of its turns like a commander deploying soldiers at a front. Only the copied text thus commands the soul of him who is occupied with it, whereas the mere reader never discovers the new aspects of his inner self that are opened by the text, that road cut through the interior jungle forever closing behind it: because the reader follows the movement of his mind in the free flight of day-dreaming, whereas the copier submits it to command. The Chinese practice of copying books was thus an incomparable guarantee of literary culture, and the transcript a key to China's enigmas.[15]

In Kafka's narration 'The Great Wall of China', the Great Wall is built in disconnected fragments; the Great Wall, as the narrator describes it, was discontinuous in its construction; chunks of wall were built, as much as 1,000 metres, with great gaps between. The writing is like the Great Wall. The reader becomes lost in its construction. The discontinuity in the writing has a solidity that the Great Wall lacks; it is almost impenetrable, a fortress of words, producing a density that thickens and hypnotises; after a while, the words cease adequately to describe; they seem to lose the thread. Significance is displaced by the writing of it. The writing, trying to find significance – why was the Great Wall built in such a manner? – causes that very significance to disappear, as if the writing cannot, any more than the Great Wall, find its joins, hence its continuity, hence a represented sense.[16]

The writing ceases to be a description of the subject – the Great Wall – as it becomes its own subject: you are not reading about the Great Wall, but reading the writing of it. The written (the Great Wall) and the writing become one. Yet this pure writing, which only becomes pure as you read it, never completely loses its figurative base. The power of the writing as pure writing depends on its purity being contaminated in a representation; representation needs to be present as a lure and a trace and a foil.

Thus, the writing retains a semiotic horizon in order better to activate its linguistic performance. This semiotic horizon, the horizon of denotation and representation, is, as Barthes has indicated, the last and least horizon of writing.

Italo Calvino was among the first writers to appreciate the Rome novels of Pasolini. Calvino saw what a wonderful linguistic feat they accomplished. In them languages – literary and slang, Italian and dialect – met and played; the novels were less a drama and parody of things described than a drama and play of describing. They constituted language theatres where the events functioned to point to the description of them. It was the contrary of representation. What was represented framed the writing. Representation was necessary, but as a condition for writing. It was not what the writing foregrounded, but rather the ground for the writing itself.

Calvino's *Le città invisibili* is set during the reign of Kublai Khan. In it, Marco Polo describes to the Khan the cities of his empire. These cities are variations of the same; in all of them there is a trace of Marco Polo's Venice. The cities are effects of languages. These effects are primarily imitative. The writing does not imitate the reality of the cities, that is it does not represent a reality; instead, it imitates its own writing, tracing cities as Kafka created walls. It is writing which invents writing in inventing cities, or multiplies writing by building into it a mirror effect. For that reason each city is the analogue of another.

If Benjamin was correct about transcription in China, then the Khan would have perfectly understood the utility, ideologically speaking, of the Venetian's descriptions. Benjamin would also have appreciated those descriptions; Marco Polo, Italian that he was, improvised.

Why would Pasolini, in *La ricotta*, the one film where he represented himself as film director, choose Orson Welles as his double? Perhaps, because Welles, like Pasolini, was an outsider, and also a figure of authority for

24

intellectuals. But perhaps, and primarily, it was because Welles acted in his own films just as Pasolini did; and Welles was fond of mirrors; and Welles was an illusionist, that is, a magician of cinema. Welles's *F For Fake* (1973) concerns forgery. What better medium to choose to express the subject of forgery than the cinema? Isn't the cinema too a forgery?

It is impossible not to recall the mirrors and reflections of Welles in *Citizen Kane* (1941); when Kane is left by Susan Alexander, he is reflected in a corridor of mirrors to infinity. Aren't the stories in *Kane* like this? Reflections on each other?

The central scene in *The Lady from Shanghai* (1946) takes place in a hall of mirrors in an amusement park. O'Hara (Welles) looks at himself in a myriad crazy distortions; nothing is real in the hall of mirrors, everything is reflected, and reflected in turn by the film; Welles is seen by, and then sees, in multiple images, Elsa (Rita Hayworth) and Bannister (Everett Sloane); Elsa and Bannister shoot at each other aiming at their reflections, which shatters the mirror. In *Touch of Evil* (1958), Quinlan (Welles) hears his own recorded voice, which, like a siren, calls him to his own death. On the one hand, identities spiral out of control; on the other, as in the search for 'Rosebud' in *Kane*, there is the lure of significance, of superimposing the reflections on each other until they add up, or become merged.

Just before Welles appeared in Pasolini's *La ricotta*, he made *The Trial* (1962) based on Kafka's novel, and acted in Denys de la Patellière's *La Fabuleuse Aventure de Marco Polo* (1964). *The Lady from Shanghai* had been made in 1946. The year before *La ricotta*, in 1961, Welles was the narrator in Nicholas Ray's biblical epic on the life of Christ, *King of Kings*. Might that have been, among others, a provocation to Pasolini? *La ricotta* cites the Passion of Christ; Ray's *King of Kings* tries to create the illusion of it, and by that fact makes it lose its real history for a make-believe history. The mirror which duplicates the character in Welles's films has a double subject: Welles, the actor, and Welles, the character. The reflections, thus, were reflections of already reflected doubles. The One was imitated – and found – in the Other, its copy. Welles, like Pasolini, was the film director, the illusionist, who put reflections into play and marked them out as fakes. The self-evident fakery gave to the language which constructed it a sharper focus.

Pasolini's special effects are always evident as effects. Nothing is hidden. The 'miracles' of Christ in *Il Vangelo secondo Matteo* are crude and primitive, whether it is the curing of the lepers, the multiplying of the loaves and the fish, or the raising of the dead. Pasolini's miracles are not like the miracles of Rossellini. Rossellini's miracles took place on the screen. In Rossellini's films, a truth was revealed to the characters in the film at the same moment as it was revealed to the film-maker and audience. Rossellini's camera waited for miracles of comprehension in the same way as the fishermen in *Stromboli* waited for the tuna to swim into their nets. It was a wait against all logic: the conversion of Karin in *Stromboli*; the sudden flash of the reappearance of love between the

Joyces in *Viaggio in Italia* (1953). It was these miracles, patiently awaited, that Rossellini found in his films and caught. He filmed the reality of the event and, simultaneously, the event of the reality of its filming.

Pasolini's miracles were already-found miracles (historical). They are not truths, but citations of truths, hence not miracles but their citational trace. There was no need for them to seem true. On the contrary, the need was rather for them to seem false. The unnaturalness of falsity guaranteed the presence to consciousness of the reality of the film's 'writing'.

Modern

Many of the most important Italian writers who wrote before the Second World War were politically to the right, and some directly implicated in Italian fascism: D'Annunzio, Pirandello, Marinetti. Was there a relation between 'modernism' and fascism?

Most Italian writers post-war and all the greats of the Italian cinema have been politically on the left, many associated with the Italian Communist Party (PCI). In the cinema: Visconti, Bertolucci, Germi; among those who leaned towards the left: Antonioni, De Sica, Rossellini, Zavattini. These artists too were modern.

Pasolini fits uneasily into the post-war situation. He was the most modernist of Italian film-makers; he belonged to the Communist Party; but he held political positions which were often conservative and sometimes Utopian reactionary. He had been a member of the party just after the war, but was expelled in 1949. One of the reasons the party expelled him was a sexual scandal involving some schoolboys. He had been a schoolmaster in Casarsa, in Friuli, and the local party branch secretary. But there were other reasons for his expulsion beyond the sexual. They were expressed in *L'Unità*, the party daily, in an editorial commentary in October, 1949:

> The incidents which have provoked grave disciplinary action against the poet Pasolini provide us with the opportunity to denounce once again the harmful influences of certain ideological and philosophical currents represented by figures like Gide, Sartre and other poets and decadent men of letters who give themselves airs of being progressive, but who, in reality, represent the very worst aspects of bourgeois degeneration.

Pasolini's sexuality gave the party a bad name. The events at Casarsa came at a moment when the PCI was seeking to be a national party. It had compromised its ideals of socialist democracy and class politics in the 1948 elections for those of bourgeois liberal democracy and a national politics as a means to gain power in the new democratic Italian parliamentary system. The party was intent on appearing more respectable than, or at least as respectable as, the Christian Democrats, who were, politically, its main rival.

But it was 'the poet Pasolini' who was more troublesome to the party than the pederast Pasolini.

The PCI was the central political body in the Italian Resistance during its military phase, 1943–5, and it retained that central role immediately after the war in the popular front coalition. The culture of the Resistance was national and popular, though not thereby socialist. Socialist ideals, because they were class ideals, split the unity of the nation and thus potentially compromised the democratic ambitions of the party.

During the armed struggle against the Nazi occupation and the remnants of the Italian fascist state with headquarters at Salò, the party emphasised national unity as a military necessity; after the war, it continued to emphasise such unity, but then as a political necessity for survival. Insofar as Resistance culture was popular culture, and the popular was associated with the national, bourgeois culture, that is literary culture, carried the stigma of being non-popular and elitist and, by that token, non-national.

Neo-realism, in literature and in the cinema, was supported by the party so long as it carried forward the notion within it of the popular and the national; this notion was not only not progressive politically, but it was extremely unprogressive aesthetically. It rejected a literary culture divorced from reality, hence from truth, the people and, ultimately, the nation; in short, literary culture as literariness, as salon literature, as avant-garde experiment was regarded at best as politically non-committal and at worst as reactionary. Moreover, bourgeois artistic culture carried with it a stigma of association and accommodation with fascism; this was true especially of the Italian avant-garde, most notably Italian futurism.

The Italian state under fascism had sought to centralise culture. Italy was predominantly rural with a very low level of literacy; most Italians spoke dialect as their first language. The issue of language was an important cultural-political issue under fascism. The fascist state tried to impose Italian, and for much the same reasons as it built roads and improved the rail system: to make the state more efficient and centralised and to extend and secure its power. The language policy of the state was not only cultural, but economic and political; necessarily it was opposed to the use of dialect.

In films of the period characters spoke a uniform, and essentially false, Tuscan-Roman Italian. The Italian was false because it was not as national as the films pretended it was or fascism wished it would be. (In the fascist period, as ever since, films were dubbed in standard Italian with a slight Roman inflection; it was part of fascist policy that, although standard Italian is based on Tuscan, pure Tuscanisms should be avoided in favour of a 'national' – that is to say, a Roman *koine*. Pasolini later argued that the new *koine* which was destroying dialects was Milanese, the language of big capital.

Under fascism, the particular was not-national. During the Resistance, tied to the reality of the people, hence to region, village and dialect, the national was represented by the particular. In Rossellini's *Paisà* (1946), as the Anglo-American armies advanced up the Italian peninsula from Sicily, each separate incident of the film takes place in a different region. In these incidents, Italian speech is notably accented or directly dialectised. The unity of Italy, and the unity of the national struggle against fascism, were expressed in the film by this fact of linguistic diversity.

Because of the peculiar history of Italian fascism, the anti-fascist populist ideology of the Resistance which the PCI promoted tended to decry experiments in the arts, especially from outside Italy. Literary bourgeois culture and avant-garde art were seen as socially reactionary. Thus, the party cut itself off not only from the best of Italian bourgeois culture, but from the best of European culture, particularly French culture.

There is no question but that a film like *Paisà* was narratively new and experimental; nevertheless, such experiment was absorbed within the ideology of Italian populism. Its modernity tended to be critically overlooked for its political content. It was the French, significantly enough Bazin and the young critics of *Cahiers du cinéma*, many of whom would later become the film-makers of the French New Wave, who recognised the modernism in Italian neo-realism; Italian critics tended to concentrate on the political-social content of neo-realism; and tended to be on guard against any hint of formalism.

Pasolini's earliest extant writing was done during his time as schoolmaster and party branch secretary in Casarsa. *Poesie a Casarsa*, a collection of poems written in Friulian dialect, was published in 1942; until 1950, most of his poetry was in Friulian, including another collection, *Dov'è la mia patria?* (1949), though he alternated in those years between poetry in dialect and poetry in Italian. Friulian was a learned language for Pasolini. Literally, it was his mother's tongue.

Pasolini's first works were written during the neo-realist period and seemed to share the neo-realist concern with dialect. Pasolini, much later, recalled his recourse to dialect as a political act within the context of the linguistic policies of fascism. On the other hand, it was a very personal one.

The links between dialect, the peasantry, the rural were connected to Pasolini's closeness to his mother; these, in turn, were analogues of poetry. Hence dialect, in and of itself, had a poetic value. Negatively, Poetry and Mother were contrasts to Father: militarist, fascist. It was the contrast, 'head-in-the-clouds' to Law and Power, the Beautiful to the Instrumental. Insofar as dialect was an illegal, even scandalous activity for Pasolini, it was because dialect was a poetic activity, and a private one.

To write poetry in dialect, for Pasolini, was to write an ideal poetry. This poetry had a greater connection with the French Symbolists than with the Italian neo-realists. The use of dialect by the neo-realists bore the marks of reality, the people, truth. It was specifically anti-literary. Pasolini's use of dialect was ambiguous. It may have carried a sign of the people, but it was not aimed against bourgeois culture; it was the perfect expression of it. His poetry may have been composed in popular speech, but the compositional gesture was 'literary' and excessively so.

Friulian was a restricted speech. Only very few Italians could understand it. It could therefore serve as a pure sign of poetry, because it could not communicate widely; it was able to qualify as pure poetic sound and rhythm. At the foot of each page of the Friulian poetry was a translation of the Friulian into Language, that is Italian. Italian thereby acquired the sign of the language of sense, of communication; dialect became instead the language before language, an immaculate chaste speech, innocent of meaning, and existing even outside History.

Dialect in neo-realism was a specifically historical speech; it was the speech of truth and reality, the social and the national; in *Paisà*, it not only signified the national, but was a principle of national unity. Dialect in the film linked the people to the regions in a New Italy unified on the basis of the reality of the people, including their linguistic reality. Pasolini was less a particularist linguistically than he was a separatist. Friulian had an absolute not relative value, a mythical not historical status. His use of dialect did not move towards progress in social-political terms; it was a regression outside history and symbolic speech. Pasolini, it seemed, wanted to take Friuli out of Italy altogether. Or so he stated in a 1947 article, 'Il Friuli autonomo', recently republished in a collection of essays, *Un paese di temporali e di primule*.[17]

Politically, his use of dialect was disruptive and uncompromising, precisely because it was mythical and otherworldly. It was not an embrace of the world and of reality; it was an opposition to the world by an extreme artistic gesture. Pasolini wanted the world to stop at the borders of Friuli, to go back forever to a 'country of storms and primulas', to a maternal pre-symbolic of Mother, to a time before one enters the world, hence to a state before language. Friulian was a prelanguage, not in fact but as analogy; it was a masquerade Edenic speech, in a make-believe Paradise filled with the sounds of Poetry. Hence, the spotlessness of Friulian. It was a hypnotic, non-communicative, pure gestural speech. Absolute Poetry.

This was a fiction. It was a myth about language. Necessarily, it could not be Edenic speech. It was only its imitation. It was language fabricated to appear as mythical speech before the Fall into symbolic language, the moment when language commenced to signify.

This gesture was modern. It was against it, in part, that the party reacted. The contentism of neo-realism had assured it a place in a political discourse. Neo-realism could be used by the party, whatever else were the intentions or merits of neo-realism. Pasolini, instead, produced a useless language, without content, whose sense was its sound and its structure. It was only 'writing'. That uselessness constituted its politics. It was an artistic politics, that is an ideal one. It knew no compromise. 'Politics' could only reject it.

Metaphor

When, in *October* (1928), Eisenstein wanted to say Kerensky was like a peacock, he showed Kerensky strutting, then he showed a peacock spreading its feathers, strutting. The image of the peacock was exterior to the fiction. Eisenstein also did this in *Strike* (1925): men were compared to animals. And he did it in *Potemkin* (1925): stone lions roused themselves like the people who had been roused to revolution.

Eisenstein's cinema used metaphors organised in this manner. He went outside the fiction to form them. The metaphors did not arise naturally from the realities in the image, but from their abstract relation to each other. It was a third, constructed sense that was not there in the images taken separately. The emphasis – and it was crucial to Kuleshov's experiments – was to arrive at a 'thought' by a juxtaposition of images, that is by a juxtaposition of realities. The thought was unnatural because it was external to those realities. It was a sense imposed on the world.

Pasolini said metaphor was a rhetorical device of literature, not cinema; a metaphorical relation might be suggested to the spectator in cinema, but not directly stated, precisely because the cinema dealt directly with realities and thus seemed to lack the capacity for abstract metaphor. The cinema, Pasolini said, was linked to archaic literature, to religious-infantile literature and to music. Its essential structural devices, as with these forms, were anaphora and repetition.

In *Che cosa sono le nuvole?* (1968), two posters of paintings by Velázquez are cited. In one, Venus, reclining, regards herself in a mirror. The reflection of Venus resembling herself, doubled and reversed in the mirror, is returned to the viewer, but with a doubly split object, Venus and her reflection. There is a further mirror of the film which contains the poster of the painting. It is a repetition of a repetition. The initial subject repeated is a subject of the repeated duplicate of Venus reflected.

The film reproduces, and also as a poster, another Velázquez painting. The poster announces the presentation of the film in which the poster is reproduced – *Che cosa sono le nuvole?*. The painting is *Las meninas*. It depicts the artist Velázquez painting the painting that you see. In the painting the king and the queen who are absent from the painting appear in the mirror at the background of the painting. They are present only as a reflection. The mirror is reduplicated in the film. The painting becomes the subject of a shot in a film which the shot points to. Like the painting, the film is mirrored in the film. It is in the same relation to the mirror as was the painting mirrored in *Las meninas*. The structure of the Pasolini film is analogous to the Velázquez painting. What holds the two together is not the embedding of the one into the other, or the multiple citations of either, but rather the similitude of their means.

Ideologically, the fact that Kerensky is a peacock, or capitalists are pigs, are natural likenesses, even if formed unnaturally. Repetition, however, is

30

something strange, even if it occurs more naturally, or at least seemingly more naturally because it is within the diegesis. In *Las meninas*, because of the inclusion of the scene of painting within the painting, it is not possible to arrive at an origin or an end, where the inside of the painting can be split from its outside, where the one begins and the other ends. Pasolini, by the fact of repeated analogies, confuses identity and boundaries. Eisenstein confirms them. The Pasolini film, like the painting, mirrors itself. There is no exteriority to the writing as there is in Eisenstein. Strictly speaking, there is no extra-diegetic to Pasolini's films.

The effectiveness of Eisenstein's films depends on the firmness and stability of the extra-diegetic. On this secure ground Eisenstein could stand and speak a political discourse. Pasolini was on less sure ground. His analogies have no outside to them. The film which contains the poster of the painting being painted is similar in structure to the original painting being painted. As in the painting, the film forms analogous mirrors of its own processes: to mirror, to repeat, to cite. The formation of the analogy (of resemblance) and the consciousness of the analogy occur at once. They are part of the same thing, not of different things (Kerensky/peacock). The lack of a gap and the formal similitudes which dissolve the gap make it difficult to disentangle the act from the knowledge of it. In fact, the act constitutes a form of knowing. Knowing is not something subsequent. Reality is lost and language born at precisely the same moment. Language records the loss of reality, remembers it symbolically, and mourns it, sometimes with sadness (*Mamma Roma*), sometimes with joy (*La terra vista dalla luna* (1966), *Che cosa sono le nuvole?*), and sometimes with sadness and joy (*La ricotta, Porcile*).

The simultaneity of being and knowledge resembles the sacred magic of the Mass where sign and reality are compounded. This is my blood (the wine) /this is my body (the wafer). At the heart of the sacred is a paradox. It can be formed, but not reasoned. Poetry, and the Cinema, contained that same sacred element for Pasolini. Reality may have become alienated in linguistic/stylistic forms, but these forms were the only ones available to return reality to itself. Reality, written in poetry and the cinema, was transmuted into the reality of artistic forms, but in such forms the Symbolic was confounded. The edges of the significant and of what could be communicated were skirted since poetry, in the widest sense, and at its most concrete, as sound and rhythm and colour, worked against the symbolic and communicative language system from which it was produced.

In Eisenstein's films, the metaphor is consecutive and consequential. The image of the peacock succeeds the image of Kerensky as sense succeeds action. The likenesses, from which sense is born, are between unlike things. As Bazin said, they are unnatural likenesses, found outside the reality filmed. Kerensky, inside the diegetic, is succeeded by an image of a peacock, outside it. The peacock provides an external commentary. Pasolini's films seldom yield such univocal meanings. Even when there is an extra-diegetic intrusion into a scene in the fiction, when, for example, in *Accattone*, Bach's *St Matthew's Passion* is heard during a fight, it constitutes less a statement likening the low life of the Roman slums to something sacred, than the actual bestowal of sacredness. It makes the squalid scene sublime, however unlikely this may be. The *St Matthew's Passion* is not something outside the scene, but directly within it. It holds a mirror to it. It is not metaphorical.

The Eisensteinian metaphor is formed in linearity. An image from one reality is followed by an image from another. Pasolini's method is the collage, the embeddedness of things, their overlap. His art is an art of superimpositions. In *Edipo re*, the music is from Japan and Romania, costumes from Arabia and Mexico, speech from Sicily, the fiction from Freud and Greek myth, the characters from the Roman slums. It is like an archaeological site. An all-at-onceness of differences which repeat and mirror each other on various historical levels, but all contained within the one fiction.

There is no outside to the fiction since it contains everything. There is no fictional world either. In the fiction what is marked out is not fictionality, but forms of writing for which the fiction is a stage. At the same time, the writing breaks the coherence of the fictional world.

In *La ricotta*, who exactly is Stracci? Who is this figure who plays the 'good thief' in a film-within-a-film about the Passion of Christ, who dies of indigestion on the cross and of whom the 'director', Orson Welles, says, 'Poor Stracci, he had to die to make us see that he existed', a comment which makes Stracci an analogue of Christ? At what level does Stracci exist? The reality outside the fiction and the multiple fictions generated from it are analogous and interchangeable. No exteriority can be firmly held on to. Stracci is played by an actor who outside the film resembles the Stracci within it. Where can you begin? The 'real' Stracci is born when he dies and becomes a sign, like Christ. This transformation goes beyond fictionalisation. It is as if Stracci enters a pure realm of language. 'Stracci' is the word for 'rags'. Stracci is that, already *in* language, a sign to begin with, the word made flesh.

Stracci is not a representation; he simply is. His qualities as a character ('written') are qualities he possesses as an actor/person (in reality). Stracci is an analogue of himself, hence the writing (the character) can be regarded as an imitation of reality by means of reality. It exemplifies Pasolini's theoretical proposition that the cinema is the written language of reality. Pasolini's characters and the actors who play them are like each other. The relation is the same as between cinema and reality.

> None of them was an actor: they played themselves. Their reality came to be represented by their reality. These 'bodies' in life were like they were on the screen. In reality, he and Accattone are the same person. Accattone is naturally taken to another level, to an aesthetic level, that of a 'solemn aestheticism of death' ... but in reality Franco Citti and Accattone are as alike as two drops of water.[18]

Eisenstein's films, like the Revolution which they sought to serve, move forward in time. By that manner they trace out a progressive temporality which is the temporality of history. History for Pasolini is always now. In it, and by means of it, a prehistory, a pre-symbolic, is born. It is born as an artistic-poetic realm. More precisely, the realm is reinstituted in time and in history. But it also stands against these as their reversal and contrary.

Pasolini's films tell the story of the birth of the Symbolic. At the end of his films, Language is born, and Reality dies. But reality, like Stracci, has been made to exist, has been given life in the story which language has shaped. Language is the instrument for telling the story of itself. In that sense, Pasolini's stories are metalinguistic. They are parables about language. They relate the story of language and the story of the birth of fiction at which language, necessarily, is in attendance. Pasolini's parables initiate a return to a time before history and before language where time is eternal, not progressive. This eternal time is the time of myth, not history. Appropriately, the form of Pasolini's films describe a circle of return, not, as with Eisenstein, a line of advance.

The parable of *La ricotta*, a parable about Stracci and language, is like the story of Christ which it imitates and parodies. In the Christ story, Christ comes to fulfil the Word. His story is a story of events already written whose writing Christ enacts. The story is the story of the return of reality to the writing, in the sense of a debt paid, but which requires the story to be told again for the payment to be recognised. It isn't that reality imitates art, but that art imitates itself.

Christ is a sacred figure born by linguistic means. He guarantees the Word and confounds it. His death, like Stracci's, gives birth to meaning, but on the condition of his death being a double textual sign. It is in writing, that is in the story, and in reality. Reality is predicated by the second story, that is the one of Christ's fulfilment of the original, prophetic story. Christ fills a potential, or, more precisely, an emptiness, the form and emptiness of language before meaning. The fact is there is no beyond to the text, no reality which doesn't return to textualisation and hence knowledge, albeit a sacred knowledge in fiction, in myth, in the paradox of the parable.

Reality can never be possessed directly. It can only be remembered in language, and its loss regretted in language. That is, the instrument which has caused reality to be lost by having translated it into a sign is the only instrument that can recover it and make us aware of it. The cinema, more than any other 'language', was, for Pasolini, closest to reality because cinema imitated reality, transparently. The cinema resembled what it 'wrote'. In a single gesture, the cinema reproduced reality and wrote it. It made reality into an object of consciousness by the fact of turning it into a sign. This was not the manner of Eisenstein who distrusted the mimetic quality of cinema, equating it with (bourgeois) naturalism. It was not that writing effaced itself before reality, as might be claimed for a naturalism, but rather that writing was affirmed within the reality *with which it wrote*. Reality was not external to the writing of it. This idea of reality was the opposite of a naturalism.

Despite Pasolini's assertions to the contrary, the duplicity at the heart of reality in its relation to cinema was the major insight and achievement of Italian neo-realism.

Naturalism is a representational art. It describes reality. Such description issues from outside the reality it describes. Neo-realism generally, and Rossellini specifically, did not work in this manner. Rossellini managed to enter the inside of the reality he filmed. Filming was part of what was filmed and it was subject to it. The scene of writing was included in the scene written. Rossellini's methods were those of improvisation and the sketch where reality was caught in its movements rather than externally fixed. As a result there is no clear demarcation in his work between the subjective and objective. The effect of reality in Rossellini's films – which for some bordered on the miraculous – was not because writing disappeared, but rather because it was featured. What you see in his films refers back to the moment of observation and filming.

In Rossellini's *India* (1958), a film which came after neo-realism, it is as difficult as it was in *Paisà* to mark out the real from the fictional. The difficulty is connected to the inseparability of the two dimensions and their simultaneous presence. For Rossellini, as well as for Pasolini, there is no extra-diegetic, nor any simple illusionist fiction.

The fact of being inside reality made Rossellini's films mimetic while still representational and semiotic. His films, made from inside the reality filmed, imitated the processes occurring in reality instead of judging and describing those processes from a privileged location beyond them. Rossellini claimed no extra-territorial rights over reality.

Modern film-makers have expanded the area of the extra-diegetic, and to such an extent as to nullify the category. It makes little sense to speak of an outside to a fiction where the writing has equal status to the written, the filming to the filmed, the document to the story, where there are no longer clear boundaries between the two, but rather edges which shift, and grate, and reflect.

When, in Antonioni's *Blow-Up*, the camera loses interest in the fictional subject, to pursue its own interests – the shape of a room, a pattern, textures, colour – to a point where the fictional subject is displaced or momentarily halted, this shift away from the subject of fiction still remains part of the subject of the film.

Isn't the writing in the film and of it, never outside it? In a naturalism, the outside would be from where commentary and description are produced. As Bazin noted, Rossellini had no comments to make.

Isn't one of the signs of the modern the presence of writing on an equal footing with the written and not simply as a function of it? Isn't the idea of the extra-diegetic tied to representation? The point about the extra-diegetic in an Antonioni film is that it is not diegetically functional, but part of the subject of the film. Moreover, unlike Eisenstein's metaphoric commentary, Antonioni's journeys from the diegetic completely take leave from it. The sense of these journeys is to define nothing, to describe nothing save their own journey of desire and fascination. It is only writing and hence it lacks all exteriority.

Pasolini was heir to the neo-realist tradition. And this tradition was neither naturalist nor an old-fashioned illusionism. How else could it have happened that Godard, Rivette, Rohmer, the French New Wave, the critics of *Cahiers du cinéma* in the 1950s, above all Bazin, so appreciated the Italians, and especially appreciated Rossellini? These critics, and Bazin foremost among them, were critics who celebrated the presence of writing in the reality of film. Godard called Rossellini's *India* a film of the creation of the world. For Godard, that meant, simultaneously, and necessarily, the creation of the Cinema. Rossellini's *India* was a miracle of cinema.

Eisenstein made his films for a Revolution being consolidated. In theory, his art directly served a society conducive to that art and aligned with it. The aesthetic and the social were not distinct or opposed as they came to seem in the West. Eisenstein's commitment was, in the long run, self-defeating since there was no permissible language for social criticism in the Soviet Union, only a language for an accommodation with the social.

It could not be stated in the Soviet Union, even if it were true, or especially because it was true, as it could be stated in the West, that the social and political were threats to the integrity of the artistic. The crime for a writer, or film-maker, or composer in the Soviet Union was to retreat to a sphere where art was self-sufficient and autonomous, not because in that sphere art failed to serve the people, but rather because in that sphere, openly or not, art served as refuge and criticism of the structures of the social, and therefore of the state which claimed the complete identity of state, party and people. At the beginning of the Revolution, the Bolsheviks may have achieved state power, but they still regarded themselves as the opposition to a prevailing conservative culture and many left artists were still free to be oppositional even within the party. But in the post-Lenin years, the political in the Soviet Union was defined as conforming with the state, the reverse of the idea of commitment in the West.

Pasolini regarded his art as political and committed, yet it is difficult to find in it a political message or a discourse of politics as is so evident in Eisenstein. On the one hand, Pasolini shared a radical modernist position towards the capitalist world: capitalism as utterly evil, vulgar, corrupt, inhumane and unregenerate. On the other hand, he retreated from contemporary society in the substance of his works towards a rural, sub-proletarian, Third World, which was essentially mythical. It was not the world of the exploited, but rather a world inhabited by those despised by capitalism, those useless to it and at its geographical and social periphery: the pimp, the whore, the savage. Pasolini's position in this respect seemed regressive and even reactionary. He wrote in praise of a romantic, primitive pre-symbolic, prehistoric, natural world.

But it was within these places that his ideas of language, of poetry, of the cinema entered, gathered under his concept of reality and of 'the written language of reality'. Against the world, Pasolini posed not simply art and language, but his idea of reality. It was because the world threatened reality (and art) that he asserted art against the world. Even as he decried the modernist and avant-garde conceits of an autonomous art, it was nevertheless the art he theorised and practised.

Pasolini was too committed an artist, or what amounts to the same thing, too uncompromising an artist, to fill his works with messages or political positions, still less a naturalism. His objections to the world required him to construct an autonomous realm from which to oppose the course of it. Messages and a naturalism – commitment in the ordinary sense – are already accommodations.

Pasolini did not belong to the avant-garde. His interest in language was not to dissolve it, but to seek the moment of its formation, its birthplace. That place where it was formed he called reality, albeit a reality he identified as outside language and beyond the symbolic, a reality whose aspects were instinctual, irrational, innocent, unconscious.

The 'writing of reality' by means of reality was a way to make reality conscious, to transmute it into forms. With these forms (from reality) he opposed current actuality (unreality). What constituted current actuality, for him, was the rationalism of economy, society and culture which had rejected and cast out the poor and the primitive and along with them the sacred, and the poetic, installing in their place an ideology of use and functionalism. Form, that is consciousness and writing, gave reality its force against the world. Artistic forms, to Pasolini, were rational forms of the irrational, symbolic tracings of what preceded the symbolic. It was the happiness of the attachment to the Mother before the responsibility of the Law and the Father; but it was also the adoption of the Law as the means to maintain, in the memory enclosed in the text, an original attachment and to mourn its loss.

Pasolini did adopt a modernist position in defence of an autonomous art, and sometimes explicitly, in his period of 'unconsumable' works – the period of *Porcile* and *Medea* – but that autonomy was founded, for him, nevertheless, in reality. His art was the formal, unnatural imitation of reality. He created forms that constituted a second-order reality with which to oppose the way of the present world, and to resist it.

> It is not the office of art to spotlight alternatives, but to resist by its form alone the course of the world, which permanently puts a pistol to men's heads ... every commitment to the world must be abandoned. (Adorno)[19]

Chapter 2

India

I

At the beginning of 1961 Pasolini travelled to India with Alberto Moravia and Elsa Morante. They went to Calcutta, Bombay, Madras, South India. As a result of that journey, Pasolini wrote a book, *L'odore dell'India* (*The Scent of India*); Moravia also wrote a book, *L'idea dell'India* (*The Idea of India*). Moravia's book explains and constructs India. Pasolini's book, as its title implies, senses it.

Moravia remarked that Pasolini's view of India was sentimental. He said Pasolini was nostalgic for a peasant-religious world that still existed in India though disappearing with industrialisation. Moravia welcomed, as inevitable and desirable, the changes Pasolini regretted. Moravia's book has the structure of an essay. Pasolini's book has the feel of a prose poem. What Pasolini offered were feelings analogous to a sense of the sacred he found in India; the analogy was a way to explain without explanation.

For Pasolini it was not by chance that Moravia explained India directly, rationalised it and at the same time welcomed its industrialisation and entry into the modern world. 'The historical world', Pasolini said, 'poses the problem of explanation. This immediately becomes a problem of negation. The negation of the magical world; the negation of homosexuality; the negation of oneself.'[1]

Almost all of Pasolini's films are journey films. In some, the travellers are a couple, as Moravia and Pasolini were in India, one representing reason, the other feeling, one sense, the other sensibility, or the couple is like Sancho Panza and Don Quixote, realistic and idealistic: the sensible Don Andrea and the excitable Pasolini in *Sopralluoghi in Palestina* (1964); Moravia and Pasolini in *Comizi d'amore* (1964); Totò and Ninetto in *Uccellacci e uccellini* (1966), *La terra vista dalla luna* (1966) and *Che cosa sono le nuvole?* (1968). The division between a rational world, which is modern, and a sensate world, which is archaic, runs through all his films, sometimes marked by the couple which gave body to the division.

These were my first hours in India, and I didn't know how to control the thirsty beast inside me, as if it were in a cage. I persuaded Moravia to at least take a short walk near the hotel and to breathe in the air of our first night in India.

So we go out, along a narrow street by the sea that runs behind the hotel, through a secondary exit. The sea is quiet, giving no sign of its presence. Along the wall that contains it are parked cars and near them those fabulous beings, without roots, without sense, filled with dubious and disturbing meanings, endowed with a powerful fascination, the first Indians with an experience which wants to be exclusively like my own.

The tone, the meaning, the simplicity are those of any song sung by young people which you can hear in Italy or in Europe: but these are Indians, the melody is Indian. It seems the first time in the world anyone has sung. At least for me who feels the life of another continent as another life, without any relation to what I know, almost autonomous, with its own laws, virgin ...

It seems to me that hearing that song of young boys in Bombay, under the Gate of India, gives it an ineffable and complicit meaning: a revelation, a conversion of one's life.

At this point Moravia decides that he is now tired and with that marvellous sense of his own bodily needs turns decisively towards the Taj Mahal [the hotel]. Not I. Until I am at the point of complete exhaustion (uneconomical as I am), I won't surrender.[2]

Morante, who played an extra in *Accattone* (she shared a cell with Maddalena), was closer to Pasolini ideologically than Moravia. The closeness was not in the way she wrote, but in her themes: the value she placed on innocence, magic, childhood, dreams, sacredness. Her novels are not merely about such values, these values constitute the quality of her writing. Her novels read like fairy tales, magical stories from the Faraway. In part this is because they are narrated by childlike, almost innocent character-narrators, whose voices Morante borrows and inhabits, the adult finding a place for itself in the soul of a child. From out of the window of that soul she regarded and retold the world, a world fantastic, wondrous, exotic, delightful, everything in it endowed with the magical.

Here is the character-narrator, Arturo, describing his childhood garden on the Neapolitan island of Procida from Morante's *L'isola di Arturo*:

About this garden (today it is the cemetery of my dog Imalcolatella), it is impossible to give an adequate description. One found there, among other rotting things around the carob tree, remains of furniture covered in moss, broken crockery, demijohns, oars, wheels, etc. And in the midst of the stones and garbage there grew plants with swollen leaves, prickly, sometimes very beautiful and mysterious like exotic plants. After the rains, hundreds of noble flowers bloomed from seeds and bulbs that had been buried for who knows how long. And it all burned, as if it had been set fire to, in the dryness of summer.[3]

In Morante, the squalid, the ordinary, the trivial become transformed into the enchanted by a narrator who invests everything with a halo of wonder and joy. It seems effortless and natural. Pasolini had not dissimilar effects. He too gave the ordinary a sacred halo. But his effects were external, intellectualist, metalinguistic. He superimposed sacred music or citations from high art on vile characters, on whores, pimps, on scenes of squalor and misery. However much Pasolini may have valued innocence, there is very little innocent charm in the ways he valued it. His attempts at humour or even grace are strained, even childish.

Many of Pasolini's films are imitations of fairy tales, or are the idea of the fairy tale, rather than being fairy tales. *Edipo re*, *Teorema*, *Il fiore* and his three films with Totò are parables or meta-fairy tales. The consciousness of the tale more than the tale is what is at stake in the telling. This was not the case with Morante or, for example, early Calvino. Though these writers took their distance from the tale and were conscious of what they did, and though neither was innocent or primitive, nevertheless their consciousness is within the tale, embedded in it, whereas Pasolini defined consciousness as an outside to the tale. As a result, he played between a diegetic and an extra-diegetic, always turning back to forms of commentary and self-reflection.

Morante and Calvino came to the irrational or the magical by not straining after it. Pasolini, on the other hand, only had a thesis about these states of being, a desire for them, an idea of them, but the things themselves escaped him, hence his agonies of frustration, his frequent breastbeating, his need to scandalise to make his internal pain evident. It was to the rational that he cleaved, not the irrational, even as he propounded his passionate love of unreason.

Pasolini in fact drew a line between innocence and consciousness, reality and significance. This line and the contrasts on either side of it were at the heart of his fictions. They were fictions about the contrast, hence about themselves, a commentary on their own self-regard.

Language for Pasolini was two-edged: on the one hand, it was communicative, conventional, part of the Law; on the other hand, it was expressive, poetic, outside the Law, a scandal to convention. Though Pasolini tried to reach the irrational, his schematism, his theorems, the poetic theories he consciously built into his work were too heavy to rise to an irrational sublime. He celebrated the irrational and the sensual, but intellectually.

Morante and Calvino told their tales lightly. This allowed them to float above the terrestrial and sometimes to fly. Pasolini's tales were weighted down with exegesis, with theory, with the metalinguistic, with self-consciousness, with his urge to speak about his love for reality. 'To make cinema with cinema or to "place within film the problem of film itself" is nothing other than to opt explicitly for a metalinguistic consciousness: and that is to opt directly for the disappointment of the viewer.'⁴

The most important theme of her writing, Morante said, was 'the difficult relation between human reason and the mysteriousness of reality'. The recourse to fiction, particularly fiction told by a narrator who retained a sense of wonder and mystery, was a response to a feeling that such mystery had been lost in the ordinary rationalist-functional world. This was also a theme of Pasolini's work, but he treated it differently. Morante wrote with generosity, gentleness and joy, free from Pasolini's indignation, outrage, his need to shock. Pasolini was in a tantrum about the loss of innocence. Morante graciously, and quietly, restored in her fictions and in the stories she wrote what had been lost and broken in the world. Her fictions were alternatives to the broken world.

Pasolini was like a frustrated child, she, like a mother making things better. It was her task, and her pleasure, to liberate in her writings the magic of reality, a magic that was not simply the subject of what she wrote about, but was in the quality of her writing.

In Pasolini's writings, joy and sensuality are qualities he invoked rather than possessed. The dynamic behind his work was a desire for a reality which eluded him and for a joy that escaped him. It moved him to continue to write to find what he could not have and knew in advance would be denied him. He structured his writing to long for what the writing withheld from him. Morante wrote to have what she could not possess by any other means save writing. Pasolini wrote to protest at what writing could not provide him with.

Pasolini's writing is nostalgic, regressive, often tortured, angry, regretful. Part of the regret involved the distance his writing took from itself by his intellectualist and modernist recourse to the metalinguistic. At the same time he never gave up the quest for reality through writing. It was a project doomed to be defeated. However much Pasolini declared his love for reality, his writing was separated from it, even fortified against it.

Pasolini wanted life so fervently, but in his work, life was condemned to be only the idea of it. Writing was the mark of an obsessive unrequited desire for the reality beyond it, losing the thing it said it wanted. Pasolini was caught between the desire to attain an irrational real, which sometimes seemed a desire to return to the womb (a prehistory indeed), and an equally committed desire to know, for which history and the Father were necessary preconditions. For him to have truly found Paradise would have been to lose the reason for his journey towards it, which was his reason to write. Only death could have freed him from the discomfort of the paradox at the heart of his discomfort with life.

In his films, journeys are taken which lead to death and the moment of consciousness just before it. For him, knowledge and death were linked. They are at the centre of his theory of film and his contrast between Cinema and Film. His idea of cinema was that it was like life itself: innocent, unstructured, infinite in its expanse, sensual, not significant; his idea of film was that it was an imposition of sense upon life achieved by a cutting into it, at once sad and exciting. Cutting and dismemberment were part of Pasolini's erotic and sadistic joy: slicing into life, reshaping its fragments, cannibalising it, fetishising it, celebrating it, consuming it, acts simultaneously sacred and sacrilegious, akin to the ambivalent consumption of the Host at Holy Communion.

Making things as he did felt to him a scandalous, criminal act, a desecration. Like the cannibal in *Porcile*, he too quivered with joy as he cut into film and reshaped it at the editing table. His indignation at the unspeakable acts of the (his) libertines in *Salò* is ambiguous for it also contained his pleasure at those acts; not only is his pleasure a scandal, but he took pleasure in their scandalousness, finding joy in the naughtiness. What is depicted in *Salò* is done without alibi, without comfort or saving grace.

In Pasolini's short film, *La sequenza del fiore di carta* (1969), Ninetto, joyful and innocent, literally dances down the Via Nazionale in Rome, encountering lovers and workmen, smiling, blowing kisses. As he dances, God tries to call him, in multiple voices, but Ninetto does not hear. The film-maker also seeks Ninetto out, superimposing on his innocence documentary scenes from the actual horrors of war, famine, torture, brutality, exploitation. Ninetto neither sees nor hears. His innocence deafens and blinds him; it becomes a form of disobedience, the opposite of the injunction in the Gospels to those with ears to hear and to those with eyes to see. The state of innocence is not to know even one's own innocence; innocence is self-centred, narcissistic; its charm and its horror are not to know the other and thereby never to know itself.

At the end of the film, God strikes Ninetto dead, just as Christ had blighted the fig tree in Matthew's Gospel.

Only knowledge can save innocence from complicity with evil. Innocence without knowledge becomes an accomplice of the devil. Who can save the innocents, the victims of war, refugees of revolution? Surely not They, not the innocents.

The idea of knowledge in the film is in the form of a parable about innocence and knowledge which Pasolini expressed in his other fictional parables equally about innocence and knowledge. The parable in its structure formally articulates the contrast. Parabolic forms are analogy, rhyme, mirrored repetition, dream, imitation, example. It provides understanding, but by a path which passes understanding, exemplifying rather than explaining. The story of Ninetto is the story of the loss of innocence. But the story itself loses its innocence, gives way to the necessity of knowledge. It is a machine for a perpetual rebirth and death: knowledge is born from the story, and the story is born out of knowledge which it exemplifies and makes manifest.

At the end of *Che cosa sono le nuvole?*, the puppets Jago (Totò) and Otello (Ninetto Davoli), having been killed by the Neapolitan audience – Jago for his treachery, Otello for his murderous jealousy toward Desdemona (Laura Betti) – are thrown down an incline into a garbage tip. The dead puppets seem to come back to life. Otello, his eyes shining and with unbounded joy, gazes up at the blue sky and the white clouds racing by. Jago is also overcome, ecstatic at the sight of the sky and of the world outside.

Otello and Jago had been puppets, born in a theatre, in play, never in reality. The moment they discover reality and the ecstasy of life, they discover their own death, unlike Ninetto in *Il fiore di carta* who died innocently.

> *Otello*: Iiiiih, what are those?
> *Jago*: They are ... they are ... clouds ...
> *Otello*: And what are clouds?
> *Jago*: Boh!
> *Otello*: How beautiful they are! How beautiful they are!
> *Jago* (in mock ecstasy): Oh, heart-rending, marvellous beauty of creation!

They are like Accattone's final words before he dies: 'I'm OK' ('Mo' sto bene').

Elsa Morante possessed the joy of writing instinctively; Pasolini sought that joy painfully. Joy was his desire, not his practice. Morante wrote about Paradise from within; Pasolini glimpsed it from the outside. He was eternally barred from its pleasures which, I think, was his joy.

II

If you have ever been to Indian cities, they seem to be like Naples only with sweetness (*dolcezza*). Calcutta and Bombay are especially so.

I was in Calcutta for the Indian film festival (1994) which honoured Michelangelo Antonioni. There was a contingent of Italians there, some for Antonioni, some on their own account. At parties, there were Neapolitans everywhere and they seemed at home. One Neapolitan, who invited everyone to Procida, the Neapolitan island of Morante's *L'isola di Arturo*, insisted from across a room that I was a Neapolitan. He kissed me, gazed in my eyes with his soft brown ones and rubbed his stubble against my cheek and invited me to Procida.

There were thousands in the movie theatre when Antonioni came in. He was still strong despite his stroke. When you walked with him, he held on to you, but it seemed that he was supporting and guiding you; though he couldn't speak, his will and force were eloquent and stronger than yours.

The Indians gave him a standing ovation of nearly ten minutes. They clapped and shouted and cried. It gave Antonioni tremendous strength and he cried as well, this mocking, somewhat cold-seeming north-central Italian, filled inside with the warmth and joy of India. He was decorated with garlands of flowers. His wife, Enrica, was given flowers too. Red streaks were marked on their foreheads.

In 1993, the Antonionis made a short film in India, *Kumbh Mela*, during a religious festival. The festival is called Magh Mela, but the most propitious time for it is every twelve years, the Kumbh Mela. The festival takes place between mid-January and mid-February at Allahabad in central Uttar Pradesh at the confluence of the Ganges and the Yamuna. The Ganges is muddy brown; the Yamuna is cleaner and green. Worshippers stand in the water between river and sky.

The film recalls others by Antonioni where water is important: *Gente del Po* (1943–7), *Le amiche* (1955), *Il grido* (1957), *L'avventura* (1959), *L'eclisse* (1962), *Il deserto rosso* (1964), *Chung kuo Cina* (1972), *Identificazione di una donna* (1982).

Persons and landscape, figures and ground, shapes and atmosphere change places in *Kumbh Mela*. Persons become part of the landscape, dissolve in it, then reappear. The film suggests the tenuousness and fragility of things and shapes, so important an element in other Antonioni films. The dissolution and reformation are the source of the beauty of his films. Reality is lost to the images of reality and images are lost to abstraction. Out of such apparent emptinesses within which subjects fade away, new figures take form, new images are born; his films, including *Kumbh Mela*, move delicately along an uncertain line between the abstract and the figurative, the image and its subject.

At the close of the Calcutta festival, the Antonionis went to a religious retreat for a month, near Bombay. I returned to Hong Kong, not the place for spiritual peace or enlightenment. Hong Kong is at the opposite extreme to Calcutta ... or Naples. It is close to the nightmare of Lang's *Metropolis*: in perpetual cacophonic renovation, the past hardly existing. It is a city in panic, without nationality or clear identity, without roots, apprehensive about an unknown future, scurrying for securities as much as possible before it returns to China in 1997.

In his book on India, Pasolini made the connection, Bombay-Naples, Calcutta-Naples. He stressed the sweetness and grace of the Hindus: the sweetness of manners and also the smell of sweetness, both sweetnesses mingling on funeral pyres. They provide the ending for both Pasolini's film on India, *Appunti per un film sull'India* (1968), and his book on India.

Morante has a passage on Naples in her diary. It almost seems a *non sequitur*. It follows a passage about feelings and the soul, and the impossibility of them being understood except through something like them: the poetic and magical, or the religious and sacred; it is a kind of homeopathy, a belief that analogy is the way to understanding ... and cure. In any case, the Morante soul was no more a subject for rational science than the Pasolini soul.

Psychoanalysis merits every consideration. But what should one think of that American woman friend of A's [Alberto Moravia], who, like so many young people from that country, go to a psychoanalyst to be cured of an unhappy love affair! How repellent. The dearest, most precious feeling taken to a doctor! It would be a thousand times more preferable to go to confession, or drink a magic potion, or consult witches. Blessed is the land where love is not yet an object of science.

... The great civilisation of Naples: the most civilised city in the world. The real queen of cities, the most gracious, the most noble. The only real city in Italy.[5]

Pasolini shifted the setting of Boccaccio's *Decameron* in his film, *Il Decameron*, from Florence to Naples. Florence was modern, had lost its pre-modern, medieval purity of five centuries ago. The faces, bodies, language of the past were gone. But Naples, like the *borgate* of Rome, for Pasolini, had not lost its purity, or had lost it less. He found an even more precise analogy for Naples in ancient Caserta, the medieval city outside Naples, beside which the Bourbons built a new Caserta in the 18th century modelled on Versailles, to be the centre of their Kingdom of Two Sicilies.

Naples is made to serve in the *Decameron* as the analogue of an ancient Florence; in turn, old Caserta became the still more precise analogue of an ancient Naples. Naples and Caserta were like Calabria and the Italian south in *Il Vangelo secondo Matteo*: the analogues of a biblical Palestine. The real Palestine of modern Israel could no more function as the real Palestine of the Bible than a bourgeois actor could have played the pimp Accattone. Pasolini required the analogy, the likeness, the two identical 'drops of water', Franco Citti/Accattone.

The squalor of Naples, like the squalor of Calcutta (Naples with *dolcezza*), in part guaranteed, and was the sign of, its archaic purity. The squalor was an exact measure of it being neglected, left behind, made peripheral. From here in Hong Kong where obedience and order are the rule, Calcutta seems filled with life and a spirituality quite other than the way of the world. There is a sparkle and mildness in the despair which is not quite resignation, or if it is, it is resignation with a sweet smile.

The reception for Antonioni in Calcutta was extraordinary. Not only on the first night when he appeared, but every afternoon and every evening when his films were screened: the same warmth, the same crowds. Every seat was taken, all the aisles filled, even the back of the theatre and the front stalls. The atmosphere was chaotic, expectant, excited, with a real hunger. The Indians seemingly couldn't get enough of Il Maestro and his works. The wonderful thing was how much they gave him. Pasolini: 'A westerner who goes to India has everything but in reality gives nothing. India instead, which has nothing, in reality gives everything. But of what?'

These are the final lines of Pasolini's India film. They are spoken just after a funeral scene of a body lovingly carried to a pyre, anointed and set alight. *L'odore dell'India* ends similarly. He, and Moravia, on a chilly wintry morning, warm themselves by the fire of a pyre at which, casually, a group of friends of the deceased are gathered.

> Thus, comforted by the warmth without giving offence to anyone, we come up very close to the unfortunate deceased being burned. Never, anywhere, at any time, in any action, during our entire trip in India, did we ever experience so great a sense of communion, of peace and, almost, of joy.[6]

III

Jean-André Fieschi, interviewing Pasolini for *Cahiers du cinéma*, remarked that while it could be argued that the mythical central part of Pasolini's *Edipo re* was a dream dreamt by Oedipus in the framing prologue and epilogue of the present, it could equally be thought, and perhaps more correctly, that the present in the film was a dream dreamt in the past.[7]

The idea had not occurred to Pasolini. When Fieschi sketched it, Pasolini was pleased, laughed, and said yes, perhaps.

The past and the present in Pasolini's work depend on each other. If the one is dream and hypnotic fantasy, the other also needs to be so regarded. The contemporary present, no less than the archaic mythical past, are phantasmagoric in his work. Pasolini played with this fact. He called the actuality of the present 'unreal', and the mythical, imaginary past 'reality'. In *Edipo re* the past is the dream of the present and the present is the nightmare of the past. The dreams are dreamt side by side by an Oedipus within a fictional past. The dream brings with it the desire to know. Oedipus becomes thereby the subject of his own regard in a present, or at least in a position of consciousness at the edge of the place in which he acts. It is a familiar conceit of modern fiction.

It is from the present that the fictional and antique past is dreamt in the film, as the present can be thought of as the imaginary dreamt from the past, as Fieschi wittily and correctly remarked.

Visconti and Fellini, unlike Pasolini as film-makers, shared with him an attachment to an irrational outside the modern, with which they associated the aesthetic and the beautiful; it was also where Rossellini found his miracles. The attachment to the irrational in a past, though it may be possibly thought of as regressive, resulted in a modern use of time, hence a disquieting position for the viewer.

In Fellini's *8½* (1962), the film you watch is the film that has not yet begun, whose beginning once found is found at the end of the film, making everything that had been seen, the entire film in fact, the film's future. The substance of that future is dreams and projections of the past. The film performs, as Pasolini's films often do, in an impossible tense.

When the Prince studies the painting of the death scene during the ball sequence in Visconti's *Il gattopardo* (1963), he is looking at his own

45

future, that is when he will become the past. The past in the future is also the quality of his present. The present slips by in the film, made out of date, internally deteriorating as it is being lived. It is, like the Prince, an anachronistic present. Everything you see in the film, and you see it in such studied phenomenal detail, is in the time structure of already being past, and not necessarily because it is set in a historical past, but because the nature of that historical past is marked internally by the erosion of time. Every object, every person, every scene exhibits a historicity, a fading, and the world is as if peopled by ghosts. The ball displays the beginning of a new era which is also the end of an old. What the Prince sees in the painting, he has seen in the ball. In both cases it is an image of himself as if no longer there, already in the past. It is that which makes his dance with Angelica so beautiful and poignant.

The film is structured by analogous mirrors of time, one of which we hold as spectators. The mirrors, as they reflect each other, establish times more easily felt than conceived: the future-past, the present-past. The mirrors of time internal to the fiction are externally reflected because the film is the evocation of a past. The present you see is only made visible in the reflection in it of a future in which it will be gone.

The fictional dimensions which characterise *Edipo re* also exist, and at a linguistic level, in Pasolini's written works. This is inherent in his poetry. Dialects in Pasolini's writings – Friulian, Neapolitan, Sicilian or Rome *borgate* slang – were languages he recruited from reality, and then rewrote, made artificial, literarised and therefore historicised. He brought spoken dialect into Literature, History and Society. In making the past present and the imaginary real by writing dialect speech and turning it into literature, Pasolini made that speech known, took languages that were outside culture and history and brought them inside culture and history. He thereby shifted the patterns of the Culture. The shift exposed cultural assumptions, not only of class and of language, but also of literature, therefore of the very construction of the social imaginary.

Dialects, though existent in fact, were mythical in the way Pasolini refashioned them. He made them into a dream speech of a time-before-history. It was with that time-before-history that he confronted history. His constructed languages were artificial and fictive. They operated within fictional worlds and were made to seem analogous to a presumed speech in Eden or in a dreamt-of primitive Paradise, the manner, for example, of Accattone's speech, whether of word or body, and also the speech of the film, its poetry of images made to resemble the structure of the speech of Accattone: a language of reality.

In *Edipo re*, the speech of characters is constructed as a pastiche of various dialects; in a like manner the music and the landscape in the film are constructed of fragments of sounds and images from Turkey, North Africa, Japan and Romania. These are made into a collage. The collage, a

46

modern gesture, bears the name 'mythical antiquity'. It also announces itself as collage, that is as language, as style.

The collage in *Edipo re* was no different from Pasolini's depiction in *Il Vangelo secondo Matteo* of Herod's men, some dressed as medieval Knights Templar, some as fascist thugs and some as soldiers from a Paolo Uccello canvas. This military-figurative pastiche, only 'language', is a pastiche that kills, slaughtering the Innocents to the accompaniment of Prokofiev's music from Eisenstein's *Ivan the Terrible* (1944–6). Superimposed on these citations is the literary citation of Matthew's Gospel almost in its entirety, visual ones from early Renaissance paintings (Piero della Francesca) and, in addition, musical and filmic quotes ('St James' Infirmary', the *Missa Luba*, Kurosawa's epics).

The collage is textual and historical. Each term is mirrored in others. The historical and ideological truth of the collage rests in its internal analogies, the repetition of likenesses: fascist thugs, Knights Templar, murderers of the Innocents. The truth and reality of the sequence does not exactly take a fictional path since the fiction is dismembered, made into collage, disjointed: rather it takes a linguistic one, more accurately a stylistic one.

Pasolini used dialect to emphasise its musical, non-signifying aspects; he turned it into an incantatory, trance-like speech. As it lost its communicative and symbolic functions, it gained a concrete reality as pure sound, pure language. The sounds had the acoustics and rhythms of dream. Similar procedures dictated the structure of individual images and the articulations between them.

Pasolini's language was artificial, constructed, mirrored, imitative, a dream language and a producer of dreams. One of its dreams was to dream the language of dreams. It was a language able to dream itself and metalinguistically reflect on itself. So powerful was the dream that it managed to overcome reality. But by being conscious of itself as dream, it was conscious of its own unreality, hence vulnerability.

Pasolini's dream language tended towards the paranoid. It was declarative, hectoring, exhibitionist, prophetic, and absolute. It declared itself as *the* reality and refused all compromise with reality.

Pasolini said of the *borgate* in his interview with Fieschi: 'Here, you see, is somewhere from the Third World. Rome is a pre-industrial city: the people live here as they do in the pre-industrial world, as in Africa, or Cairo, or Algiers, or Bombay.'

Though such worlds existed, they were in tatters, their values disintegrating, their physical character disappearing. In his quest for primitive authenticity Pasolini went from Friuli (in the 1940s), to Rome, to Naples, to Calabria (in the 50s and 60s), to Dar es Salaam, to Calcutta, to Bombay (in the 60s and 70s). Finally, he moved to myth, to never-never lands, lands of dreams, the Faraway. They are the worlds of *Il fiore, Porcile, Teorema*, constructed from the shards and remnants of a vanishing reality.

A collage made from fragments of reality is like the mechanism of dream. Pasolini regarded cinema as inherently dreamlike. His films were made as collages. They became voyages through labyrinths of false likenesses, through a maze of reflecting analogies. In some films tales were embedded, superimposed, as in *Il fiore*, the traveller caught by the narratives, unable to find an outside or beyond to the vortex of fictions which bound him.

Such worlds were phantasmagoric. They existed in a non-time, a before-time. They erased time, made it and history into phantasms. The speech of those worlds, more than of the characters within them, that is the speech of the film, was designed to resemble language-before-Language, a non-symbolic, mythic, impossible, yet poetic speech.

What could such a language say?

In the analytic scene, dream is the subject for analysis. In a film or novel it is the subject of the work. It is the way the work speaks. Such speech is not primarily representational but linguistic, that is a structure for the production of meaning, rather than necessarily a structure with a meaning. Such speech could hypnotise.

What of the bourgeoisie and bourgeois speech? The bourgeoisie seem unreal in Pasolini's work, and nowhere more so than in his last, posthumous work, *Petrolio*. He could not speak them or represent them. They were literally unspeakable for him, unutterable, indescribable and therefore absent. When he thought of them he suffered a bulimia of language, a physical revulsion. He wanted to vomit out the bourgeoisie, expel them from his system. It was a way to cleanse himself of their corruption. By birth and education, however, and in practice, he was a bourgeois writer.

Though Pasolini idealised a primitive world, it was to the bourgeois world that he spoke. He railed against the bourgeoisie for its sins with gestures of an Old Testament prophet, outside the society he scourged with his words and also part of it. His Christ in *Il Vangelo* was a prophet, another Isaiah and just as unpleasant: hectoring, confronting, unyielding, uncompromising, unsmiling. His mother was played by Pasolini's mother.

In his films Pasolini's bourgeoisie are played by professional actors (Girotti, Mangano, Stamp, Wiazemski) unlike his sub-proletarians and peasants who play themselves (Citti, Davoli). In his films, the bourgeoisie are grotesque: the Milanese family in *Teorema*, the German industrialist family in *Porcile*. The representations were dreamlike, albeit horrible ones. They are the reverse side of the primitivism Pasolini romanticised. In *Porcile*, it is the cannibal segments, outside any history, that are realistic and the historical segments, the bourgeois parts, that are nightmarish and artificial. In them, the characters speak verse; in the cannibal segments, they hardly speak at all.

The funereal, hideous nightmare of *Salò* is Pasolini's most unreal film. In it, fascism and capitalism are triumphant. Reason dominates to the point of the complete destruction of all that is pure and innocent. Reason turns into the horror of a demonic, fascist unreason. It is Pasolini's most compelling film visually and his least watchable one: the shit his characters eat, the scalping, the tongue-cutting, the castrations, genitals burned, eyes gouged, masturbation, buggery, incest, killings, mouths bloodied with razors. It is hallucinatory, a Dante's *Inferno* but one made mad by the excessive rationality of the Marquis de Sade. It is not the classical reason of Dante, based on Aristotle and Cicero.

The sub-proletariat is only apparently contemporary with our history; the characteristics of the sub-proletariat are prehistoric, directly pre-Christian; the moral world of a sub-proletarian has no awareness of Christianity. My characters, for example, have no idea what love is in a Christian sense; their morality is the morality typical of the whole of southern Italy, which is founded on Honour. The philosophy of these characters, although in rags, with only its minimal terms still intact, is a pre-Christian philosophy, a type of Epicureanism, coming from the Roman world and surviving undamaged through the periods of Byzantine, Papal and Bourbon domination. In practice, the psychological world of the sub-proletariat is prehistoric, while the bourgeois world is obviously the world of history.[8]

Where dialect speech still existed in fact, and where there were poor people to speak it, Pasolini felt himself in a linguistic dreamland: the Rome *borgate*, Calabria, Sicily, the rural Third World. Even if such worlds were disintegrating, he could piece their left-over fragments together, make with them his own World-before-Language collage. The collage he assembled was constructed of such 'realities': language, gestures, faces, bodies. It had an infantile quality, like building castles of shit.

Pasolini felt the speech of his peasants and pimps to be closest to Poetry and to an earthy real, and he made his collages resemble that poetic speech. It was a homage to the primitive and also a contestation of the communicative, unreal, functional, unpoetic languages of the bourgeoisie: the languages of reason, of modern society, of capitalism, of exploitation, of politics.

I used to walk through Rome and Rome smiled at me. ... The people of the *borgate*: full of life with a speech full of life. The words, the phrases were a continuous, joyous invention, everything that came from their mouths was a pearl. ... A world of fierce and generous instincts.[9]

Naples most of all possessed for Pasolini that language of pure music.

Naples has remained the single great dialect city. Adjustment to the models of the centre, to norms imposed from the top on language and on behaviour, is only superficial. For centuries the Neapolitans have adapted themselves mimetically to those above them, but in substance they have remained the same, preserving their cultural models. ... Luckily. What nation would a Neapolitan feel part of? At least in Naples, something authentic remains. Only Naples has its dialect and its own world.[10]

Pasolini's speech, freed from the necessity to mean and to represent, is palpable, concrete, sensate. It is fleshy, sonorous, rhythmic, bodily. In part, it is composed by the eruptions of laughter or farts from his actors, the sudden glow of a smile, an uncontrolled tumescence. It is also like these things in being outside convention, undisciplined, a brute fact rather than part of a meaningful stream. The sensateness of his images is not by that token sensual or seductive. More often they are repellent, like the pock-marked, fatty flesh of an actor, the ungainliness of a clumsy realistic fuck, a dick pissing on banqueters, mouths drooling shit. They are less shocking than they are strident. They seem like the cry of a frustrated child wanting attention. Often they are merely regressive, an infantile idea of the shocking.

IV

Calcutta is very polluted. Broken-down taxis, buses, lorries fill the streets spewing out diesel fumes and the city is ringed by ramshackle industries. The poverty is unimaginable. At partition, millions of Hindus fled across the border into West Bengal and into Calcutta from East Pakistan (now Bangladesh). The infrastructure could not cope and it still cannot.

At night the air is cloudy with the grease and dust of pollution. You can smell it during the day, watch it pour out of motors; at night you feel it, see its particles in the air. It mesmerises as it envelops everything, coats and mantles the world. The light is beautiful as a result, extraordinary, unreal; the streets seem like film sets of the Apocalypse; there is nothing on earth, nothing like the night light of Calcutta. Everywhere there are rags, piled along the arcaded streets, and empty markets. At first, you don't realise these rags are people even when they begin to move and moan and thrust out to you leprous hands and feet. They seem to be ghosts.

At Calcutta a dreadful vision. One must go and see the temple of Kali, one of the few sights in that grim city without hope and with one of the greatest concentrations of humanity in the world.

We arrived, got out of the taxi and were assaulted, as if by swarms of mosquitoes, by a throng of lepers, of blind people, of cripples, of beggars. We managed to reach the small central courtyard of the temple (without being able to see it, so great was the awful crowd around us: it was a modern construction without any stylistic value), and, getting there, amidst a vortex of rags and emaciated limbs, we saw someone dragging a goat kid towards a kind of scaffold, a divided structure of wood planted on a pavement. A curved blade was raised, the head of the kid rolled on the ground, and the circle of its neck filled with a foaming, boiling of blood.

Life in India seems unendurable. There is no way people can avoid eating a handful of dirty rice, drinking filthy water, in constant threat from cholera, typhoid, smallpox, plague; they sleep on the ground or in horrible shelters. Every morning getting up must be a nightmare. Nevertheless, the Indians do get up, and with the sun, resigned; and with resignation, they begin to do things: to move in an empty void all day long, rather as one sees in Naples, but here the effect is incomparably more miserable. It is a fact that Indians are never happy: they smile often, it is true, but the smiles are smiles of sweetness (*dolcezza*), not of happiness.[11]

V

Deleuze argued that Pasolini's films suggest a potentiality of cinema, an ideal cinema which actual films can only approximate.[12]

On this point there is no essential difference between Pasolini's theory of cinema and his practice of cinema: both point to the same ideal, both are theoretical or metalinguistic. For example, Pasolini's 'Cinema of Poetry' ('Cinema di poesia') essay discusses a raw, brute, primitive ideal cinema which ran beneath the actual existing cinema. His ideal cinema corresponds to his idea of a pre-symbolic, a language-before-Language. His cinema of poetry was a cinema which returned to a primitive writing of cinema, a cinema which directly reproduced reality as reality was before it signified. This idea of cinema rested on the transparency of film, its iconic, reproductive capacity.

The cinema of poetry also contained, necessarily, a subjectivity, the personal feelings of the director, and an ecstatic, poetic celebration of art. Subjectivity and reality were aligned insofar as the objective real was necessarily viewed from a perspective. Subjectivity was the opposite, however, of sense or meaning; it was sensibility, emotion, passion, not signification. It aligned the irrational of emotion with the rawness of the real. For Pasolini, both were prior to any symbolic necessity.

His idea of a cinema of prose was an idea of a narrative cinema whose forms functioned to produce sense. His idea of a cinema of poetry was of a cinema that was more purely art and language, more form, hence more aesthetic and expressive, rather than meaningful:

> ... the prevalent artistry of the cinema, its expressive violence, its dreamlike physicality.
> ... all of its irrationalist, dream, basic and barbaric elements are contained beneath the level of consciousness: they are exploited as unconscious elements of persuasion and contrast: and above this hypnotic 'monstrum' that is always part of film, narrative conventions were quickly constructed.
> ... Visual communication is at the base of the language of cinema and is ... extremely raw, almost animal-like. Just as mimicry and raw reality are almost pre-human facts, at the limit of what is human, so too are the signs and mechanisms of memory: they are pre-grammatical or directly pre-morphological. ... The linguistic instrument therefore on which the cinema is based is irrationalist: and this explains the

profound dreamlike quality of the cinema and also its absolute, unavoidable concreteness, let us say, object-ness.

The 'Cinema of Poetry' ... thus has ... the characteristic of producing films of a double nature. The film that one sees and one normally accepts uses a 'free indirect subjective' ... due to the fact that the author avails himself of the dominant psychological state of things in the film – which concerns a protagonist who is ill, abnormal – and makes of it a continuous mimesis which permits him a great deal of stylistic liberty to be provocative and anomalous. Beneath such a film, there is another film – the one the author would have made if he had not had the pretext of the mimesis *visiva* of his protagonist: a film totally and freely expressive-expressionist.

It is the moment, namely, in which language, following a different and more authentic path, frees itself from function and becomes 'language in itself', style.[13]

The cinema of poetry was what the cinema might be, not what it was, even in the films of Pasolini. It was a theoretical ideal. As Deleuze noted, it was a 'potentiality', and thus a criticism of 'actuality' and an artistic goal. The contrast in the 'Cinema of Poetry' essay between reason and unreason, the objective and the subjective, communication and expression, the real and the ideal formed a familiar Pasolini structure which he played out on a variety of registers and in varied substances.

Much of his lament at present reality revolved around the need to recall the ideal, tempered with the knowledge that it was after all only an ideal, a myth, a dream, a fiction, a memory, desire, longing. But these qualities were precisely the critical strength of the ideal. The potentiality his work pointed to could only retain its critical and theoretical-reflective dimensions, and its political force, by not being realised, by remaining theoretical and metalinguistic.

For example, Cinema theoretically was the 'writing of reality with reality'. It corresponded to Pasolini's 'infinite shot-sequence' which would exactly duplicate the space and time of reality. Film, on the contrary, cut into the seamless writing that was Cinema by disrupting the infinity of time and space of the infinite shot-sequence, by in effect reshaping reality and reshaping the ideal. Film rewrote Cinema, brought the ideal down to earth. The rewriting bestowed significance on reality, gave it a historical and social sense. Film provided a knowledge of reality, but at the cost of reality's disappearance. The knowledge of reality included, and even primarily included, the knowledge of the loss of reality engendered by the fact of it being rewritten in film. Film represented, then, or rather Pasolini's films represented, a consciousness of a lost reality, lost to the effort of making reality known, that is of retaining it.

It is in this sense that Pasolini's films are theoretical. They reflect explicitly on the relation of Cinema to Film, ideal to real, insofar as they reflect on the relation of reality to language.

All films present images of scenes which no longer exist. The cinema plays on a paradox of presence–absence. Images are the memory traces of an absent reality which can only exist again by being memorialised, carved up, disrupted and reprojected. Most films seek to make the absence present by an illusion of presence. Pasolini's interest was not to exploit the paradox, but to point to it. In that sense, his cinema was less language than metalanguage; it emphasised the loss and absence of reality, rather than creating an illusion of its existence. In his melodramatic and reductive association of knowledge and death, significance and loss, the disruption of reality by its symbolic transfer to language, he simultaneously expressed the (sad) loss of reality to language and its (joyous) restoration to consciousness, that is to text, to writing.

What saves Pasolini's cinema from simply being a dream cinema or a romantic poem to the irrational was his theoretical, metalinguistic impulse to bring irrationality to consciousness, hence by that means to create an intensely rational and intellectual cinema, albeit one regretting what he and the world necessarily had lost in the process. But his cinema was not a poem to reason. It was, on the contrary, an attempt to recover a lost reality and irrational subjectivity in the concreteness of an art which was essentially poetic and expressive and whose expressiveness was constituted by artistic analogies of realities he felt reason had lost.

It was a reasonable approach, but not one rationally argued. Pasolini's metalanguage is demonstrative not explicative, analogical not discursive. What makes writing about Pasolini so difficult is that the only effective way to grasp his thought is to find in one's own writing an analogy of it.

In a scene from *Il fiore delle Mille e una notte* a king (Harun) and a queen (Zeudi) are equally struck by the beauty of a young boy and girl, the king with the boy, the queen with the girl. The king and queen each assert that their object of admiration is more beautiful than the object of the other's. What excites them is the desire for another whose sex is the same as their own. What also excites them is the desire to watch.

To decide who is more beautiful ('The girl of whom you speak is a jar of piss compared to my branch of myrtle') and win the wager of their desire, they drug the boy and the girl and wager that the one who wakes and falls in love with the other will be declared the less beautiful because 'it is always the less beautiful who falls in love with the more beautiful'.

They wake the boy (Berhame) without revealing their presence. He sees the girl, spreads her legs, mounts her, enters her, falls back to sleep. Then they wake the girl (Giana). She sees the boy, rubs his penis, makes it hard, mounts him, takes him inside her, falls back to sleep.

Harun and Zeudi watch the double scene of love, from a raised stage above the action. They exit as if from the theatre. Zeudi says: 'Neither I nor you have won. They are equally in love with each other and in the same way.' Harun replies: 'Each is the mirror of the other, two full moons in the same sky.'

Pasolini wrote a short piece at the time of *Il fiore* (1973): 'Sopralluoghi o la ricerca dei luoghi perduti' ('Locations, or the Search for Lost Places'). He referred in it to the scene with Zeudi and Harun:

Unless you are dealing with a *voyeur*, the look of someone regarding two nude bodies making love is not self-sufficient, does not resolve itself in oneself: rather it implies an identification with one or other of the two protagonists in the love-making, and, at the same time, an impossible movement of desire towards the other. The pleasure in looking at a sexual act reproduced – a sexual act which one has experienced – involves also the pain of realising that one is inevitably excluded from it. Thus, to watch an act of love reproduced is like watching something lost which returns, something dead which comes alive. It is to recognise with one's reason what has been experienced in one's body.[14]

The scene from *Il fiore* reproduces sexual acts of voyeurism and love-making. The acts are more emblematic of sexuality, and a lost sexuality, than they are sexual in themselves. The sexuality is transferred to consciousness. It is the idea of it. The king and queen, who view the couple from their balcony like spectators in the cinema, are necessarily excluded from what they see. It is the sense of exclusion, the loss, that is the subject of the scene, not the love-making. This exclusion reflects back on the paradox of presence-absence in the cinema. It is a nostalgic, sad fuck for the spectator-author condemned to contemplate the death of what he kills in order to make it come alive. Eroticism thus goes to the heart of death, and, for Pasolini, to the heart of language. Sexuality, 'at least has the quality of being innocent, prior to conditioning by the social which tends to vulgarise and impoverish it ... the brown Eritrean cock of **** and sweet cunt of **** ... are the most ingenuously beautiful things in life.'[15]

Il fiore is not a film which celebrates sexuality. It is a lament at the loss of eros. The film recalls the erotic as an absence, in much the same way as Pasolini earlier had recalled the lost primitivism of the sub-proletarian in the Rome *borgate* in *Accattone* or the lost brute simplicity of the Calabrian peasantry in *Il Vangelo*. They were records of a presence fading out, becoming past, almost like the impossible sad tense of Visconti's films: the future-past. Pasolini confirmed the absence of eros by turning it into myth. Myth is a second-order discourse on reality, a statement of reality's absence.

Il fiore is the myth about eroticism. Since the erotic and the sensual were what Pasolini regarded as that which flowed beneath the surface of cinema, an expressive reality always there, but repressed by the conventions of narrative, *Il fiore* becomes a (radical) essay, in the form of a mimetic myth, on the instruments of cinema. It is not a film about sexuality which the film converts to myth, but a film about the cinema which presents a myth of a lost sexuality. At the same time, the film, by its very practices, exemplifies that myth. It encloses and embalms a loss. It is a cinema pointing to death.

The subject of all Pasolini's films was the third world whether it was the slums and ghettos in the First World, or the slums and ghettos of the Third World at the borders of the First. This Third Worldness was not a reactionary retreat from modernity or a populist sentimentality, as Moravia said it was; the Third World was no more the primary stake in his films than was sexuality in *Il fiore*, even when Third Worldness was exploited by him to indict the functional rational norms of contemporary modern society.

The Third World in Pasolini's work figures as part of a problem for a European artist of what to speak and how to narrate. It was not a problem particular to Pasolini nor was his recourse to the Third World unique for dealing with it. The Third World was first of all an idea and one that posed itself linguistically. Pasolini always returned in his work to the terms of making cinema and writing, that is to making his films or poetry discourses on language, metalinguistic essays. It was not simply that his writing was reflected in the tale, but that his writing was known by the tale, comprehended. It was the writing cognisant.

Pasolini's social regressiveness and reactionary positions were linked to an artistic modernism. He was not simply, or even primarily, in search of a lost innocence, but rather used that search to pose the problem of how to write, that is the relation of writing to reality in the contemporary world. This problem was particularly poignant for an Italian intellectual who called himself a communist and a Marxist, but found himself out of place and out of step in the new Italy. It was the problem of the commitment of the writer as old as the Italian Resistance, indeed older still.

> What can one narrate and represent? There is a lot that no longer exists: men, feelings, things. ... To enjoy life (in one's body) signifies to enjoy a life that historically has been lost: to live it therefore is to be a reactionary. I expressed for some time now reactionary propositions.
>
> I have resought an old reality in places where I have found a moment where Eros was in some way authentic. Even if I have made it into a fable, it nevertheless has to it the substance of the real.[16]

Pasolini was not the first to seek in fiction the way towards truth and reality even though his fictions directly framed that search since they were mythic, metalinguistic, at a distance and at odds with themselves. Discursive reason and practical politics as he experienced them had failed as writing and as politics. They were part of the modern world that needed to be changed, not the means for change. He turned to a pure, functionless, highly wrought, artificial writing as the only way to resist. For him, those means were uncompromising, absolute and revolutionary, especially his decadent assertion of art over the real, and they made him a modern artist.

VI

In Calvino's *Le città invisibili*, Marco Polo describes the Great Khan's empire and its glorious cities to his emperor and master. The cities are textual effects, stylistic, linguistic, the consequence of a discourse. And they bear the traces of Marco Polo's own city, Venice. The Khan's empire in Marco Polo's description of it in the Calvino book are variants of his (but whose?) Venice. They are transposed nostalgic memories.

The Khan's empire, reported and made literary by Marco Polo, was, in the original medieval travel book he wrote, a European empire resited and narrated. Marco Polo's medieval text was a report of a sojourn most of which was made up but governed by conventions of European travel writing of the period. Calvino's book imitates Marco Polo's which he appreciatively rewrites as a modern homage not dissimilar from his presentation of Italian fairy tales.

In Morante's *L'isola di Arturo*, Arturo lives virtually alone in his father's dilapidated castle on the island of Procida. Arturo has brought himself up. He is his own mother and father: 'So, you have spent all your life without a mother!'

His father, Arturo's hero, is a distant, infrequent, taciturn visitor. He seems a father invented by Arturo, not a real being. The novel is narrated by Arturo. Nothing much seems to happen. What is narrated are his thoughts. Arturo not only seems to have given birth to himself out of nothing – and there is a startling birth scene in the novel in which he seems metaphorically to have done just that – but he has given birth to the language which bears and nurtures him and which has come from out of a silence and an unknown. Stories and language must have been born on the same day.

One of the most dramatic events in the novel is the arrival one day on Procida of his father with a young wife from Naples. She is sixteen years old; Arturo at the time is fourteen and taller than his father's new wife. Arturo tells her of his plans, when he gets older, to travel the world and see its marvels in the company of his hero father. She – her name is Indi – becomes irritated. She tells him that all the marvels in the world are in Naples. There is no need to go further. He believed Naples was a starting point. For her it was the sum and total of all things against which everything could be measured and to which everything would return.

It seemed, for her, that beyond Naples and its immediate hinterland there was nothing that would be worth the trouble to explore, so much so that listening to me celebrating far-off places offended her jealous sense of Neapolitan honour. And she continually interrupted me, in her proud, but simultaneously bitter accent, that there was this in Naples, and also that. ... It was as if all the existing wonders of the world, were, fundamentally, second-hand, provincial goods; a citizen of this first city of the world could save himself the trouble of travelling; it was sufficient simply to be born since the best of everything could be found at his doorstep.

And I began to praise the Crusader Castle in Syria, where in ancient times, up to 10,000 knights had lived! But she, immediately, told me that in Naples there was a castle (fifty times larger than my father's), which was called *of the egg* because it was completely enclosed, almost without an opening, like an egg; and within it lived the kings of the Two Sicilies, the Bourbons. ... And I cited the huge Sphinx of Egypt that thousands of groups of travellers from all the continents on earth came to see. And she responded by telling me about a church in Naples where there was a statue of the Virgin in marble, as big as a giant, who sometimes, when she was shown a crucifix (even a tiny one, like the ones you wear sometimes around your neck), had tears in her eyes. She assured me that many had witnessed this miracle: not only Neapolitans, but Americans, French, and even a duke; and that this statue was visited by thousands of pilgrims, who made offerings of precious crosses, hearts and chains which had transformed the church into a gold mine. ...

I told her about Indian fakirs, and she immediately praised champions of phenomena no less marvellous who lived in Naples! In Naples, in the sacristy of a convent, there was a nun, delicate and slight in her person, who had died more than seven hundred years ago; but she remained always beautiful and as fresh as a rose, and within her glass urn, she seemed to be a doll under glass. ... And in Naples, in Piazza San Ferdinando, there was an old man, with black lips and a black tongue, who could eat fire. He gave his performances in front of cafés, eating handfuls of fire while his grandchildren went around with offering plates and thus this old man supported his family.

'Ask my mother if I am telling lies. You can ask all of Naples if what I have told you are my inventions or the truth.'[17]

Pasolini's written descriptions of Calcutta, Madras, Bombay are marvellous. They are exact and redolent. They have the feel of India, the perfume, the touch of it, the softness of smiles, the gentleness of eyes, the sweetness of flowers, the scent of burning flesh. It is the same with his India film, especially in the panning shots of faces in the streets, hand-held, at street level, everything immediate, palpable, bodily.

His India is like his Naples which is like his Yemen, his Harlem, his Calabria, his Rome *borgate*, the Sassi di Matera, the alleys of Palermo. They evoke earlier descriptions and memories of the Paradise he lost in Friuli which blurred with another maternal paradise, even further back.

Many of Pasolini's films describe a return. They don't move forward but circle around, turning on themselves and revolving on a central rhyme. Their ends resemble their beginnings, or they end exactly where they began, as in his India film, with the same images, at the same place. These circular returns relate to the paradox formed at the interstices of his work between Being and Consciousness, the loss of one for the gain of the other, life in death. In the two symmetrical, interwoven yet separate tales in *Porcile*, one ends with the death of language (the modern), the other with its birth (the ancient). Weird as it may sound, the film recalls Griffith's *Intolerance* (1916). Perhaps it's the image of the cradle.

There are traces in Pasolini's India of his attachments not only to Friuli and Naples, but also to his mother, Susanna, with whom he fled Friuli to Rome and whom he lived with until his death. Pasolini's arrival in India was a return, a repetition of something ancient and sacred, the renewal of what had been dreamt and had now come true. It was just as things had been for Oedipus. There is an eternity in the return. Time is erased. Past and present commingle. In India Pasolini sensed the scent of the analogy.

VII

Many of the things Pasolini thought valuable were ambiguous, contaminated, hybrid in their nature (like the Sphinx). They are thus hard to grasp, as a riddle and paradox would be. They are not one thing or the other, but rather in transition.

For example, his idea of the script was of 'a structure wanting to be another structure'; it is written language, but a writing written to efface itself in images. It moves from a completely symbolic medium (writing) to a seemingly less symbolic one (images). And there was his notion of Film, underneath which flowed that other, rougher, language of reality which was Cinema and which existed not only as a potentiality for film, but as a stylistic/linguistic disturbance of it. And there was his notion of Film as the consciousness of Cinema and therefore a herald of death as it cut into the infinite continuity and pure being of the Reality-Cinema, the infinite sequence-shot.

Pasolini's terminological world was unstable. An attempt to make a lexicon of his terms and keep them in their place would fail. His terms are relational, and the terms shift in their sense, as repetitions do in changed contexts. There is a problem not only in theorising Pasolini's ideas and theories, but in theorising their theoretical practice in his films and writing.

His India film is an example. The film is notational and preparatory. It is not a film in its own right, any more than a script can be thought of as a film. His India film is a film in search of faces, bodies, ideas for a film to be made on India. The film you see is not that film; it is rather 'a film for a film to be made' ('un film su un film da farsi'), as if the script was a structure wanting to be another. They are in an ambiguous time zone which erases its own trace. It is analogous to his sub-proletariat whose passing he fixes as it ceases to be, almost like a death mask put in place just before the last twitch.

This search for things in reality to be included in a future fictional film is explicitly the subject of the film he made in Palestine, *Sopralluoghi in Palestina*, which is a record of his search for locations and actors for *Il Vangelo secondo Matteo*, which he in fact filmed in Calabria because he failed to find the biblical reality he sought in Palestine. He found the past instead in Calabria ... analogically. Most of his films pose this analogic relationship between past and present. What he sought in Palestine, India, Calabria or the *borgate* of Rome are these analogies from a past for a future ideal use, just as his idea of reality was in and of a past, and film and text the future of this past, its writing, with which he could criticise the present. He criticised the present because it had lost the past, that is it had lost the analogy, the only relation possible for Pasolini with which one could approach the real.

The film Pasolini wanted to make in India would have begun before Indian independence and continued through its attempts to modernise and industrialise. He went to India to find the sites of such a film and the people to play its characters: the maharaja, his wife, their children, Untouchables.

The film-to-be would have been a parable on the transition between the old India and the new which would centre on the theme of hunger in the Third World. India, a land of frequent famine, would have been exemplary. It was the example, then, the analogy, and from the beginning, which told.

In the old India, in the film-to-be, the maharaja was to have been out surveying the borders of his lands when he encounters hungry tiger cubs in the snow. He dismisses his retainers, dismounts from his elephant, takes off his clothes, gives himself to the hungry cubs, who devour him. His family is left destitute by this act of generosity. India becomes independent. The family become beggars in a country where famine is endemic. One by one they die. The last one, the youngest son, is burned on the banks of the Benares in South India.

This type of maharaja no longer exists in India. In *Appunti*, Pasolini goes to a modern suburb in Bombay to interview an actual maharajah and his wife. They are bourgeois: sweet, but awkward, stiff, shy, not as a romantic, old-fashioned maharaja ought to be. Pasolini asks the maharaja whether he would offer himself to the hungry cubs and asks himself whether 'my film can begin with this episode or not'. The maharaja says that the compassion of the maharaja in the story and the religious feeling that had been its motive would not occur in today's India. Pasolini then speaks to the wife about whether begging for food in the film-to-be from an Untouchable would be repellent to her.

And you, madam: if your husband should become poor, or better perhaps, if you were to be an actress in the film playing the part of the wife of the maharaja who had become poor, how would you behave among the poor? Would you feel any inhibition? Would you feel reserved because of caste, or not?

The maharaja's wife says she would feel no reserve, and that caste would not inhibit her. But as she speaks her body stiffens, constrained and taut. She holds herself rigid, her face expressionless. She cannot smile. Her voice is barely audible.

The questions Pasolini put to the maharaja and his wife, which he also posed to others in the film, are from a hypothetical, somewhat absurd story which he invented. There is no truth to the story, nor was it designed to be true.

> It may not be true and the family that I imagine does not in fact exist. But it is a working hypothesis which may become poetic: that is to say though it is something purely conjectural, it nevertheless may become paradoxical and scandalous, and thus bestow reality on a 'realism' which is merely verbal and one-dimensional in the documentary part.

The story of the maharaja and his family is a parable. The parable has the power to reveal the truth which lay in the documentary facts gathered in the *Appunti* film. Similarly, the truth of the parable in which an older, sacred India is contrasted to a new modern one is revealed in the interview. It is not revealed by what the maharaja and his wife say, but rather by what they are: nervous, reserved, repressed, conventional bourgeois. The film-to-be-made, for which this India film is the notebook, is present in this unusable segment for the future film. The maharaja is too modern. India has already changed. The sacred has been lost. This was the entire sense of Pasolini's *Sopralluoghi in Palestina* where nothing at all in the film was of use for the film-to-be-made that was made, *Il Vangelo secondo Matteo*, made in Calabria, an analogous biblical Palestine. Reality points to the absent ideal within it.

The first image of the film is a full frontal close-up of a magnificent Indian in a turban with a neatly trimmed moustache and impeccable beard. He is Pasolini's choice to play the maharaja in the film-to-be-made. He is not a real maharaja, but he has the look of one. The look is analogous to antique representations of maharajas in Indian miniatures highlighted by the film. These are like the Mannerist paintings, the Giotto frescoes, the Piero della Francescas which were the models for Pasolini's choices of actors, costume and gesture in *Il Vangelo*. It was the likeness to an image that told, not the likeness to a reality. And in *Il Vangelo*, the actors, the real faces and bodies became citations of Art from one universe and characters in an art of another. The real maharaja from Bombay was beardless. He dressed like Nehru. He wore glasses. He was without grandeur or grace. The person Pasolini chose for the maharajah seemed a real maharaja because he conformed to a figurative citation, a remembered image: reality was in the analogy.

60

In another part of the film Pasolini searches for someone to play the young daughter of the maharaja. His camera, slightly above the faces he scans, goes from one to another: 'This one? Or this one? Or this one?' At last he finds the right one. She looks at him, sweetly, shyly smiles with great softness. 'Yes, this one. This sweet tender little lamb.' But why? There is no reason. Any more than there is a reason for the smile.

As with the Bombay maharaja, the body speaks the truth. It is that truth Pasolini embraced. It is a truth that simply is, and is irresistible.

VIII

Pasolini's interview with the maharaja and his wife in *Appunti per un film sull'India* might have been included in his projected, never made film on India. The hypothetical, conditional tense of his questions corresponds to the conditional nature of the *Appunti* as a whole. If the scene with the maharaja's wife had been included, it would have alternated with its fictionalisation which might have seen the maharaja's wife on the streets of Bombay begging for food, not in a luxury Bombay flat offering it.

Had this been the case – I am convinced that it would have been partly– it would have retained a temporal and narrational structure familiar from other Pasolini films where the present time of the narration would have made itself felt within the past of the fictional story. Pasolini's projected India film would have had a double structure composed of two voices, two styles. It would thus have been like his Friulian poems which were written in dialect but with Italian at the foot of the page, the one pure expression, the other explication. Or it would have been like his Rome novels composed in literary Italian and Roman slang, side by side, insinuating themselves into each other, creating a monstrous, hybrid, contaminated language of mixed substance and history, like the figures of the sphinx in *Edipo re*, the centaur in *Medea*, the man-monkey in *Il fiore*. Insofar as the real constituted a language for Pasolini these monsters were also linguistic monsters, the modern figures of the plurilinguistic.

The search for the person to play the wife of the maharaja in the film-to-be-made is not confined in the *Appunti* to the interview with the real wife of the real maharaja. Just before Pasolini selected the sweet little lamb to play the maharaja's daughter, he finds the mother, the woman to play the maharaja's wife. And before that, there are images of mother and child from Indian miniatures, then images of miniatures which are part Hindu-Indian, part Christian-Western. The choice of the mother is dictated once again by analogous models in figurative representations, in what is already style and language, pre-existing images to which Pasolinian reality was meant to conform.

It would have been, then, this mother, who smiles at Pasolini, who would have played the maharaja's wife in the fictional segment of the projected film, while alongside her, in a documentary segment, and in another voice, would have been the real maharaja's wife playing her awkward, unnatural bourgeois self, being questioned by Pasolini as in the *Appunti* film.

The projected film would have maintained two distinct voices: a fictional one and a documentary one. The fictional segments would have been shot with the conventional illusions of fiction; the documentary segments would have been spontaneous, illogical, realistic, immediate. More or less, the documentary segments would have consisted of the *Appunti* film as it now exists. These segments would have been edited into patterns with the fictional segments of alternation and rhyme between the real locations and bodies in the document and the displacements of them in the fictional narrative.

> The fragments of the episodes in which the story is told will be narrated according to conventional rules. They will be shot and edited conventionally. The fragments relating to the search for locations for 'the film to be made' will maintain its casual and immediate quality.[18]

The double-voice structure is less a technique than the subject of Pasolini's films. It is their language whose principal function is to exhibit itself. In that sense, Pasolini was a neo-realist, as was Fellini, and Visconti, and Antonioni, and certainly Rossellini. It was not simply that neo-realism concerned itself with the edge between fiction and documentary, but that it marked the edge of languages. Hence in the films of these film-makers there is the marked presence of the film-being-made in the film that has been made and that we watch. Is not that the drama of *8½*, and also *Morte in Venezia* which contemplates the passing of Aschenbach as it contemplates the passing of its own melodramatic form in which Aschenbach is entombed? Isn't it the language of these films that is their subject? Isn't this the case in the films of Antonioni when the camera strays away from the fiction to an interest which is formal and abstract, later to return to the fiction to find something has changed, or when it arrives at a scene before the characters do, or departs after they have left? It is made to appear that there are two films in one, as in the beautiful moment in *8½* when Guido, the film director-author, enters the circle of his own film to begin the film that is about to conclude and to disappear, truly liberated.

The maharaja's wife in the *Appunti* film reveals her true social-cultural class position not by what she says but by what she is. Reality, for Pasolini, was always primarily concrete physical reality. This would have been the case also in the fictional segments. A function of the document, especially the document cut into the fiction, would have been to make any fictional synthesis and integration impossible. Thus, even if the person to play the mother would have been an apt mother in the fiction, the fiction would have been so denaturalised by the document as to make the mother reappear not as a figure in a fiction, but as a figure who exceeded it.

Thus, by making the mother in the film-to-be-made fictionally unreal, that is discontinuous and disarticulated from within the fiction, she would have been made to appear in her actual reality in the present. The fiction would have served to dramatise reality by separating reality out from it, as one might trace elements in a chemical solution. It would not have been reality as part of a fictional illusion, but reality as physical fact distinct from illusion. The Pasolinian emphasis on the facticity and physicality of reality, its brute concreteness, is a stylistic, linguistic consequence, more precisely a commingling, where reality is known by the juxtaposition of languages where reality is differentially represented to the point where the real appears in its fullness from beyond the confines of all language, reality as no longer symbolised but purely itself.

The reality of the real wife and, by extension, the reality of contemporary India are revealed in the wife's unsuitability to serve as wife in the fiction film. Similarly, the reality of the woman in present-day India who was to play the wife-mother would have stood out from any attempt to absorb her, seamlessly, within a fictional past. Her reality would have been too strong for any fiction.

Because, in *Mamma Roma*, Anna Magnani was such a strong fictional character, she vitiated Pasolini's desire to star reality as a presence outside fiction yet by fictional means. Magnani's real presence absorbed the fiction of *Mamma Roma*, overcame and dominated the film, as if she possessed it. Pasolini therefore lost the necessary reality gap to form an analogy.

Fellini had wanted Magnani to play Cabiria in *Le notti di Cabiria*. Magnani turned it down. 'Can you imagine me', she said, 'quietly accepting being locked in a toilet all night by a fading film star?'[19]

A central figuration in all of Pasolini's films is the insinuation of past into present and present into past as in *Appunti*. It defines a particularly modern position for the narrator. Pasolini, strictly speaking, is not a narrator of fiction, or if he is, that position is overtaken by his obsession with the language of narrating until the film or writing becomes less a story or work 'about' than a story of the 'writing about', like his *Appunti* film on India. It might also be argued, and I think it is true, that to write about Pasolini directly – given his manner of writing – is to force one towards a writing-about-a-writing-about-Pasolini, which is the manner of his own writing.

There is a built-in metalanguage to all writing, but Pasolini's forces it to the surface, turns it into the subject of his works.

In the compound hybrid of past and present, Pasolini explicitly rejected any place outside his writing from which he might write 'about'. There is no location in his work from which he tried to dominate time and events and turn them into a past, either the illusory past of a fiction or the illusory past of history.

Despite claims to the contrary, I think this is also true for the films of Visconti though in an entirely different manner. And it is true no matter how historical his films are since the melodrama he employed, and which contains the facts and objects of history which he displayed, is pointed to as an equal historical fact: a historical form. Visconti literally reflected the past in his films as in a mirror: he could only do so by inserting into every historical object he so carefully filmed not only its passing but its future, including the future-present of his regard of it, when it would become only a form of the past, a looking glass which would reflect above all forms and time.

In *Appunti per un film sull'India*, Pasolini calls up the past into the present, turns past into actuality, not fictionally, but in fact.

He does so by finding the deposits of the past in bodies and faces which have not yet been obliterated by history. Though he converts what he finds into language, it is, nevertheless, a language constructed upon things still living. It is upon this living language – the 'written language of reality' – that his fictions directly attach. This is what occurs in his *Appunti*, as the film searches for actors and places. The film is simultaneously a social-historical search and a lexical one. The lexical search is for a type of pre-grammar, in the sense given in his 'Cinema of Poetry' essay, that is seeing reality as constituting the basic units of Cinema: the brute primitive reality of objects, locations, bodies, memories, gestures, faces. Upon it, this language of reality, he sought to fashion the grammar of his films. It is the place at which the animal and the human join to form a linguistic centaur.

IX

The story of the maharaja who gives himself with compassion to the hungry tiger cubs and whose own family as a result starve to death in modern India was to be at the centre of the film-to-be-made for which *Appunti per un film sull'India* was the preparation. The film-to-be-made was meant to contrast a magical ancient world, almost dreamlike, and a modern, rationalist one, old India and modern India.

In a section of *Appunti* devoted to sterilisation and the problems of overpopulation and famine, Pasolini interviews workers in Delhi. All, save one, are in favour of sterilisation. The reason for the investigation is that famine and overpopulation are linked to the fictional fate of the maharaja's family. The organisation of the film-to-be-made would have juxtaposed documentary elements, like the discussion with the Delhi workers, with the wandering of the fictional family through India, begging and starving. This was to be the structure for the entire film. The dramatic moments in the fiction would have been 'extended and made to come alive by the documentary apparatus'.[20]

After Delhi, the film moves to Bhavani, a village in the countryside, near Bombay. The scene perfectly expresses the theme of the contrast between an ancient and a modern world. It was a contrast Pasolini saw everywhere and expressed in nearly all he did. It was like the Venice Marco Polo had found in all the cities of the empire of the Khan.

The camera enters the village silently, stealthily, tentatively, not wanting to disturb its ancient sleep. In Bombay, it literally careers its way through the city, tracking, panning, zooming. The voice-over:

> Here is the village of Bhavani. We entered it almost secretly, afraid of breaking who knows what kind of spell. The village was immense. It was immersed in a deep afternoon peace. It was a prehistoric peace not without a certain sweetness which was almost elegiac. The villagers greeted us, smiling. With great sweetness and with a spirit of hospitality that was very moving, they smiled at us. They showed us how they worked, what techniques they used, which were exactly the same as they were two or three thousand years ago. But when we asked them to speak to us about sterilisation no one wanted to know about it.
>
> The villagers scattered, angrily, smiling no more.

At each moment of Pasolini's *Appunti*, there was a reflection back towards the parable of the future film-to-be-made. The juxtaposition of workers and peasants, and the contrast between the ancient peace of the village of Bhavani and Pasolini's disturbing questions about sterilisation in the documentary sequences, would have appeared alongside the story of the maharaja's family forced to contend with a modern independent India into which they are cast from out of their traditional kingdom. Parable and document would thus have mirrored one another, like reversed analogies.

In the Bhavani incident, two realities and two languages would have been placed beside each other rather like the presence of dialect and Language in Pasolini's Friulian poems, or of slang dialogue and Italian narration in his Rome novels, that is as disturbances. These, in turn, would have been redoubled in the central structural contrast of the film between document and parable. The artifice of the fiction would have exposed the truth of the documentary and the documentary would have given sense to the reality contained by the parable. The reality of the Bhavani village would have simultaneously exposed the artificiality of the story and its truth since involved in the truth of the parable was the loss of a world and a world literally unrepresentable because it was gone. Hence, to document that reality, including its disappearance, required fictional means, but of a very special kind.

Like the Bhavani incident, the parable required an external contrast to mark its reality and also an internal contrast as a parallel mark. The external contrast would have been provided by moments like Pasolini's entry into Bhavani, or his meeting with holy sadhus at a monastery, the scene with which *Appunti* begins and which would have corresponded to the sacred world of the maharaja and of an India before the modern.

The internal contrast would have been provided by the inclusion of locations, gestures, persons, faces, in short of bodies and places, in the very texture of the parable: the face of the 'sweet tender little lamb' who is real and who plays the maharaja's daughter; the face and bearing of the man who plays the maharaja; Bhavani as a model village, and so on. These remnants of an ancient reality would have been the lexical material of the story. In the story the ancient reality as remnants would have been made visible. Remnants have a double face. They are the presence of the ancient because they exist and the sign of its absence because they are only left-overs though as irrepressible perhaps as the signs of the unconscious in the body. In the document, Pasolini searched for a lost reality. In the fictional parable he wrote that reality with the reality he had found and which contained its loss.

The parable is a story which is not true, but nevertheless contains the truth, in this case of lost realities. It contains them at a level which is not simply of substance but of form, the form of the parable. Its artificiality and unreality would have bestowed on the story, according to Pasolini, an atmosphere of make-believe, even of magic. Thus, it would have directly expressed the truth of a fabulous and magical world being destroyed. Therefore the parable would have been the truth of modern India. In a similar way the contrivance and artificiality of settings and the narrative in *Il fiore* express the fabulousness of things in that world, and also their actual absence in the contemporary Arab world, except, once again, as shards and left-over fragments from the past. This is exactly expressed in the Indian film. Such left-overs are like holy relics or fetishes. They excite Pasolini with a devotion both lyrical and erotic.

The bodies framed by the film have been dismembered on the editing table like the body of the maharaja torn by the tiger cubs in the winter snow and then devoured. The act of dismemberment upon the film, mirrored by acts of dismemberment within it – and these occur in other Pasolini films: *Medea, Porcile, Il fiore* – are linked to a scene of compassion, of self-sacrifice, of giving yourself to others. It is compassion, but compassion within a world that has lost compassion.

Involved in the eroticism, the editing, the dismemberment are analogies with the sacrifice of Christ and his martyrdom, and also, as with that sacrifice, an exhibitionism, a scandal of the body, of sacrifice and cannibalism, and a social scandal which accuses a world of no longer caring. There is too perhaps the pride of martyrdom, the will towards it.

The parable of the maharajah would have been formed as analogous to the substance of the story those forms evoked. How else to write about the fabulous if not by means of a fable? And how else to write of reality if not with reality? It is the lesson contained in the fable. The maharaja lives in a magical realm and doubly so: by the substance of the fable and by the structural fact of it which reflects that substance.

The maharaja, living in a place which is outside daily, normal reality (a kingdom), and being nourished by an ancient culture (which is lost and contaminated in the modern world), is in some measure outside history.

... In the world (... in the first scene the world appears to us as unreal and fabled: a world where religion is everything and which conforms with all the outlines and all the folds of reality): we are now in the modern world – it is like a degeneration or a deep and general corruption.

Is this not the sense and form of *La ricotta* when Stracci dies of indigestion on the cross having been driven to overeat by a modern Rome which starves him into an *imitatio Christi*? And is not *La ricotta* a modern parable of the ancient parable of Christ's Crucifixion? And does not the Indian story have the same sense as Pasolini's mirrored parable of Matthew's Gospel in his *Il Vangelo secondo Matteo* which imitates Matthew and becomes a type of meta-gospel?

Who crucified Christ in *Il Vangelo*? And who erased the sacred in contemporary Palestine which 'forced' Pasolini to find his locations for *Il Vangelo* in analogies in contemporary Calabria? And who caused the death of the maharaja's family?

These were acts of the modern state. In *Appunti*, in independent India, no one, save a lone sadhu, considered self-sacrifice to the hungry tiger cubs as an act of sweet compassion. The documentary becomes thus the condition for knowing the sacred truth of the story which is the truth of the loss of the sacred and the end of the marvellous except as parable and in the concrete details of its language, of the faces and gestures from out of a past where the sacred had once been the condition of life.

Pasolini recalled two early (homo)sexual experiences, one when he was three, the other when he was five. In both stories dismembered limbs are erotically framed and fetishised. The stories were linked to a secret joy in the idea of being crucified, as Christ was, and so regarded (and worshipped) by others as Christ-like. To be martyred, and in such a scandalous manner, was for Pasolini the ultimate in sensual pleasure.

In the first story, Pasolini was watching some boys playing football in a park near his home in Belluno:

> More than anything else what struck me were the legs and especially in the convex part behind the knee, which was bent while running and which tensed the nerves in a gesture at once elegant and violent. I saw in those released nerves a symbol of life that I wanted to have: that gesture of youth in flight was a sign to me of growing up. Now I am aware that it was an acute sensual feeling. If I recall it I can feel precisely within my very bowels the sweetness, sadness and violence of desire.[21]

In the second story:

> Now I can remember something else, the second step on my journey down there *(quaggiù)* [homosexuality]. I was five years old and my family was living in Conegliano. ... One Sunday evening, mum and dad and I had just come back from the cinema. I was waiting for dinner to be ready and I leafed through some advertising handouts that had been

given to us at the cinema. I recall only one illustration but I remember it with an exactness which still disturbs me today. How I was riveted by it! What suggestions, what voluptuous pleasure it gave me! I devoured it with my eyes and every one of my senses was excited as I tasted it to its depths. ... The illustration represented a man upside-down in the paws of a tiger. Only his head and his back could be seen; the rest of him had disappeared (as I imagined it) in the jaws of the beast. But I believed that the rest of him had been swallowed, just like a mouse would have been in the jaws of a cat. ... The young adventurer seemed still to be alive and aware that half of him had been eaten by this magnificent tiger. Lying with his head back in a position almost like a woman, defence-less, naked. Meanwhile the animal swallowed him up ferociously. Looking at this picture I had feelings similar to those I had when watching the young boys in Belluno two years before, but it was now more pressing and troubled. I felt a shiver within me almost like abandon. Meanwhile I began to want to be the explorer eaten alive by the beast. Often, from then on, before I went to sleep I would fantasise about being in the middle of a forest and attacked by the tiger. I let myself be devoured by it. ... And then automatically, although it would have been absurd, I tried to think how to free myself and kill it.

The link with the Passion:

In my fantasies there was expressly the desire to imitate Christ in his sacri-fice for others, to be condemned to death and killed although innocent. I saw myself hanging from the Cross, nailed to it. My thighs were scantily covered by a light piece of cloth and a huge crowd was looking at me. That public martyrdom became for me something voluptuous and sometimes I was nailed to the Cross completely nude. ... With my arms spread out, my hands and feet nailed, I was utterly defenceless, lost.[22]

These stories, about dismemberment and which dismember, describe an eroticism which connects with the act of cutting and framing in film. The cut is tender and painful, compassionate and creative, and also, of necessity, violent. It violates a wholeness. On the other hand, the viola-tion is the condition for re-membering what had once been whole and intact but was no longer so. Thus the fragments of lost worlds evoked in films like *Appunti per un film sull'India* have an affinity with the pro-cedures of cinema as Pasolini theorised it: the loss of the wholeness of reality (the infinite shot-sequence) in order to reaffirm the past presence of that wholeness in consciousness and writing (montage), the acts that dismembered. Eroticism was this cultural act of writing and violation. It was culture in part as scandal. The sensual did not therefore reside in reality for the artist, but in its dismemberment and later re-formation, even if such anti-real, artificial acts become tinged with a false and entirely fictitious regret.

Wholeness, unity, reality belonged to something theoretical for Pasolini. They belonged to his metalinguistic inventions, and also to his Oedipal sorrow: the loss of the mother, the loss of an undifferentiated real, the necessary and intensely exciting entry into the Symbolic, that extraordinary act of the birth of Language and of writing, and perhaps the act more extraordinary still to Pasolini: the birth of the writer.

> For the sake of expression I have to cut into the shot-sequence, but in so doing I reawaken the consciousness of having done so, of having lost it by creating a sign and yet the sign is the necessary condition for registering the loss.[23]

Wholeness may have been lost and the loss regretted, but the cultural act of the cut was full of joy for him. Pasolini not only cut as other film-makers do, but he disarticulated what was cut, as in the India film where languages clash, disrupt, grate. If other film-makers cut to join and to replace the wholeness they had disrupted by a make-believe unity, his cuts stood out, declared themselves, like martyrs, asking to be lamented and grieved. But the loss that the cut had engendered was not simply to be mourned; it was also to be celebrated, as the cannibal celebrates in *Porcile*: 'I have killed my father. I have tasted human flesh. I tremble with joy.'

The violence of the act lay in the refusal to rearticulate the cuts. Instead, Pasolini framed the consequences of the cuts in order to recall the act of cutting itself. Thus he violated a linguistic and social code by forming an anti-language language, a disarticulation, a language of pre-signs aimed specifically against the Symbolic, albeit with symbolic means. It was an act of personal and thus social disobedience, an act against the Father, and against his father.

More crucially, it was a way to return to the Mother (historically) and to his mother (personally) by gathering up the crucial instrument of procreation of the father in an act first of delicious castration and then of an even more exquisite cannibalism. Pasolini's films are filled with scenes of eating inedible foods, of razor blades in a polenta, of death by indigestion, and by poison.

> I find at the moviola ... an almost sexual pleasure in breaking the code, exhibiting something violated. It is a feeling that I also have when I write poetry, but the cinema intensifies it to infinity. It is one thing to be martyred in your room, quite another to be martyred in the piazza, in a 'morte spettacolare'.[24]

One way to understand Pasolini's return to the Mother through a cultural act of murder and cannibalism which deprived the Father of his power may be in Pasolini's myth about homosexuality. The myth has the same degree of falsity as his parable about the maharaja and the tiger, and therefore the same force of emotional truth.

In Rome, Sicily and, generally, throughout the Mediterranean, homosexuality had its roots in very particular social relations. In the societies of this civilisation, in which an archaic substratum still exists, 'homosexual freedom' is now becoming extinct. It has, however, very deep historical roots. This tradition is constituted from a specific sociocultural reality. Originally, it related to the social hegemony of men which palaeo-Christian and then Catholic and Roman cultures defined in law. This male hegemony doesn't itself explain the freedom of homosexual practices in Ancient Greece and overall in Graeco-Latin societies. Certainly, slave society was a society of men and of the segregation of the sexes, above all at the level of the ordinary classes where women were an inaccessible good, a luxury. Finally, taking all these things together, there is the enormous power of the mother, her archaism, her secret sovereignty. ... In all the countries in which homosexuality is endemic or publicly recognised, the relation with the mother, with the maternal signified, determines a fundamental inversion in the relations with women. Perhaps the homosexual has the sense of the sacred origin of life more than those who are narrowly heterosexual. Respect for the sanctity of the mother predisposes him to a particular identification with her; I would say, in fact, that at the core of the homosexual there is, unconsciously, a reassertion of chastity: the desire for purity. In a rather obscure way the homosexual seeks himself in the other (the other-same), a partner with whom he does not risk reproducing the terrible power of the father, of the profaner. I would say that the homosexual tends to preserve life, not contributing to the cycle of procreation-destruction, but rather substituting the coherence of a culture, the continuity of consciousness, for the survival of the species.[25]

Pasolini's homosexuality involved an ambivalence towards his mother (Mother) and his father (Father). That ambivalence and its paradox were expressed in all his work the subject of which was the paradox. He called it 'the unnaturalness of reality'.

The court cases, scandals, trials for obscenity, moral offensiveness, blasphemy that shadowed his work were, from his point of view, the consequence of having violated the Code, and not only in the body of his work, but in his actual body, in his homosexuality. It was that body he thrust forward in composing works formed of the dismembered limbs of others into which he entered. Among other things, as every martyr and prophet possibly experiences, it made him feel good, righteous, sacred even, like the obedient-disobedient Son of God who gave Pasolini the symbolic to eat as his flesh and blood.

If a maker of verses, of novels, of films, finds himself honoured, accepted or understood in the society in which he works, he is not an author. An author can only be a stranger in a hostile land: he in fact cultivates death rather than accustoms himself to life and the feelings he provokes in others are feelings more or less strong of racial hatred.[26]

X
Rossellini:

> One must get to this extreme point where things speak for themselves. Which does not mean that they alone speak, but that they speak of what they really are. When you show a tree, it must speak to you of its beauty as a tree, a house of its beauty as a house, a river of its beauty as a river. Men and animals too. A tiger, an elephant, a monkey, are as interesting as a gangster or a society lady. And vice versa.[27]

In the tuna-fishing sequence in *Stromboli*, however narratively relevant the sequence is and however much it is therefore fiction, the actions of the fishing for tuna overpower the narrative and become pure fact, like a document: the laying of the nets, the wait for the fish to swim into them, the hauling in of the nets, the scramble of the tuna as they are caught, the prayer of thanksgiving. The beauty of the event as real stands out against the event as fiction. It escapes a fictional grasp long enough to speak of what it really is.

This is also true in the final sequence of the film on the slopes of the volcano. The grandeur of the volcano not only overpowers Karin, but overshadows the fiction in which she is caught. It is as if in the presence of reality everything crumbles.

Fiction is a Rossellinian means to approach reality. Rossellini acted not unlike his Stromboli fisherman who established conditions for the tuna to be caught, then waited for the miracle of the tuna's appearance. The miracle in Rossellini's films is of this type. Reality appears suddenly and inexplicably from within the heart of the fiction to the degree that the fictional is momentarily cancelled out. It is a matter of a stage being set with the help of fictional conventions (language) to enable reality to enter until those conventions are lost before the force of the reality they have been instituted to find.

The miraculous appearance of reality coincides with the disappearance of the language which was present at reality's birth. It seems that at that instant all signification, indeed the Symbolic itself, is overwhelmed.

In the late teens and early 1920s, Robert Flaherty spent nearly ten years, in part as explorer, among the Eskimos in Canada's northwest, at Hudson Bay. He made a film of Eskimo life. The footage ignited in the editing room and was completely lost. Flaherty returned to Hudson Bay. He spent two years with an Eskimo family. The result was *Nanook of the North* (1922). The film follows Nanook and his family in their normal daily activities.

The narrative is extremely slight. The protagonists of it were as much the ice floes and windswept snow and bleak environment of Hudson Bay as they were Nanook and his family trying to cope with that environment.

Most of the scenes are of practical activities: hunting seal, catching fish, killing a walrus, building an igloo, feeding the huskies, protecting the husky pups. The hunting and fishing scenes, like the tuna sequence in *Stromboli*, depend on patience and waiting. The walrus has to be slowly and carefully stalked. At the moment it tries to flee, Nanook springs with his harpoon. And the walrus has to be fought while still in the sea until it dies, the walrus herd wailing in anguish, at a pitiable short distance, one of the female cows locking tusks with the male to free him from death. Slowly the Eskimos pull the two-tonne walrus to shore, slice it up, there and then begin to eat it.

The fish are speared with a small trident harpoon. Nanook waits above an opening in the ice, jiggling a shiny lure, then spears the fish as they come near it, hauling them out of the water, digging his teeth into the space behind their gills to kill them, then smiling at the camera, as he does when he eats the walrus.

The hunting of the seal is perhaps the most famous of the sequences in the film, in part because it fits with a realist notion which argued that montage was the enemy of the cinema and that true cinema, as Bazin enunciated the concept, 'depends upon a simple photographic respect for the unity of space'. The entire process is filmed in a single long sequence-shot: waiting for the seal, harpooning it, fighting it, hauling it up through the ice. In fact, the scene was faked. The seal Nanook struggles with was already dead.

Helen Van Dongen, who worked with Flaherty as an editor on *The Land* (1942) in the 30s and on *Louisana Story* (1948) after the war, grew exasperated with Flaherty:

> As a realistic matter of time was involved, I could not forever let him indulge his enjoyment of unarranged rushes. Sometimes I suspected that he would be perfectly content to do nothing but shoot, screen whatever he shot, and bewitch everyone with his enthusiasm about 'what a wonderful film this will make'.[28]

Flaherty spent day after day, and hours each day, watching the rushes for *The Land*. The film was meant to celebrate the agricultural achievements of the New Deal. It became a film poem to the victims of dust-bowl agricultural devastation. Flaherty was unable, or unwilling, to edit the rushes into a clear pattern or narrative shape. It was as if any pattern of meaning might disturb the images from having their say. He watched the rushes waiting for a sense to emerge, rather like Nanook waited for the walrus.

Most of the scenes in *Nanook* actually occurred and were not staged, and were typical of Eskimo life. Indeed, they were a necessary part of that life. The animals the Eskimos killed and ate in front of the camera had to be killed in order for the Eskimos to survive. It was the same with the igloo they built. In one instance, Nanook and Flaherty travelled 600 miles by kayak and dog-sled to hunt polar bear. They never found bear and nearly died trying to get back. Two years after the film was made Nanook died of starvation.

The matter of staging was extreme in *Man of Aran* (1934). The bleak rocky Aran islands lie off the coast of Ireland. The islanders were suffering economic hardship largely to do with conditions related to absentee land-lordism. It was 1934, the midst of a world depression and political reaction. Flaherty ignored the social issues, and social issues generally; for this John Grierson and Paul Rotha, who felt they had responded to political and social realities in their films, condemned him: 'a reactionary return to the worship of the heroic'. 'Surely we have the right to believe that the documentary method, the most virile of all kinds of film, should not ignore the vital social issues of this year of grace.'[29]

Though Flaherty's film privileged the archaic against the modern and for that reason might deserve to be called reactionary, something else was at stake: an aesthetic which he attached to the archaic and the elemental, and from which his aesthetic derived its power. That aestheticism verged on a social meaninglessness, on values which were timeless and mythic, whereas Rotha and Grierson wanted their films directly to signify socially. Flaherty's work was doubly useless in this regard. He had composed a film poem to a primitivism that no longer existed or, if it did, existed so marginally as not to matter historically or socially. In the circumstances of fascism and depression, Rotha and Grierson felt something more muscular was required, certainly more clearly committed.

This was a similar situation with the editing of *The Land*. The film was commissioned in the late 1930s. By the time Flaherty released it and had made his mind up about the editing and its patterns, social events, including a world war, had bypassed its social relevance. The agricultural administration had long since lost interest in the film.

Fifty years before Flaherty made *Man of Aran*, the islanders had hunted basking shark for lamp oil. They hunted from small rowing boats using harpoons – not unlike Nanook. The barren harshness of the Aran landscape and the struggle with it also recalled the earlier film. The island was windswept, the seas extraordinarily rough and dangerous. Nor was there soil on the island. Women and donkeys are shown in the film piled high with baskets of seaweed which the women had gathered at the shore to be rotted down for soil to grow potatoes. There was no grass, no trees.

Flaherty hired an expert in basking shark hunting to teach the islanders their lost skill. The hunt for the shark – vast schools numbering in the hundreds swim past the islands once a year – was at the centre of the film. It was not only staged, like the seal hunt in *Nanook* and the tuna fishing in

Stromboli, but it no longer had any contemporary social reality or importance, even less, perhaps, than the story of the maharaja and the tigers did for contemporary India in Pasolini's film.

Nanook and *Man of Aran* are in a film tradition where documentary truth depends on distortions of reality not unlike the procedures of fiction. But whereas the fictional film – including *Stromboli* – tended to incorporate reality into a story, Flaherty's stories were devised primarily to link natural occurrences. His slight narratives were pretexts for the framing of reality even if that reality was often invented. His narratives were settings for scenes from the real. Reality was not given to the fiction to make the fiction seem more true, but rather fiction was on loan to the real in order for the real to be brought out. Flaherty engineered his scenes, but not for illusory effect. He was concerned not with factual accuracy, but with 'the truth': 'One has often to distort a thing to catch its true spirit.' This tradition also belongs to Rossellini, especially his *India*.

Man of Aran directly inspired Pasolini's proposed film on India for which *Appunti per un film sull'India* was the pre-text. Pasolini said *Man of Aran* was the technical and stylistic model for his India film: 'The film ought thus to be, above all, a documentary whose images, arranged in a dramatic rhythm, insert themselves into the story, making themselves one with the story, in a double function of justification and liberation.'[30] The other model was Rossellini's *India*.

In Rossellini's *India* the event has an original, pristine power. It is as if what is being seen does not issue from a form or a language, but is prior to any form, or rather it is formed in that instant. The image is always fresh. It is not simply that you see it for the first time, but rather that it seems to be the first time it has happened. Few images in the cinema are ever that spontaneous and particular. The event is as if stripped of anything but itself including the camera that brought it into being. Rather than watching a film, it seems you are watching the universe begin. Godard said that *India* was 'as beautiful as the creation of the world'. The Creation is difficult to describe.

In a Pasolini film, though the event often has the quality of being part of a parable, or a fairy tale, or make-believe, it is only these things metalinguistically. The Pasolini event has already lost its innocence. At best, there can only be a parable of innocence in Pasolini, never innocence itself. This is especially so because his parables, more often than not, are about lost innocence.

There is an excess in his films. The fact that the parable is metalinguistic involves a deficiency. The innocence within the parable must be pointed to as an example of innocence. Innocence without understanding risks being missed. Pasolini needs to lose it in order to retain it. His sacred frames, citations from high art, analogies, imitations, masquerades, feints, mirrors are devices to explain something which is not self-sufficient even though Pasolini's explanations take the form

74

principally of mimetic examples. His events, then, are second order. They have been refashioned, thought over and are always declarative of their linguistic-stylistic texture.

The Rossellini event seems genuinely pure. There is nothing beyond it as a metalinguistic excess or anything less than it for which it is the compensation. In short, it does not seem to function like a sign. It is not the expression of a reality greater than itself or more particular than itself, nor does it invite commentary, nor does it represent. It seems simply 'to be'. The event puts a stop to language and signification because of its total adequacy. This is the sense, I think, of Godard's remark.

Take the scene in *India* of the elephant trainers scrubbing down the elephants, and later working with them for logging. Or take the scene of the old man in harmony with the simplicity and sublimity of nature. These scenes of harmony between people and nature, where culture is devoted to nature rather than committed to alienating it, present a world as pure and innocent as that of Rossellini's Franciscans in *Francesco, giullare di Dio* (1950). This purity has to do not with the subject, but with the 'fact'. This fact is aesthetic. It is a certain way of creating a scene irrespective of its content. Or, more exactly, the reality seen is seen for what it is. The aesthetic and the content are virtually the same. For that reason it seems that the sign as representation has disappeared. Quite simply, it ceases to be necessary. It is the redundancy of the sign that indicates the adequacy of reality to the image.

Only in *Nanook* does Flaherty come close to Rossellini. In *Man of Aran* there is too much aestheticising, too much a sense of beauty and the romantic. They tend to overcome the reality being romanticised, as if Flaherty had sensed Rotha and Grierson's criticisms. Hence the need for justifications even though Flaherty didn't agree. His images have built-in alibis, albeit the alibis of photographic beauty and the primitive simplicity of Man.

Flaherty's protest against modernity in the choice of his unmodern subjects and his lyrical photographic romanticism was probably the source of much of Pasolini's admiration for him. In the specific case of *Appunti*, however, and the projected Indian film, it had to do also with the visibility of that line in Flaherty between the fictional and the documentary, especially since the line had been formed, if not by making his subjects sacred, at least by making them heroic. In any case he sketched a halo for them, as Pasolini had for his pimps and whores.

The man of Aran, dressed in his tam-o'-shanter and sailcloth trousers, and Nanook in his polar bear furs and wearing the sealskin boots his wife had chewed soft that morning, are Greek heroes, epic warriors, legendary paladins. The killing of the walrus, the hunting of the basking shark are tales from Homer. These heroes are made of more than they are in order to be who they are. It was exactly the contrast, and paradox, that Pasolini was fond of. It was instructive.

Pasolini:

> The non-violence, in short the gentleness, the goodness of the Hindu. They perhaps have lost contact with the direct sources of their religion (which is evidently one that has degenerated) but they continue to be living examples of it. Thus, their religion, which is the most abstract and philosophical in the world in theory, is, now, in reality, a totally practical religion: a way of living.
>
> One reaches a kind of paradox: the Indians, abstract and philosophical in their origins, are actually a practical people (though of a practicality that allows them to live in an absurd human situation), while the Chinese, practical and empirical in their origins, are actually an extremely ideological and dogmatic people (permitting them practically to resolve a human situation that seems unresolvable).[31]

In *Chung Kuo Cina*, a film nearly four hours long recording the journey of Antonioni's camera through China, there is seldom a smile. Occasionally, there is the spark of one, but this is generally as rare in the film as is the infrequent flash of colour in it. China is either without colour or has been drained of it in Antonioni's images.

Colour, and smiles, only fully enter *Chung Kuo Cina* in the final sequence. The audience file into a theatre in Shanghai to watch a theatrical-acrobatic troupe, much as the audience take their seats in Vertov's *The Man with a Movie Camera*. The screen erupts with colour. In life, in Antonioni's China, it is misty grey, soft blue, pastel green. In the theatre, it is red, yellow, bright blue and filled with joy. During each act and after the incredible displays of plate throwing, acrobats leaping, acts of balancing, the actors smile and laugh and so do the audience. Balance and equilibrium are Antonioni themes, sometimes literally represented: the black nightclub entertainers in *La notte* (1960), Aldo falling to his death from the tower in *Il grido*.

It is not fair to generalise about an entire people, especially one you can only know from the outside. To many Westerners the exterior of most Chinese is like a wall behind which everything may go on, but not much registers on the surface. There are hardly any apertures or gaps left open for the internal to become visible.

On the street, in shops, on public transport, in most daily contact, the Chinese body seems a casing holding itself in, keeping it firmly intact, pressed in on itself. There are rarely smiles, flirtations, acknowledgments, looking, exchanges of glances, a touch of eyes, even the most minimal politenesses. There are beautiful bodies, often exquisite bodies, but few relaxed ones. Often, you feel yourself invisible amid the crowds around you in a world from which you are systematically excluded. But the Chinese also seem excluded from the world, as if there are no bodies, no life despite the frantic activity.

Chinese physical reserve is difficult to become accustomed to. It is a reserve which seems to have resulted in an extraordinary productive power.

What does not come to the surface is concentrated internally. It produces enormous energy for work, responsibility, effort, devotion, self-sacrifice and gain. Hong Kong is an example of it, as are Taiwan and Singapore. Now it is China's turn.

A fragment of the second intertitle from Flaherty's *Nanook of the North*: ' ... the most cheerful people in all the world, the fearless, happy-go-lucky Eskimo'. Nanook grins from ear to ear as he eats the raw flesh of the walrus he has just killed. As Nanook teaches his son to use a bow and arrow, they both smile. Nanook laughs as he hunts, ecstatic as he fits a block of ice into his newly made igloo. The final block which completes the igloo is crowned with Nanook's beaming grin, as when he eats walrus or fish. His wife smiles perpetually.

Nanook is a film that glows with the warmth of the Eskimo smile. The grace and simplicity of the film are attached to the graciousness of that smile and the physical suppleness and poise of the Eskimo body. It is a body relaxed even in the most tense situations, and however swathed in furs and sealskin.

From Pasolini's *L'odore dell'India*:

In the meantime there was someone near me who I observed. He was an old man with long hair bound in a fetid turban who had a great black beard; he was wrapped in white rags and looked at me, with a kind of grin ...

I understood that it was a smile of complicity.

It is correct that the Indians are never joyful; they smile often, it is true, but these are smiles of sweetness, not of joy. ...

Seen from the distance of time Indians fix themselves in your memory with their gesture of assent and with that infantile and radiant smile in their eyes that accompanies it. Their religion is in this gesture. ...

Now he was there beside us, looking at us with a shrewd and sweet smile: it was somewhat askance, as he ran obliquely, with his white clothes of an angel fluttering around him. ...

He followed us, and while he left the rickshaw we went towards the shops on the waterfronts. He watched us as we bargained with a boatman, and, when we were getting into the boat, he was there, looking at us with the whites of his eyes and teeth fixed in a sugary smile. ...

And he continued to say no, with his happy smile. ...

All the joy of the hour and of the moment were contained in those dark eyes which glowed from out of those dark faces, and in those tender and humble little faces. They looked at me and Moravia, slightly askance, and then turning on us the fullness of a smile. They didn't dare speak to us and we were also silent, almost for fear of interrupting that current of sympathy, which, by being silent, was full. They seem to have also understood, both masters and students, that the best thing to do was to look and smile, in silence. …

'But how many roads are there yet to travel! Our villages are made of mud and the manure of cows; our cities are only markets without form, all dust and squalor. Diseases of every kind threaten us, smallpox and the plague are in our houses, like snakes. And hidden there are so many small brethren for whom we cannot find even a fistful of rice to share. What will happen to us? What can we do? However, in the midst of this tragedy, there is in our souls something which if not joy is almost joy: it is a tenderness, a humbleness towards the world, and love. … With this smile of sweetness, you, happy foreigner, once returned to your own country, will remember us, we poor Indians.'[32]

There are passages like this on nearly every page of Pasolini's *L'odore dell'India*, filled with the smiles of India. It is the case too for Pasolini's India film, a film of smiles, grins, smirks, giggles, laughter. The smile is irrepressible. It wells up in bodies involuntarily and breaks their surface. It comes from a psychic-social interior which changes the face of things. It is the body out of social control, brightened by laughter; in extreme instances, it is distorted by laughter.

The smile is the most frequent and ubiquitous sign in Pasolini's films. They are displays of laughter, of faces brought to tears by laughter, characters convulsed with it, their bodies rolling on the ground, arms flailing about: the scene in *Accattone* of Cartagine responding to the joke about his smelly feet; Mamma Roma at the opening banquet mocking the Last Supper, leaning in her chair, roaring with laughter, banging the table, her head thrown back, grabbing little Ettore, wheeling him about, laughing and smiling. In a final eruption of her body, she dances with Ettore in her joy at liberation from her pimp, in her happy love for her son, for the ecstasy of her physical release. It is her body which speaks, and through it, principally, her laughter.

A slightly embarrassed smile from an extra in one of the two Deposition scenes in *La ricotta* grows into a laugh until it sets off the entire troupe into uncontrollable gales of mirth. Not only are they unable to contain their own bodies, but they lose hold of the body Christ who tumbles down from the Cross, cracking up with laughter like the others. It is the neuralgic bodily point of the laughter that causes the film of the Passion and the Christ of that Passion to fall from their fictional places towards the reality of the set, outside the rules of fiction and the boundaries of the diegetic. From the set the fiction was initiated. Now, from the set it is convulsed with laughter. Laughter becomes a scandal of the body against its fictionalisation.

Anna Magnani's body is forever bursting its boundaries in *Mamma Roma*: laughter, anger, hysteria, dancing, song, grimaces, tears, anguish. It is a body which gets the better of her even as she tries to discipline herself and her son into the repressed controlled ways of lower middle-class respectability.

In the Last Supper sequence which begins *Mamma Roma* characters are eating and drinking. Nourishing the body has the effect of liberating it from necessity and the practical. The celebratory banquet is also a celebration of the body. To eat and drink to excess and for no reason but the pleasure of it is a means to lose control of the body – being fed as if food and drink were generating a life force within it which the social cannot fully contain.

Mamma Roma's behaviour is not only a travesty of proper behaviour and all the disciplines of the body, but it is a travesty of the Last Supper which frames it and of the form of that supper in the Leonardo painting. The life that is expressed by Mamma Roma is made of vulgarity, excrement, food, dance, digestion, sex, song, poetry, a vital force that belongs in the film with the people. Laughter is the people expressing itself – it is never polite – and in a language not only earthy, but mixed, plurilingual. Her body, and it is the body of a whore, is against convention, social repression, against all that is one-directional and functional. Her body goes beyond the bounds of the necessary.

The bodily excess of the characters, which is a linguistic-stylistic excess of the film, is a feature of the composition of the scene which contaminates high art with low life, the figurative and the cinematic, the spiritual and the terrestrial, the diegetic and the extra-diegetic. However much the scene of the Last Supper is high art, it is also structured as a homage to the language of the characters and social world they fictionally inhabit: the characters overwhelm the boundaries of the fiction with that other language, which Pasolini considered natural, real, corporeal, and which bursts forth towards the reality of the set, hence to the reality of the characters as persons, as whores, pimps and thieves, as the real-life figures of the *borgate*. These realities form the fictional scene, but, as in *La ricotta*, they return to their origins and so belie the fiction, explode it.

The smile, as Pasolini used it, is that which is socially uncoded, hence a disruption of the social. Insofar as he associated it with life, the people, the real, the irrational, it was a perfect sign for, and parable of, the Third World. The smile is that which remains even after the facts of modernisation and industrialisation have done their repressive work and it is that which he seeks in *Appunti*, and which he seems to find. To write of it is to share in that smile.

XI

In *Salò*, the bodies of the innocent young are humiliated, besmirched, torn apart, violated, entered, solely for the pleasure of the bodies of the decadent old. It is the exact opposite to the celebration of bodies in the *Trilogia di vita*: *I racconti di Canterbury*, *Il Decameron*, *Il fiore delle Mille e una notte*. The society formed by the law of the libertines in their *palazzo* of sadism in *Salò* is hermetically sealed against the outside world. The laws are absolute and anti-social. And they are rigorously, obsessively enforced. The laws govern the body in the smallest details and avenge themselves against the body, all its surfaces, openings, functions, desires. To shit without permission was a crime, certainly to fuck, especially a heterosexual fuck.

Il fiore is composed of embedded tales whose pleasure is in avoiding the law in the pursuit of desire. In *Salò*, only the fascist libertines are permitted to desire. Their captive children can only suffer it, forced to obey the law of it. That law is instituted from the beginning as the libertines read out the codified terms of their will. Everything is measured, calculated, annotated, described, written down, catalogued. It is the rule and madness of reason.

Il fiore tells the magical tales of a magical universe. It is not the rational law which prevails but its contrary. Men become monkeys, carpets fly, mountains move, and the devil appears from nowhere. The film depicts a magical world and exemplifies it. The Law is broken in the telling and in the told. Magic is not only depicted, but governs the manner of depiction. Tales beget tales and just as the devil's flight defies logic so too do the tales. They connect by fantasies, improbable inventions, by fabulous analogy, not a rigid calculus. The stories are wonderfully untrue. In *Salò* the story is unwatchably real. It is a film-poem to death and the perversity of reason. *Il fiore* belongs instead to to happy pleasures, sexual exuberance, irrational, unexpected, unplanned desire.

Il fiore is based on a medieval Arab text. The locations in the film are in Africa, the Middle East and Asia. It is a mythical collage of an ancient world when, Pasolini believed, there was still magic, a sense of the sacred, the ability to write tales like the one he had transposed into images, a world which thought and wrote in fables, not yet fully committed to function, where there was still the presence of realities in language, where things had the power to conjoin and conjugate as if objects generated a grammar. It was a time for Pasolini still at the edge of history before the full institution of the symbolic, a mythical time of innocence and play. It was a lost world of his invention which he saw from the distance of the loss, hence it was tinged with regret and nostalgia. It was an invention of joy, but invented to lament. He brought the world to life, but it was marked by its death.

The soul Pasolini found in the Third World and composed poems to, he had found earlier in the Rome *borgate* and with the Calabrian peasantry. He also found it among blacks in America. Much to his surprise, because his idea of a capitalist, uniform, homogenised America was so negative, he was delighted with New York, particularly with Harlem. There he found not the First World, but the ghettos of the Third. He made friends with Allen Ginsberg and given time he would have discovered Whitman.

In Harlem, in Addis Ababa, in Sana'a, he found replicas of the Rome *borgate* and its sub-proletariat. They in turn were replicas of a lost, mythical Friuli which in turn had other associations: the maternal home, the breast of his mother, the undifferentiated closeness of infancy before the weariness of an Oedipal journey and the interminable need to record it.

> When I leave for a country in the Third World, I do it for my pleasure, for pure egoism, because I feel better when I do it. ... It is a sentimental rather than ideological impulse. I hate everything that belongs to 'consumerism' and I loathe it in a directly physical sense.[33]

His journeys of pleasure to the Third World were erotic and infantile, in search of an Eros Pasolini believed contemporary society had irrevocably lost and that he had lost too, at least in its purity, its infant innocence. 'Thus I gathered up this old reality in whose sphere I have rediscovered a moment of Eros that was in some way authentic. Even though I made a fable of it, its substance is real.'[34]

Flaherty had gone to Hudson Bay in search of a purity and simplicity that modern society was losing or no longer had. In order to express this simplicity, he had to stage it, turn back the clock, give Nanook his harpoon, teach the Aran islanders to hunt shark, so as to make a fable in a fabulous land, as if it were true. He asserted the truth of an illusion against the false values of reality. That was why Pasolini loved him. He had a similar need to stage the substance of truth by reinventing in fictions vanished forms of reality.

In 1968, Pasolini sketched out a plan for a film in five episodes on the Third World. Each episode was to take place in a different part of the Third World: India, Africa, the Arab countries, South America, the black ghettos of the United States. All the episodes were to have the same theme: the price of the integration of the Third World within a global capitalism, and the spiritual price of that integration, though each episode would have had its own particular emphasis. For India, it would have been religion and famine; for Africa, white rationality and black preindustrial consciousness; for the Arab countries, nationalism; for South America, guerrilla warfare; for black ghettos, dropping out. The film was to be called 'Appunti per un poema sul Terzo Mondo' ('Notes for a Poem on the Third World'). It was never made. It would have had the form of *Appunti per un film sull'India*: a central fictional story interrupted by documentary commentary.

Had the India film that was not made and the Third World film that was not made both been made, they would have been themselves films for a film to be made. The form of the proposed film in either case was based on the assumption that the fiction within it could not be told adequately and that ultimately fiction could only exist as the idea of fiction, not its practice.

Pasolini insisted on a reality and equally insisted on its absence since his reality was a reality lost. He reinstituted the reality in fiction, but continued to contend that it was still real, albeit a reality within a mythical fictional language, his virtual Cinema, his 'written language of reality' which 'wrote reality with reality'. His insistence on reality was in direct proportion to the lack of substance, the lack of reality to the reality he insisted upon. Just as Pasolini invented the idea of a virtual Cinema, and of a virtual language, he invented virtual films and virtual places. Like his language of reality, these were ideals. To maintain them, to maintain their ideal purity, they needed to remain virtual. Pasolini was condemned to imitations of Cinema and Reality, to actual films.

Chapter 3
And Africa?

Africa! Unica mia alternativa ...

I

Fellini's *Prova d'orchestra* (1979) takes place in the choir of a medieval church. The caretaker sets out the chairs and music stands with their sheet music as he relates the history of the famous conductors who have played there. While he speaks, setting out the sheet music, a slight breeze, seemingly from nowhere, blows an occasional sheet to the ground. He picks it up, replaces it on its stand, then another blows off. The incident is repeated a few times. The orchestra players gather, and a television crew (unseen) who interview them. Each player asserts the superiority of his or her instrument and its pre-eminent place in the orchestra. The earlier order so meticulously established by the caretaker begins to come undone. Chairs are moved, music stands shifted. What had been organised, symmetrical, balanced, becomes disordered and chaotic.

The rehearsal commences. The conductor is German. His attempts to impose a sound order fail. The music is uncoordinated and awful. The instruments will not respond to each other. The spatial disharmony the orchestra created is matched now by a musical disharmony. All aesthetic control has been lost.

The orchestra takes a break under the insistence of the union organiser. When the conductor returns he finds an orchestra in revolt. The walls have been spray-painted with radical political slogans, the conductor is booed and shouted down, portraits of Beethoven and Bach are besmirched, fights break out, a gun goes off. All ties, all linkages and connections disintegrate. Suddenly, without apparent motive or explanation, as if it were a natural fact, an iron ball, used by wreckers to break down walls, crashes through a wall of the church. Dust and rubble are everywhere. The disorder is total. Everything is in ruins. The orchestra becomes silent. The conductor resumes control. The rehearsal begins.

The film constructs contrary poles of order and disorder. They are not simply contrasts in the action of the film, but a feature of the film. The film charts its own becoming, its skirting of disorder, its source in chaos, its movement to an edge of formlessness even as it forms itself, towards the ecstactic joy of disintegration. Is that the pleasure, the spectacle of a Fellini film? The action of the film is a mirror of the process of its representation, as if it were looking at itself. The film is its own duplicate, a story of its own production. This is absolutely the case in *8H* when the character/film director (Guido/Marcello/Fellini) finds the order of his film from the chaotic life that surrounds him and which is the film itself, the film that we have just seen and that Guido/Fellini now join. At that instant of order, the film disappears from sight.

All the pleasure of the film is in its chaos, its blindness, its not yet being formed which is what composes it. The camera darts about in the disorder, to which it contributes and within which it plays, picking up moments of glow, a sudden incandescence that only chaos can produce, that can only issue from the dark and from non-seeing and in which the film revels, spectator at its own spectacle. It is a *festa*.

Fellini was not an Italian neo-realist. But he shared with the neo-realists a tradition that also included film-makers like Antonioni and was a sign of the modernity of the post-war Italian cinema. It involves the sense that the film is being made as you watch it, that film is a process in which it seeks its own shape as it forms itself rather than imposing a shape beforehand: Rossellini's notational spontaneity, his expectant patient wait for it. This aspect of Italian cinema relates to Bazin's remark on neo-realist films that they had an *a posteriori*, not *a priori*, sense, finding the reality they were part of, not constructing reality in order to fill a concept or express an idea from outside reality in some privileged, safe place.

Though everything is artificial in Fellini's representations – the Via Veneto of *La dolce vita* (1960), the medieval church in *Prova d'orchestra* – the films which form such artifices are the subjects of the filming. The Fellini camera turns on itself. This may not be conventional social realism, but it preserves, indeed features, the reality of filming which it catches, as Dziga Vertov, in an utterly different manner, caught the traces of reality in his *The Man with a Movie Camera*.

The reality of filming and the reality of film, and more importantly the reality of creating a film, become Fellini's subjects. For that reason, in part, characters in Fellini films, including Fellini (*I clowns* (1970), *Intervista* (1987)), sometimes speak directly to the camera, are interviewed off-stage, seek to make sense of their position, their place in an order, as the players in *Prova d'orchestra* vainly seek to do. It is also why too, notably in *8½* and in *Intervista*, Fellini's films have a dizzying, vertiginous quality as they seek to find themselves, but wander off, or are fooled by their reflection in the mirror of the film and become lost within its maze. Often his films become lured into their own *festa*, the circus and spectacle of film, its energy and possibilities, its variety of characters and centres, its fascinations, movements, its becoming and metamorphoses, what Deleuze called the crystalline quality of Fellini's films, a shimmering of light, changing of shapes, the multiplication of entrances and exits. The film is dragged into its own spectacle, as Guido is in *8½*.

Disorder is not what threatens a Fellini film. It is the heart of it, the source of its creation and energy, the moment of its happiness. Fellini has been able to incorporate chaos into the structural order of his films, almost making of it a structural principle. Insofar as chaos is also a place of unconscious dreams and desires, Fellini brings an unformed consciousness to the centre of his films, though not in order to be unravelled, but to reproduce that formlessness and to make use of it.

Nothing can be extracted from a Fellini film independent of the experience of the film. What the film 'is' attaches to the viewing of it, outside which there is nothing at all. There is no sense that can be dislodged from his films. His films become their own necessity. If it were possible to take sense from out of their structures then the films would lose not only their necessity (and sense) but their concreteness. Fellini's emphasis on artifice guarantees the concreteness of his films. The artifice is without any pretence and thus displaces any kind of representational illusion. The sense of Fellini films is in the structures that form them.

Because the processes of his films are their own subject, the films have no existence prior to their becoming. They are what you see as they concretely take shape, and include in them the risks and temptations towards formlessness which they encounter and display.

A film-maker like Kieslowski who tells moral tales within a pre-ordained and rigorous order is at the opposite end of film-making. Rather than using film to investigate and discover, including the discovery of itself, the charting of its own becoming, Kieslowski uses film to state what he knows independently and outside of the film he is making. His films are the expressions of that something: an ethical lesson. Morality is recruited by film. His films, as a result, are as distanced from their representations as his characters are from their lives. Such a distance would have no sense for Fellini.

II

Appunti per un'Orestiade africana (1970) is set in Tanzania and Uganda. There is a discussion in the film about the film with African students in Rome and there is a jazz sequence performed by American blacks in a Rome recording studio; some documentary footage comes from the war in Biafra. That war is intended to serve as an analogy with the Trojan wars.

The film follows the pattern of Pasolini's other *sopralluoghi* films – searching for locations – (*Sopralluoghi in Palestina*, *Appunti per un film sull'India*) whereby the film you see comprises notes for a film to be made later. As in these other films, there are two principal figurations in the *Orestiade*. The first is a contrast between an ancient world and the modern one taking shape within it; the second is an analogy between terms, each of which contains the contrast. In the *Orestiade africana*, the analogy is between Aeschylus's tragic trilogy and contemporary Africa; in *Sopralluoghi* it was between Matthew's Gospel and modern Israel; in the India film, it was between a pre-independence fable about tigers who ate a maharaja and the new, developing India where famine and death remain unavoidable limits.

The past/present analogies are between classical texts and actualities. The connection with ancient Greek texts and contemporary reality was used in Pasolini's finished films, *Edipo re* and *Medea*; the analogy of text to actuality was a permanent feature of all his films, notably *Il Vangelo secondo Matteo*, *La ricotta*, *Teorema*, the films of the *Trilogia della vita* and, of course, *Salò*.

Two related themes intersect in these films. One concerns the relation of parents to children, particularly sons (*Edipo re*, *Medea*, the *Orestiade*, *India*, *Teorema*, *Il Vangelo* and God and his son in *La ricotta*); the other, more broadly, is the relation of adults to the young, dramatically treated in *Salò*; that same relation is the dominant motif of Pasolini's political-cultural writing of the period. It includes his stand against the legalisation of abortion and his denunciation of the student revolts in 1968 (in the poem 'Il Pci ai giovani').

Aeschylus's trilogy begins with the return of Agamemnon to Greece at the end of the Trojan wars. Ten years earlier, just before the wars began, the Greek fleet was unable to sail to Troy to bring back Helen because of unfavourable winds. Agamemnon sacrificed his daughter Iphigenia to please the gods and change the winds. This act of murder initiates a cycle of revenge murders which are the main action in the Oresteian trilogy. When Agamemnon came back to Greece he was murdered by his wife Clytemnestra (for the murder of their daughter); she is murdered in turn (in retribution for the murder of his father) by her son Orestes.

The murders are urged on by the ancient and primitive Greek gods, the Furies. In the last play of the trilogy, at the behest of Apollo and Athene, Orestes is put on trial before the Athenian court, the Areopagus. He is condemned, but pardoned. The Furies were part of an archaic Greek religion which predated the advent of Zeus and the new religion of the Olympian gods to which Apollo and Athene belonged. The pardoning of Orestes in the Athenian court ends not only the blood feud, but the power of the Furies connected to it; it ushers in a new realm, no longer of primitive justice and revenge, but of rationality and the state.

The Furies, heretofore actual presences of horror and cruelty, are converted into the Eumenides who, in Pasolini's understanding of Aeschylus, become dreams, irrational forces existing by the side of the rationality of the state and within it. They now can be comprehended and dealt with, rather than simply suffered. The transformation of the Furies to the Eumenides was not primarily a defeat of the old, more pagan, elemental

Greek religion, but rather its conversion and absorption by the new religion, much as Catholicism absorbed rural pre-Christian cults.

The Furies changed from real beings to imaginary ones, psychological presences, memories of something ancient and terrible, no longer the real thing, but the dream of it, its representation. Thus, the shift to the Eumenides represents a shift towards the symbolic, towards the sign; the Eumenides are more linguistic than actual in their aspect. Because they are encompassed by language, they become more confined and bounded by the social than the Furies were, hence tamed, subject to the laws of society more than society is subject to them. Literally, the passage to the Eumenides is the taming of the ancient gods.

The contrast in Aeschylus's *Oresteia* of old and new, real and symbolic, irrational and rational are also present in Sophocles's *Oedipus Rex* and in Euripides's *Medea*. There was an affinity between these Greek works and Pasolini's work which caused him to call upon them and create works analogous to them. Greek themes are present in all his works, especially *Porcile*. *Porcile* enacts the simultaneous birth of society and the birth of the symbolic, that is the birth of language. The birth is signified when the cannibal speaks for the first time, exulting in the murder of the father. A similar birth, attendant on the substitution of the imaginary for the real, is the subject of Aeschylus's final play in the trilogy: the pardon of Orestes and the institutionalisation of the Eumenides. Along the way, as the price for the social and the need for it, a father, a daughter and a wife are sacrificed.

Deaths, certainly fictional deaths, no matter how brutal and senseless, can carry a lesson of sense fictionally, as they do in Pasolini's *Salò*. They become thus, and as well, part of a new order in which language, not action, is central. Action can be imitated in language rather than duplicated in fact; repetitions become linguistic and objects of knowledge, rather than, as in the realm of the Furies, an infinite repetition of murder.

Aeschylus's *Oresteia* was a mirror analogy, for Pasolini, of the contemporary history of modern Africa. That history involved, for him, the taming of what was real, primitive, terrible into the rationality and controllability of signs and language. It brought the primitive under the control of civility, reason, order. In so doing, the Furies remained, but with their irrational force now a force for poetry, or more exactly a poetic force.

The Furies are the Gods of a tradition – a savage tradition, grounded in blood and pervaded by terror – who in the end are not destroyed by the Goddess of Reason (Athena), but transformed: they remain as irrational, archaic divinities, but rather than presiding over horrible, obsessive, degrading dreams, they preside instead over works of poetry, of fantasy, of feeling.

The Oresteia synthesises the history of Africa over these last one hundred years: the sudden passage from an almost sacred society to a civil and democratic one. ...The terrible and fantastic divinity of

African Prehistory must submit to the same process as the Furies did and become the Eumenides.[1]

Pasolini's idea of poetry referred to all the arts: it was the Poetic. The idea owed a debt to Croce which was unacknowledged, to the distinction Croce made between the poetic or lyrical, and the non-poetic. Pasolini thought of language and poetry as structured by two contradictory elements. One element was primitive, a substratum of the irrational; the other element was civilised, a surface of the rational. The value of each depended on the presence of the other in a relation of opposition.

Pasolini and Fellini share a common ground in a view of a creative irrational which, though it threatens disorder, promises delight and can be identified as the source of the poetic. This view in part derives from Catholicism and the presence within Catholicism of an earlier paganism. The idea of the creative irrational is linked to a contrary yet complementary aesthetic and linguistic need to govern the irrational in order to bring it under the sway of consciousness and make it productive and alive for civility, that is to turn it into poetry and art and by that means to bring pleasure. Visconti equally came out of this culture. The central dilemma faced by Von Aschenbach in *Morte a Venezia* (1971), Ludwig in *Ludwig* (1973), and the Professor in *Gruppo di famiglia in un interno* (1974) revolves around the conflicting claims of passion and duty, art and reason; it tears these characters apart internally and it dooms them as the more externalised conflict of these elements doomed Rocco and Simone in *Rocco e i suoi fratelli* (1960).

The delight of the irrational is to be within it and also to be safe from it, to enjoy it but at a distance, converted into signs. The Greek myth which records the conversion of the Furies to the Eumenides (the Kindly Ones) can be thought of as a parable of the birth of poetry. It is that birth which Pasolini constantly oversees and restates.

The fact that the Greek myths (European) and African life were analogous mirrors for him could be extended beyond Africa and Greece to Europe generally in the past (pre-Renaissance) and to a Europe of the present in the poor areas of southern Europe where a peasant, rural life and society were still existent. It was the point Pasolini stressed in *Il Vangelo*, setting the Gospel in Calabria, and also in *Edipo re*, where he relocated Sicilians in Morocco.

Pasolini's work, conceived of as poetic in the widest sense, obsessively repeats, and thus re-enacts, its own birth as part of a universal and historical birth. The fact that much of his writing and film were scandalous and strident was an indication of the sense of danger he felt for his writing. If the ancient and primitive world disappeared, so too would poetry which had been born from that world.

The sacred, in modern society, might never reappear in fact, except as isolated traces (Calabria, Africa, India), but it could reappear as idea, that is as writing and memory. The birth of poetry had to be reiterated, adamantly, by Pasolini, as something difficult and obdurate the more it came under threat from a modern consumer society that seemed to him to be swamping all sense of the primitive and the irrational as he understood it.

The safeguard of poetry, for him, lay in the retention of its opposition to rationality, not the triumph of one or the other. For poetry to exist as a primitive, real, sacred source, it required rationality to textualise it, to help to write it, and it required rationality to be its permanent foil. It was the Eumenides who were wanted, not the Furies. But modern society – for Pasolini, capitalist and consumer society – appeared to be bent on destroying the difference, the opposition, hence the values not simply of the irrational, but also of rationality, of the social and the civilised. Not only was the ancient world being destroyed by modern capitalism, he believed, but also the humanist world which could recall it and hence preserve it textually as poetry and as literature.

Literally, it was the end of a fruitful opposition between the irrational and the rational, life and art, reality and language, by the loss not of one term, but of both. The oppositions and differences upon which language and thus, ultimately, poetry depended, included the language in which poetry was written and the source that inspired the writing.

Pasolini's defence of poetry was a political act of complete commitment. It was the defence of a politics of writing as the defence of a certain kind of order of existence, in fact, for him, the only existence worth living, a life of beauty and intelligence. The new society which was being formed had nothing left in it of the primitive (the real) or the humanist (understanding). It was no longer civilisation. It was barbarism.

Pasolini's opposition in 1975 to the legalisation of abortion in Italy was part of his defence of poetry. It was connected to the perception that consumerist society was destroying poetry as it was being born. The physical act of abortion was symbolically analogous for him to his fear that poetic language was at risk and he defended both, the unborn and the language which could give birth to poetry, with all his pained passion.

He called the legalisation of abortion a sickness of modern society. It had converted natural and beautiful occurrences into anti-social acts; it made the natural unnatural; it instituted the murder of the unborn as a precondition of social life. Children were no longer blessings, but curses. Even when they were born, they weren't always wanted. And the children knew it. It made them sad, for ever. This is Pasolini's story of Oedipus and the motive for all of Oedipus's crimes.

To Pasolini the legalisation of abortion constituted a reversal of the values of an older society, before consumerism, when births were a joy and a *festa*, when nature was wondrous and sacred, not, as now, he said, functional and calculated. Abortion had a mad rationality to it. Society murdered its unborn in order to maintain itself. What it killed was, in every sense, for him, the real, reality. What occurred in clinics was occurring in society at large. The real was being destroyed in the name of reasons that were reasons of consumerism, not humanity. Abortion, I think, symbolised for Pasolini everything that was brutal and insane about modern capitalism.

Often, repetition, even the repetition of the most painful and awful things, gives us a sense of security. The story may have been terrible, but it is, nevertheless, the story that we once experienced. It becomes thus the true story:

> 'Once upon a time, Little Yellow Riding Hood.'
> 'No, Red.'
> 'Little Red Riding Hood went to her grandfather's house.'
> 'No, "grandmother's".'
> 'Her grandmother's house …'

We may wish for another story, but it is sometimes difficult not to return to the one we first had. Pasolini behaved so petulantly, insisted so painfully on being the rejected son that he established the conditions of that rejection in his actions, and in his writings (so many of them banned). He thereby established the truth of the story that he was rejected. At least, however miserable he may have been, he could comfort himself that he was right.

I wonder, particularly since Pasolini could be so infantile at times, whether he felt such a rejection very privately, in the family, and whether he was the unwanted, though tolerated (suffered) child, at least by his father. Towards the end of the war, Pasolini's brother Guido joined a communist unit in the Italian Resistance. Guido was the favoured, adored son. He was killed, not by the Germans, but by Yugoslav communist partisans fighting the Italian communists for bits of territory. Guido was a hero who met a tragic end, and he was beloved. Everything he was, Pasolini was not. Everything Pasolini was, his father disliked: a poet, a homosexual, an intellectual, head-in-the-clouds, mamma's boy.

The feeling of the rejection of the baby and the rejection of poetry met in the rejection of the poet. It became universal to Pasolini, one reason why his personal position was politically exemplary: martyred by the world as his gift to save it, and the son sacrificed.

In 1975, Pasolini wrote a chilling essay 'Vivono, ma dovrebbero essere morti' ('They are Alive but They Ought to be Dead'), lamenting that the entire younger generation of Italians was unwanted, a generation too many. The sense of not being wanted was felt by them, he said, immediately, at birth. They were as a consequence children afflicted: weak, ugly, sad, pale, forever ill. The world had become, as Pasolini made clear in *Salò*, a world of a living dead: miserable, rejected children, hating hateful fathers.

The legalisation of abortion represented, for Pasolini, a historical, ideological, hence, terminological shift. It was more than a change in reality. It was a revolution in it. And therefore a revolution in sense and language. The legalisation of abortion destroyed, for him, the oppositions within which he worked and which structured his thought: the natural and not-natural, the irrational and rational, the sacred and profane. It was as if his world had collapsed. The sacred was gone even as a memory.

The Furies (the primitive) had gone from it, and also the Eumenides (reason) who retained the Furies in consciousness and thereby sustained poetry, the creativity of language. Pasolini's world, and therefore Pasolini, was displaced from within *the* world. He could only outrage it now, accuse it from his prophet's bunker, remind it of the sacred that he claimed had been forgotten, assert his self, even his body, his outrageous identity as realities in protest against reality.

Pasolini insisted on poetry as the preserve of what had been lost in modern, consumer society. His position recalled Symbolist and Hermetic poetry whose forms Pasolini in part repeated: the idea of a purely poetic, aristocratic language, even an obscure one, as a sign of absolute difference (and absolute purity). Because the sacred had been lost, his poetry was constructed as a poetry of scandal: impossible, often horrible, strident, weary, angry, even childish, 'bad verses', to protest and cry out against the absences he felt. It was a poetic tantrum in despair for a world where the poetic was dying and where there seemed no longer a place for the Poet.

He could not, I think, accept the fact that to break out of the world as it was being constituted was impossible. If you don't believe in the impossible there is nowhere to go, nothing to do except try as hard as you can to be like everyone else. On the other hand, where he wanted to go could only be, because it was impossible, written and imagined. Given the way he thought of things, Pasolini had no choice. He had to protest absolutely, that is uselessly and idealistically, by means of impossible ideals, primarily by impossible, unreal, head-in-the-clouds, out-of-the-world means, by poetry. Reality could only be contested by poetry and refused by poetry which was the alternative to the real. There was nothing that could be hoped for from reality, for it was that that had been lost.

Pasolini seemed to have hated contemporary society with such passion (but which included the passionate love of what it was not and might have been) that perhaps, in an absurd parody, like the comic-sad death of Stracci in *La ricotta*, the only analogy left was to imitate the Passion of Christ. After death the continuity of life is at an end; in its stead is its *sense*.

There is the 'pleasure' that one has in every realisation of the desire for pain and death. ... If a writer of verses, novels, films finds acceptance, honour, understanding in the society in which he works, he is not an author. An author can only be a stranger in a hostile land: he in fact invites death rather than accustoms himself to life. And the feelings he evokes towards himself, more or less strongly, are feelings of racial hatred.

I have no regrets: whoever loves reality too much, as I do, ends by hating it, rebelling against it, sending it to hell.[2]

III

In 1963, Pasolini wrote the script for another film set in Africa, *Il Padre selvaggio* ('The Savage Father'). He wrote it nearly a decade before his *Orestiade* and in the same year that he made *La ricotta*. In part because of the trial for blasphemy against *La ricotta* and problems of finance consequent on it, *Padre selvaggio* could not be made and never was.

Like Pasolini's *Orestiade*, and like so many of his films, it concerns the passage from a primitive, pure state of society, to a modern, rational, civilised society, and what followed from that. In this regard it is like an *Accattone* or a *Mamma Roma*, but set in the African bush. At the centre of the story is an African student, Davidson, torn between two worlds: the one he comes from (primitive) and the one he is going towards (modern). In the one he comes from, his father is crucial; in the one he is entering, it is his teacher, an Italian, who is crucial.

At the beginning of the film script, the teacher and Davidson speak about poetry. Each of them says the other 'people' possesses true poetry:

> 'You are an African, you are immersed in poetry!'
> 'No, poetry is a matter for the whites.'
> Davidson is seized by the urge to sing and dance.
> 'Ah ha', says his teacher, 'that is poetry.'[3]

There are two kinds of poetry: one is instinctive, immediate, sensual, belonging to a primitive Africa; the other is conscious, rational, mixed, belonging to civilised Europe. One is superior because it is innocent; the other superior because it is not. Davidson's poetic language is in song and dance; the teacher's poetic language is in Language. European poetry can never reach the springs of the other poetry, the soul to which it belongs, but it can know it and can create an analogy for it in its language. It is poetry as a second-order language, a metalanguage. It is not reality as Davidson's language is, but the knowledge of reality as Davidson's language is not. African poetry is innocent of language, even as it uses it. Its purity is a consequence of its lack of knowledge. It is therefore more purely expressive and therefore more essentially 'real'.

In the script, and off-screen, there is a tribal war going on. A United Nations peacekeeping force is involved. Davidson takes part in one of the raids of his tribe against another. The raid is murderous, brutal, savage, primitive. Davidson obeys his father and together they kill. Davidson has reverted to his other primitive self. Among those murdered is an Italian serving with the UN, Gianni, with whom Davidson had made friends. Gianni was almost a brother to him. It is unclear in the script, but Davidson, directly or indirectly, shares the responsibility (and guilt) for Gianni's death.

Gianni is a brother to Davidson, by analogy almost his white twin. Gianni comes from the Italian countryside and Italian peasantry. At the moment of his death, he recalls his *paese*, in images, not words. The analogy between the two boys is in their way of thinking – in images more real than words, and which predate the symbolic. Gianni plays the music of Bach and he dances to it, just as Davidson had danced to his tribal music. Both have inside them a sense of the sacred only felt in the peasant world, the world before the history both have entered and found in death.

After the raid the teacher reads out a lesson to Davidson:

> I will seek an understanding, a historical understanding ... you must try to understand me. ... Only through history can one explain what came before it, what is within us.
> Only then will prehistory be victorious again, humble us with its terrible, triumphant incomprehensibility. ...
> I know everything, all those simple little things that you don't want to know. But only reason can save you, and reason rejects all sentimentality, mystery, pain. ...Reason is healthy. ...
> You forgot how to be a modern civilised person. ... Oh, no, it wasn't your fault. ... You went back centuries ago, surrendering to it. You were drugged, participated in rituals that are no longer yours. Thus you are guilty. You have killed, tortured, participated in massacres of your friends, of the boys from the UN! [4]

Davidson shouts out it isn't so. He assaults the teacher, tries to kill him with a knife. Davidson is subdued, things calm down. At the end of the script, in a last class, Davidson, shyly, surreptitiously, leaves something on the teacher's desk. It is a poem.

The teacher reads it and is overjoyed. He says to himself:

> It is very beautiful, very beautiful ... poetry, and poor Davidson, poor poet, how much it has cost him to become one! ... I will see that it is published, yes, in a European journal ... it is very beautiful, Davidson, it is very beautiful.

It will not be a poem of joy, of 'pure life'. Instead, it will be of pain, disappointment, and criticism. Uncompromising feelings coming out of a rationalist passion – still somewhat shy – for the sweet feelings of the things alive in Africa. The celebration of a civilised life being born. The horror of massacres.[5]

IV

Art offers the possibility of correcting the imperfections of life. It can create Paradise, Utopia, perfect though impossible worlds. The impossible world, which is only textual, can serve to criticise the actual world, but by unnatural and ideal, that is artistic, means. Naturalist art is illusionary because it seeks to create a simulacrum of reality which erases any trace of the simulacrum as artifice. It is a simulacrum which denies itself in order to ensure the effectiveness of the illusion that it is not a simulacrum, but the real thing.

Pasolini's art was non-naturalistic. To follow reality would have been to reproduce its imperfections and in so doing be complicit with them. Such an art would have been on the same level as the reality it reproduced. To make the natural an object of consciousness and therefore of criticism, unnatural means were required. Naturalism is a form of acceptance, of compromise, even when it talks reform or revolution. A revolutionary art, as early Soviet artists taught, must make reality strange. The gap between art and life that naturalism seeks to close by its illusions, revolutionary art needs to reopen by its truths.

A problem faced by the neo-realists was that the Resistance, its populism and will to social reform seemed to require an accessible and familiar art, one able to represent current reality. Neo-realism was always threatened by a naturalism it embraced for political-social reasons yet also needed to criticise for aesthetic-cinematic ones.

Pasolini, with not dissimilar ends, chose very different means. In his theory of cinema, cinema ideally is a duplicate of reality, but at the level of language and in such a way that the language was marked out, starred, almost self-quoted. Cinema was no more than text and as such provided in its duplications a knowledge of the original which it duplicated. This double operation occurred within the gap formed by reality and text, reality and language. Cinema may have been the language closest to reality because it most exactly duplicated it, but the closeness was exemplary and analogic only.

His films work on analogies: Africa (real) to Greek myth (text), actor (African) to character (Orestes), Biafra (real) to the Trojan wars (fiction). The analogy establishes the terms of the opposition, real to text, turning the text into an exemplification of reality, which is only made possible by means of the distance created in the text from reality.

This gap figures as a permanent paradox in Pasolini's work. He finds reality by means of writing, thus necessitating the death of reality as the precondition for reality to live in consciousness. Reality becomes something lost whose loss is not recovered in the text, but remembered by it, hence the nostalgia for reality in his work. Beyond any substantive lesson of politics or ideology which his works teach, they teach a lesson about necessities in art, by reflecting back on its own processes. This is the sense of Pasolini's frequent emphasis on poetry as *always* metalinguistic, *always* a reflection on the language of poetry.

The language of poetry, as *Appunti per un'Orestiade africana* and *Padre selvaggio* make clear, is a mixed language which contains the paradox as a structure, reproducing it in its representations. Representation and writing in their reflections form a mirrored analogy of the paradox which each expresses exactly as Greek myth and African reality duplicate each other, but as textual positions and textual figures. Davidson is caught between two worlds in *Padre selvaggio*, but so is the poet and so too the script which tells the story, simultaneously a story about Davidson and a story about poetry. The script is not simply a narrative about Africa, but a narrative of its own becoming. Pasolini's most eloquent narrative of this kind is *Porcile*.

Primitivism, then, just like Cinema, is a term within a paradox whose opposite pole is the consciousness which thinks or reveals the sense of these terms. It is necessary for the ideals to be directly translated into the text in order to be seen and their value recognised. And it is also necessary that they exist in opposition in order for them to be seen side by side contaminating each other, that is informing one another.

There was no difference for Pasolini between 'poeticamente' and 'metaforicamente'. The metaphor was the paradox and the paradox the central structure of poetry which could only encompass reality unrealistically through a text that yielded up a consciousness of language. Thus, built into the Pasolinian text was the refusal of reality as the precondition for understanding it, in effect, possessing it. What was possessed proved to be realistically empty, impossible. That impossibility was embodied by poetry which served, by that very fact, as the political and ideological criticism of any reality whatsoever. Pasolini called this work 'scandalous': he thought that poetry was always a scandal because it broke with the conventional codes of representation and naturalism, because it was unnatural, perverse.

In almost all of Pasolini's films the act of coming to consciousness is linked to death. Death is the price of knowledge (Ettore, Accattone, Ninetto, Stracci) and the precondition for compassion (Christ's Passion). It is also the precondition for the existence of language. Pasolini's Cinema is nothing other than a consciousness derived from film which represents a cut into reality, thereby pointing to reality (to Cinema), in the gaps with reality film creates. The ideal Cinema is made a subject of consciousness by the activity of actual films, metalinguistic means for reflecting on the language of cinema, and above all for reflecting on its vocation as duplication and mimetic example.

Oedipus violates the social-symbolic order by killing and dispossessing his father and marrying and fucking his mother. Parricide and mother-fucking may be against nature, but as actions that are also in and part of nature, hence the social prohibitions instituted against them, that is to say, the incest taboo. Oedipus is also able to penetrate the riddles of nature posed by the Sphinx, a paradoxical monster who repeats his nature in paradoxes. Oedipus seeks to discover his own nature by anti-social – hence socially defined – means. Such unnatural means are crimes committed upon nature to uncover nature's secrets. As Nietzsche asked: 'How should man force nature to yield up her secrets, but by successfully resisting her, that is to say, by unnatural acts?' And he concluded: 'The edge of wisdom is turned against the wise man; wisdom is a crime committed on nature; such are the terrible words addressed to us by myth.'[6] Of course, it does not follow that *all* crimes against nature produce wisdom. The metaphor, the analogy, the paradox are never innocent; they are the means to know innocence, but the knowledge is perverse.

Davidson has two fathers: a natural father who is tribal, and an unnatural one who is his European teacher. The act of murder committed by Davidson is in obedience to his father and motivates a lesson from his unnatural father which teaches him the history and consequences of his obedience to his natural father. To write poetry, as opposed to merely performing it, symbolic murder is necessary. Two things die in the script for the proposed film: the chain of murder and the chain of obedience. Only by breaking with his natural father does Davidson understand his relation to him and to himself. It causes him to be born again as a poet to practise unnatural linguistic acts to comprehend natural relations. In effect, Davidson has entered language and history by means of poetry. These rational instruments make it possible for him to preserve an understanding of irrational forces. It is the reappearance of the Eumenides.

V

If Poetry for Pasolini was a form of knowledge, it was knowledge of a peculiar kind. What it knew was primarily itself and its own processes and structures, notably the metaphors and oppositional paradoxes of which it was composed. Pasolini knew Africa, India, the Middle East, Calabria, the Rome *borgate* only poetically, not actually. They were terms in poetic constructions. He used the Third World as a poetic figure, not a real place. As his work never tires of reminding one, the duplication of reality is an unnatural practice: it textualises.

It was important that Pasolini not know the Third World too well. It needed to function as distant and innocent for his poetic purposes. He needed it to remain poor and primitive. If it were other than that (modern, knowledgeable) it would cease to serve as a terminological referent. There is a lament in his work about the end of primitivism, the expulsion from Eden and Paradise, the loss of reality. It is a lament internal to his structures. Innocence is what does not know but also what he does not know, therefore he can call it innocent. The innocence is not a truth about reality but a poetic and analogic truth, textual at its beginnings.

Pasolini's works begin with the death of reality. It is their precondition and principal subject. From that point reality ceases to be reality in any conventional social or political sense, or even a historical one, and becomes simply language and poetry. Reality is what he forever refused and never knew, or knew insofar as it duplicated the paradox between reality and art, reality and language, sometimes translated as mass-consumer-capitalist-society vs. poetry. His poetry may have had a political yield, as did his Utopian renunciation of present reality, but it was a politics of writing and language, not a politics of politics: fundamentally, Pasolini had no interest in actual politics.

No matter what political situations existed, whatever country Pasolini found himself in, from as early as the late 1940s, he would always return to the same set of structural ideas, the same structured paradoxes. His structures were indifferent to actuality. They remained the same irrespective of the reality involved: India, Africa, Naples. The structures reflected back to him what he projected on to them. The relation created a self-contained mirror-effect, produced structures in which nothing could be learned that was extraneous to them, since the structures were designed not to learn. They were defensive, nostalgic, reactionary and self-justifying.

If you compare Pasolini's *Orestiade* or the script of *Padre selvaggio* to Jean Rouch's *Les Maîtres fous* (1955) or *Jaguar* (1958–67), it becomes evident how fundamentally uninterested Pasolini was in the Third World. He used the Third World without knowing it and needed not to know it in order to use it as he did for his poetic ends. The Rouch films are organised to understand Africa by trying to understand the way the Africans seek to know themselves. The films are about the narratives the Africans invent and enact as ways to come to terms with the changes affecting their world in contact with the West. Their subject is the myths Africans create and hence the structures of African self-consciousness. It concerns African sophistication, not ignorance. For Rouch, African myths, ancient and modern, are not exemplifications of innocence but forms of knowledge. It is not he who possesses that knowledge, but they. The Western myth of primitive innocence and Western rationality, essentially a rationalist myth of the superiority of reason, is rejected by Rouch in all its forms including the one Pasolini adopted, in praise of innocence.

Pasolini's films are self-centred. They are not about Africa and African consciousness, but about Pasolini and a poetic consciousness. Pasolini recruited Africans for a poetic work about poetry and language in which they remained essentially dumb, inert. They were his innocent foils of innocence. Rouch, on the contrary, sought to expand a notion of language by seeking with his films what could not be known without them. The films become their own necessity and justification. Fundamentally, Africa is superfluous to Pasolini's films about Africa. It is *his* Africa, confined within a structure which it serves without affecting or altering actual Africa in any way.

Pasolini wanted to preserve an idea of primitivism and the irrational unthought. His works were organised not to know, but to maintain. What he maintained was the permanent status of the not known. The entire area of the irrational, what could not be possessed but only invoked, and most often as reality, had to be retained in his works and poetics as a thing lost, irretrievable, dead. In valuing reality, he wrote a poetry at the doors of death. Among the paradoxes he manipulated was the one which contained the contrast between life and death, reality and meaning, as poetic preconditions for each other. Much of his work, certainly his films, and particularly his last ones, the *Trilogia della vita* and *Salò*, are devoted to death. It is death which motivates the life and movement of the films.

Pasolini valued knowledge at a level that was neither discursive nor rationalist, but poetic and sentimental, knowledge that could only be poetically expressed. He was disarmingly frank about it:

> When I go to a Third World country, I do it for pleasure, out of sheer egoism, because it makes me feel better. I have found myself sometimes in a country where I lose sight of the misery and of the reactionary regime in charge. My reaction is more sentimental than ideological. I detest everything to do with 'consumerism', I hate it in a complete physical sense.[7]

Sophocles's Oedipus is horrified at the incest he committed. Freud understood the horror as ambivalent. It contained a secret wish. Pasolini's Oedipus opens the secret up. He knows it is his mother while he is fucking her, and he likes it, revels in it, calls out her name as he comes. The pleasure is heightened by the social violation. The unnatural act makes him vibrate all the more. It is the vibration of crime.

Pasolini's Oedipus blinds himself not because of the incest, but because of its consequences. Jocasta kills herself. It is then that he takes the pins from her dress and pierces his eyes. He lost his mother by demanding too much, an absolute acceptance. Either it was too late, or he was too driven, but he could not suppress a wish or symbolically transfer it. He had to perform it. Oedipal desires, from a Freudian perspective, are infantile ones. They never leave you. But they do need to be readjusted as the necessary price for maturity.

The fear of growing up is in part a fear of losing what pertains to childhood, or perhaps, more regressively, to infancy. When you grow up, you know that the only way to keep what you are afraid to lose is to lose it, to stop seeking it any longer in experience, in repeated scenes of childhood, and instead to find it where it really is and where it can be productive, as dream and as memory, and for some, as writing. To place it there is to allow one to care for it. It is a way to care for oneself. It allows for compassion and forgiveness, the Eumenides, the Kindly Ones.

The homosexual knows that the heterosexual is sexually ambivalent. How? He knows it because he is sexually ambivalent. We all are. I can only speculate on Pasolini's motivations, try to imagine them.

Pasolini did replace his father. In 1949, when he was forced to flee Casarsa, accused of molesting schoolboys, he fled with his mother Susanna. He always lived with her. His homosexuality was a protection against ancient desires.

His homosexuality operated on a switching mechanism. In his work, Pasolini maintained the paradox of wanting an experience he had lost but couldn't have again. He constantly re-evoked the desire for that experience, but the re-evocation was the symbolic transfer of it to language. It became a paradox within a text, and the motive and subject of his work. Pasolini's works contained mirrors of themselves. The paradox reproduced itself in a switching between represented fact and the structures of writing which produced the fact. His signs were broken, divided, ambivalent. The signified was derided by the signifier, the signifier taunted by the signified. It was a play and burlesque of artifice to avoid the real. It never settled in the sign.

It is difficult not to respond to Pasolini's lament for what he had lost in becoming a writer. It is the subject of his writing. Somewhere, even as he wrote about the loss, he could not accept it: hence, he went on lamenting it, looking for it, however much, on that other side of the search, he knew it was fruitless and what he sought impossible. It was like never completely growing up. At some point, I think, you have to accept the loss and cease to lament it. To do so is not to renounce the paradox central to living and writing, but rather to accept it, but from the other side of the paradox, by admitting that what is lost is lost for ever and irrecoverable. If you admit that, you can contain the experience and to that extent have it, and in such a way that you can look forward. The lament is to look the other way, to regress.

The character of Pasolini's work looks backwards away from reality towards a longed-for, impossible ideal whose recession from Pasolini's attempt to grasp it was guaranteed by the way he sought to take hold of it. That was why, I think, he never sought to know what he said he loved, whether that love was for Africa, or India, or the global sub-proletariat, or his mother, or life, or reality. He needed what he loved to be far away and not known in order to be ideal and, therefore, to fuel his system of perpetual desire which was the paradox and motor of his writing. To know was to risk losing the impetus to write which was the means to find what pre-existed writing and was, literally, an impossible knowledge. Pasolini loved where he was not and did not know and hated where he was and knew. He loved Africa and hated Italy. He hated the bourgeoisie and he loved the sub-proletariat.

Antonioni is eighty-two. He had a stroke, walks with difficulty and hardly speaks. But he makes his will known. He can construct scenes with objects: though virtually mute, he continues to act as a *metteur en scène* and film director, and has just begun a film with Wim Wenders. His assessment of Pasolini? Antonioni looked straight at me, and then, turning his head repeatedly, he looked over his shoulder, backwards.

VI

In the year Pasolini wrote the script for *Il padre selvaggio*, he wrote a poem called 'E l'Africa?' ('And Africa?'). The verses are dated 30 January 1963. *Il padre selvaggio* was only published by Einaudi in late 1975. The *Il padre selvaggio* project was directly connected to the 1963 court case brought against *La ricotta* for blasphemy.

La ricotta caused Pasolini and his producer, Alfredo Bini, problems in raising money for *Il padre selvaggio*. Bini was a courageous producer and had produced all of Pasolini's early work. Bini and Pasolini quarrelled over the problems attendant on the blasphemy case: perhaps Pasolini really had gone too far.

Africa, the primitive alternative other to Italy, became unreachable as a consequence of the *La ricotta* trial. The hated near (Italy) denied Pasolini access to a beloved far (Africa). Consumerism had defeated primitivism, the present had buried the past. Pasolini had lost yet another opportunity to approach Paradise.

The court case against *Ricotta* for blasphemy prevented me from making *Il padre selvaggio*. The pain it gave me – and I tried to express it in these ingenuous verses of 'E l'Africa?' – still gives me pain. I dedicate the script of *Padre selvaggio* to the Ministry of Justice and to the judge who condemned me.

And Africa?

The yellow and red face, vanishing
up into the baldness, down into the smooth
round chin: with a red half moustache,
in profile, cruel, like a
middle-aged Lansquenet,
descended from Lands of spired roofs and frozen rivers ...
It was this face,
which, behind a desk, in rustic style,
for important bureaucrats,
fixed me with his blue but classic eyes,
while outside atomic bombs burst
in the yellowish sky one afternoon twenty years ago.
Then he began – swollen
with hysteria, and red
like a bloody foreskin –
to scold me, to call me mad ...
And I ... innocent, offended ... listened,

mixing in my throat of an adolescent dressed
by his mother,
tears and protests: uselessly! He,
a practical man, was right:
I had spent too much money on useless luxuries,
and, besides, I had touched upon the susceptibilities of
important people,
innocents, even they, in their splendid private lives.
I listened to him. He did not yet lose his temper:
Even his Lansquenet throat was the throat of a boy,
and, also there, while scolding, were mixed deaf tears.
The yellowing pout beneath the red moustache,
was evidence of something sacred
that was happening within him.
And I: 'I did not know how I could
know it, and I have been doing this work only for a year!'
And other confused, offensive words that I don't remember.
And, meanwhile, his face splits:
rather, at first, for a moment,
he was another, who appeared at a threshold,
not far from the table, in the light
of that ancient afternoon from a faded war.
He was the real master, and in fact, he said
to the soldier (for a while, thus, silenced):
'What does it matter, some extra expenses, now
that I have stopped production!'
And I was a bit relieved.
But that other, there, who by osmosis
came from the chest of Bini, was my father.
The father not named, nor remembered
since December of fifty-nine, the year he died.
Now he was there, an almost benevolent master:
but immediately he again became my contemporary from
Gorizia
with the red skin, hands in his pockets,
heavy like a paratrooper after taking his rations.
Resolving thus, partly to my advantage
the question of the other film
– dreamt a bit earlier and persisting
with rural and desert images in the new dream –
there was a brief silence, full,
seemingly, with consolation, in reality, with a limpid hurt.
I went towards him who, meanwhile,
just behind me, was leaning absorbed in silence
against a wall of the room,
I went towards him, and timidly almost to his face ...

which by now was simply the face of my father,
with its grey skin of a drunk and someone on the verge of
death,
I murmured to him: 'And ... Africa?
And the flamboyants of Mombasa?
Red branches against green leaves,
stylistic model of red on a green background,
red and green
without which my soul could not survive?'
Oh, father now no longer mine, father who is nothing other
than father,
who comes and goes in dreams,
whenever you want,
like a wild boar suspended on a hook, grey with wine and
death
coming to say terrible things,
to reinstate old truths,
with the zest of he who has experienced these,
dying in the old cheap nuptial bed,
vomiting blood from your guts on the sheet,
travelling for a night and a day
in a casket towards the inhospitable Friuli
on a sun-soaked winter day in fifty-nine!
The world is the reality that you have always paternally
wanted.
And I, the son, systematically trying everything,
every heart-rending thing that sons must try,
I find myself here, first guinea pig of an unknown pain
prefiguring the impossibility
'of expressing oneself out of necessity';
things which a poet, stern possessor at least of a humble pen,
never had to fear in the past.
Martyrdom, a bit ridiculous like all martyrdoms.
But in this great paternal normality of dreams and of life
above all, how moving is it,
my wish to die, in the dream,
for the disappointment of a lost red and a green! [8]

The images of Bini/the father are unpleasant ones: a monstrous fairy-tale-like ogre, hideous, bloody. Inside the memory of the poet is a frightened child and also a stubborn adult. He will express himself despite the father. 'The yellow and red face, vanishing/up into the baldness, down into the smooth/round chin: with a red half moustache,/in profile, cruel, like a/ middle-aged Lansquenet'.

   Bini is a prick: 'Then he began – swollen/with hysteria, and red/like a bloody foreskin'. The prick is divided into two: Bini and Pasolini's father

– 'his face splits'. Pasolini's father emerges out of Bini's chest, displacing him, a biological, primeval ooze.

The father is ghostly, ashen grey, like death. 'I went towards him, and timidly almost to his face ... /which by now was simply the face of my father,/with its grey skin of a drunk and someone on the verge of death/. . . like a wild boar suspended on a hook, grey with wine and death/coming to say terrible things,/to reinstate old truths,/ ... dying in the old cheap nuptial bed,/vomiting blood from your guts on the sheet'.

Bini and Pasolini's father are men of affairs: producers, soldiers. They berate the Poet for being a poet: impractical, abnormal, head-in-the-clouds, dreamy. The Poet resists, justifies himself, but it is painful. There is a lament, a groaning complaint: their anger threatens his soul, wants him to be different. His difference was who he is, his very soul: ' ... without which my soul could not survive?'

The pain is irreconcilable. It is the conflict between wanting to be yourself and reluctance to displease those who would have you be other than yourself, be like them. Pasolini's disobedience in the poem to Bini is not something new, but a repetition of past disobediences to his father, all fathers, *the* Father (the *La ricotta* case). 'E l'Africa?' is a filial poem, a son-father poem and thereby political.

Mr Lincoln, in John Ford's *Young Mr Lincoln* (1939), is equally tempted by the apple pie and the peach pie in the pie-judging contest. Tasting the apple, he wants the peach; tasting the peach, he wants the apple. The choice between the pies mirrors the choice faced by the mother of which of her two sons to save in the accusation against both of murder. If she saves the one by saying he is innocent, she will doom the other. An impossible choice. Lincoln saves both brothers by miraculously discovering the truth that neither of them was the murderer. Lincoln is not above a bit of cheating to get to the truth.

In the medieval epic poem *Sir Gawain and the Green Knight*, the lord of the castle gives the knight hospitality, but the lady of the castle wants to extend the hospitality by offering him herself. A knight does not refuse a lady, but neither does a knight violate the hospitality of a host. He saves the social code by literary invention: he tells her a story, just as Scheherazade tells stories to save her life, fiction coming to the rescue of reality. The knight's story is provoked by the need to obey the social code and be safe, and the desire to violate it and have fun. He switches levels towards the fictional. Pleasure is found and even intensified not by the consummation of a seduction in reality but by redirecting it into fiction.

In *Il padre selvaggio* Davidson is caught between two disobediences: to his father by becoming Westernised and to his teacher by remaining primitive. He resolves the problem by writing poetry. In that manner he is neither obedient nor disobedient. He breaks the code only fictionally. It is an ideal, not a real break. Reality is textualised, turned into language. By that fact, by abstracting reality until it is only a trace and memory, and then displacing it with what for Pasolini is not its representation, but its analogy, Davidson has moved away from his real father towards his adopted, fictional one. He has become Westernised without, however, losing the presence of the primitive and the irrational. He has found his head in symbolic writing, but retained his soul by finding a poetic writing. If poetry imitates reality in the sense of an irrational sacred before language, it retains that reality in language. It is the paradox of what he does that saves him. He can choose the two contraries. Davidson writes between the poles of a reality lost and a symbolic gained. Writing is not wholly in one place or the other.

The symbolic is overcome by reality because poetic language can subvert its ordinary communicative function. It can turn language into an aesthetic object, making it a thing of beauty and at the same time rendering it useless by compromising its vocation for meaning. Isn't the most beautiful thing the most useless thing which has no other use than to be beautiful? Poetry returns language to its primitive concreteness, to all that belongs to sound, colour, rhyme, metre, but only grazes sense.

Reality, in turn, is overcome by being transferred from reality into its analogy in language, an imitation of reality and a metaphor of it: 'the written language of reality'. It is a first step towards understanding and consciousness, yet it is not completely one with these. The Furies are displaced by the Eumenides, and, in part as a consequence, the father is displaced by the son.

In Aeschylus's *Oresteia*, Orestes is pardoned and the Eumenides assume their new-found social-ideological place and their place as poetic stimulus. The father, Agamemnon, was murdered when the Furies and the old religion still ruled. Orestes had been the obedient son. He avenged the murder of his father by killing his mother, Clytemnestra. In being pardoned, he has displaced his father, without thereby being disobedient. Davidson resembles Orestes. Poetry was a way of cleansing him of having killed his 'brother' and a way of reconciling him to his father, in language not in deed. Davidson is the beginning of a new Africa, as Orestes was the beginning of a new democratic Greece. Davidson has been loyal to his father and loyal to himself by the shift to the linguistic and fictional.

To break with the codes of language by writing poetry – poetry in the widest sense – was an erotic thrill for Pasolini. It was incestuous (languages were mixed) and patricidal (he broke the Code). By means of poetry, he obeyed the symbolic (he wrote) and violated it (by writing poetry). Poetry subverted the symbolic and adhered to it. Poetry belonged to the mother because it imitated the irrational. Language belonged to the Father because it belonged to the social structure.

Poetry displaces the father fictionally, not in fact. In writing it was possible to play happily with the consequences of the displacement by touching forbidden places, in effect mixing categories of the law with the urgings of desire. Pasolini called his languages contaminated, corrupt, incestuous languages. They performed in a space bounded by the symbolic and the irrational, by sense and its loss of sense, representation and the purity of the signifier. That space was defined by these terms as if they were its border, and also constituted that space, filling the border. The tension of these contraries, their contamination and paradoxical relations were the stakes of Pasolini's poetic game. Their performance produced poetry and the poetry produced the terms. It was a system which generated itself.

What was important was never to win, to keep the stakes in play, maintain their contradictoriness, refuse any resolution. It was necessary in order for the writing to continue that it be written within a paradox and it was equally necessary to maintain the continued force of that paradox in what was written to ensure that the writing never died.

Incest and patricide are closely related, not because to rid himself of the father makes the mother more available to the son, but because the patricide involved is fictitious. It is a wish, not a reality. Desire is realised by a fictional detour. The wish is not mother to the deed, but mother to language and story. The crimes of incest and patricide are more fun to imagine than to enact. In any case, imaginatively, they are productive of drama, poetry and all the beauties that language is capable of.

When Oedipus solved the riddle of the Sphinx, things were not over. Solving one riddle, he generated another and a more obdurate one. It had the same mix which constituted the ambivalent, paradoxical structure of the Sphinx and the riddle it posed which combined and contaminated the natural and the artificial, nature and the unnatural violation of it. The same ambivalence is reproduced when Oedipus murders his father, more especially when he fucks his mother. The more Oedipus exercised his reason, the closer he approached a realm which compromised it. From out of that compromise, or rather within the riddle of it, the poetry of tragedy was born.

Nietzsche commented that Oedipus had to break the natural order as the only way to discover it. Oedipus's exercise of reason, by approaching the irrational secrets of nature, risked his own disintegration. Reason was a crime against nature. Yet the artifice of it and the knowledge such artifice produced about nature constituted a cultural victory. A result of that victory is the Oedipal myth which represents, as in a mirror, its own becoming, tells the story of its own generation. The myth is a reproduction in fiction of a paradoxical relation between language and reality which the myth can only restate and duplicate, but never resolve. That is, the myth is mythologically productive: its truth requires a mythopoetic and essentially paradoxical structure to be known.

Oedipus was a son not wanted. He tried to be loyal to his father and mother, the king and queen of Corinth, but these were fictitious parents. His real parents, the king and queen of Thebes, had given him to servants to be killed when he was born. The awful truth Oedipus learns as he tries to save Thebes from ruin concerns not only his inadvertent crimes against nature, but the purposeful unnatural crimes his parents committed against him. Oedipus is a rejected son. It is his father who is murderous, not he.

Oedipus's father seeks Oedipus's death because it is prophesied to him that Oedipus will do what he ends up doing: killing his father and fucking his mother. A threatened, imagined violation of nature (what it is imagined Oedipus will do) creates the conditions for the realisation of what is fearfully imagined by his parent and itself constitutes an unnatural crime (the attempt to murder Oedipus). That the father is murdered by the son and the mother is punished in turn are not altogether unjust occurrences.

Pasolini often acted like a rejected child: difficult, demanding attention, scandalising the adult world. If he can be believed, his father rejected him. 'E l'Africa?' is the expression of that rejection and the felt pain of it. But let us suppose, nevertheless, that Pasolini wanted to remain an obedient son, even if sometimes he courted martyrdom and rejection in not being so, repeating endlessly the scene of his rejection ... by being impossible, by being disobedient. His way out of this lived dilemma is to become a poet like his Davidson does, even if it is as a poet that his father, *the* Father and Bini reject him (*La ricotta*). In poetry, he can write the condemnation, express the pain, turn it all into language and thus, in part, escape being condemned for writing by the beauty of it.

The ideal state for Pasolini was not the contaminated scene of writing, or the paradoxical situations Davidson or Orestes find themselves in, but the one before that: the simple, primitive, prehistorical, pre-symbolic state, when poetry was natural and automatic, when people lived in myth and spoke in parables, when there was no difference between language and reality, no split, no paradox, when sons, without difficulty, that is without thinking, obeyed their fathers.

Pasolini's ideal, his Utopia, political and poetic, was not simply a rural primitive world but, as a result of being rural and primitive, one in which fathers and sons are reconciled, where sons follow their fathers without question and fathers accept their sons without condition. This was the bliss of Pasolini's Oedipus before he left home. It was because Oedipus wanted to maintain that bliss that he left, in order not to hurt his father, in order to remain a loyal son, in order to avoid the evidence of his dreams.

Utopia, then, is the Utopia of absolute love and absolute acceptance without the pain of disobedience and separation. It is to be eternally a happy child, always loved, never disobedient, never completely growing up. This Utopia, marked by infantile wishes, relates to an issue of immense importance in Pasolini's work: the issue of Revolution.

VII

In the penultimate sequence of Pasolini's *Orestiade*, which interrupts the film like a choral break, there is a dance sequence. (It is reminiscent of the dance at the bar in *Uccellacci e uccellini*.) It is shot live; the dancers are in various everyday dress; though rhythmic and intense, it has a higgledy-piggledy, often burlesque character, like their clothes. It is not completely serious.

> We are among the Wa-gogo tribe … where I have shot this dance. It is an ancient dance … up until a few years ago it was a ritualistic one with its own precise meanings – religious, perhaps even cosmogonical. Now, to the contrary, as you can see, the Wa-gogo, in the very same places where they had once taken these things seriously, are repeating them; the repetitions, however, are for the fun of it, to enjoy themselves, but the gestures and movements have been emptied of their ancient sacred meaning and are being redone almost out of sheer joy.

Earlier in the film, and constituting a major break with its documentary style, albeit a style into which the *Oresteia* tragedy by Aeschylus is woven, there is a precisely scripted performance by two American black singers who chant segments from the *Oresteia* to jazz music composed by an Argentinian (Gato Barbieri) and played by an Italian jazz trio.

The sequence is marked as serious art. The modern jazz music and the choral chant are like sacred ritual music, similar to the feel of the Congolese *Missa Luba* mass in *Il Vangelo secondo Matteo*. Like it, and like so many of Pasolini's other works and the citations in them, the sequence juxtaposes the ordinary – the document – with the sublime of high art. The art is performed by American blacks. Though they are not, like Franco Citti and the pimp Accattone he plays, sub-proletarians from the slums, they can stand for children of the ghetto, framed by high art as Accattone–Citti is framed to appear like a Masaccio saint. American blacks are children of Africa. The high art they sing and perform is like Davidson's writing of poetry. Africa wells up in them and becomes not the savage but the sublime, yet sublime for being in touch with a savage past.

The ordinary in the film is invested with a sacred quality, and a sacred high art is overlapped, like a rhyme, with the everyday and the popular.

> A sudden idea seized hold of me to interrupt this kind of narrative, tearing into its style without style which is the style of the documentary and of the notational film …
>
> It is very clear, in fact, to everyone, that the twenty million black subproletarians in America are the leaders of all the revolutionary movements in the Third World.

Though, as can be seen in the dance of the Wa-gogo, a sacred tradition is disintegrating, it is fictionally restored in the film by high art and its sacred analogies. What is not possible in fact is made possible in art. Art restores the Ideal. Pasolini, American black singers and Aeschylus are made to seem closer to ancient Africa than real Africans, the Wa-gogo, dancing their higgledy-piggeldy burlesque of cultural decay in tattered underwear. If the people are no longer what they had been, the Italian poet can re-evoke what they had been, in poetry, in the myth of a myth, in sheer artifice, and then fictionally he can enter its circle as if it were real.

If primitivism and myth are indeed, as Pasolini repeatedly emphasised they were, in an ideal and critical-revolutionary relation to modernisation and hence to the West because primitivism contained a sense of the irrational and the sacred which modern societies had lost, then it was the poet, and a modern one, who more than any other had inherited the revolutionary cloak of primitive Africa. It is he, aware of the loss of the past in the modern, more conscious than any primitive of the consequences of that loss, who can recall those traditions and repeat them in highly wrought artificial imitations and analogies, in poetic techniques of a post-modern art. The poet Pasolini is like what the poet Davidson becomes, but in reverse. He is the bourgeois writer who finds within him an ancient soul. Davidson is the primitive African who discovers in writing his self-consciousness. They are mirrors, self-reflections the wrong way round.

The poetry involved is conscious of primitivism, but not primitive itself. It can rescue the world because it can appreciate the loss of a primitive soul. It possesses the memory and consciousness of it and the fictional, mythological means to repeat it, virtually rescue it from decay and oblivion. The metaphor, the paradox, the citation are self-conscious, not innocent. Pasolini presumes to restore to Africa its past and to the world its lost humanity: the mythic, psychoanalytically rich history of the *Oresteia*. He brings back the past to revolutionise the world in the antique forms of the myths of Africa and Greece, the savage ancient world and the classical ancient world mediated by the poet.

The poem, 'E l'Africa?', juxtaposes the disobedient poet/son to the conformist father/film producer. The poet/son opposes the father/film producer, and, because the latter represents society, the poet's opposition is a generalised one, as Africa is a universal sign of what opposes the Father and modern Society and the conformity which the Father demands, prick that he is. It is conformity that the poet resists by means of his Africa, the Africa the father/film producer seeks to crush in the poem. Africa is the poetic means to contest conformity. And the Africa that contests it is the Africa of *Il padre selvaggio*, the savage father posed against all the fathers who have instituted the society to which Pasolini will not conform.

The poet is a revolutionary by the fact of his loyalty to a (mythic) past and his disobedience to an (actual) present. The loyalty is essentially a poetic loyalty, to a mythic ideal only possible in writing, in poetry, not in reality. Pasolini's loyalty was to the language(s) that could evoke and recreate his ideal, the languages of myth, the parable, poetry. He was not loyal to Africa, but to the film of it and to the poem of it which laments the impossibility of realising the dream of it.

Africa had no real existence for Pasolini, any more than India, or Calabria, or the *borgate* did. They were critical and radical 'functions', not realities. Their purpose was to oppose reality. They were poetic metaphors for what was missing in the modern world, not real locations, not actual places. They were created by Pasolini as forgotten Paradises Lost. They were an other, a contrary, the ideal opposite which he restored. His love for the ideal other, like all real passions, was impossible and necessary, hence the need to write it.

In the final sequence of the *Orestiade*, a group of African peasant farmers hoe their land. They stand in a straight line and, rhythmically, like a *corps de ballet*, in perfect unison, their hoes moving up and down, their bodies swaying, take up, by a natural measure, precisely the same quantity of earth. The rhythm of their movements is punctuated, as if choreographed, or perhaps rhymed, with the sounds of a Soviet chorus singing a Soviet revolutionary song. The finale is the same as that of *La rabbia* (1963).

The Revolution, for Pasolini, was constituted by these physical gestures from out of Africa framed by a revolutionary Soviet song, the Soviet Revolution in fact and the African past in spirit. By means of the one (Soviet, conscious), the other (African, innocent) found its force. The reality of Africa is mythologised by the song of Revolution. The juxtaposition is the myth of a myth. It restores, rather invents, a relation, as with the analogic relation of Aeschylus's *Oresteia* to contemporary Africa. Both are the idealisations of reality, 'poeticamente e metaforicamente'.

Pasolinian reality had two dimensions: itself and its writing, reality and art, document and consciousness. Reality needed metaphor and art to transform it and thereby make it known. The need to artificialise signalled that the the reality so altered – though often simply by being cited – was anachronistic and no longer in existence. Like the photograph, it mimicked what was gone at the moment of being possessed in an image. The image and the analogy were the records of a loss, and one not only recorded by the analogy but formed by it.

Pasolini's documentaries were feigned. His past was not real, but a fragment framed, cut out. Reality was mutilated to make it all the more beautiful. His poems to life are remembrances with the sweet smell of a funeral pyre. What he made known was that the past was dead, keeping it alive in poetry, which imitated life, like a death mask. What had disappeared in reality became present in memory and language. Consciousness was a consciousness of the impossibility of all that he desired (the past, reality) and of the need to keep the desire alive and himself alive: the desire was the desire to write all that remained of the lost reality. Impossibility and necessity – the centre of desire and passion – were the reasons to live. He was in pursuit of the impossible, and he refused ever to it give up as if poetry was his protest against life and the guarantee of it. It also marked out the boundaries and force of his courage.

VIII

Pasolini knew, I think, that his ideal worlds and the past which he evoked (where these ideals were said once to have been) – Utopia, paradise, prehistory – never existed. They had a mythological, hence hypothetical, value, not a real one. He invented worlds and languages to go with them. Both of these, place and language, were fictional. The myths from the past accused the actual present, and thus had a critical function. They were also a defence against the present, a make-believe world to play in, which stood guard against the reality at its borders that threatened to deny it. It was a perfect world. Nothing real could enter it and nothing from it could escape into reality. It was the world in which Pasolini wrote. He wrote so that his invented world would retain its singular function as the only place where he could be fully himself, where the world could be his and where he could write.

In the novels of Elsa Morante, the main characters – especially in *Menzogna e sortilegio* and *L'isola di Arturo* – are alone in the world. In their isolation and loneliness they create imaginary worlds. They create stories about the world in which they live, that is they fictionalise reality as the way to make it bearable. The novels are these fictions. What you read is the attempt by the characters to reason out their world by fictionalising it. Horrible as the world often is for them, when veiled in fiction it becomes ideal, that is no longer reality, but writing and invention. Reality becomes a pretext for their imagination rather than the goal of it. Morante's novels, though lengthy and seemingly naturalistic, are the reverse of a naturalism, though by the gentlest of means. Her sensibility is kindly and soft. The characters who tell the tales in her fictions are telling them out of the same motives as she had in writing those characters. The characters in her novels populate their world with characters and she populates her world with them.

Earlier, I noticed a sentimental and ideological closeness between Morante and Pasolini, despite their stylistic differences. I think, perhaps, there is something more. Fiction is not only a way to understand for Morante but, by understanding, a way to grow up. The ideal and the real, imagination and actuality, are mixed without becoming confused. They help each other like two drunks on an icy road. Fiction is a means to escape from reality and therefore it is a private happiness. Reality is public, symbolic, repressive. But fiction is also a means to approach the things and experience of the world again, to re-encounter them imaginatively.

Pasolini's structures of ideal worlds and real worlds were relatively rigid. They defined the space for his writing and the writing remained within these borders. Morante wrote to escape the world in order to reapproach it. Pasolini's works were more determinedly set against the world, less fantastic yet more escapist, because more Utopian, more complete and self-contained. He wanted to criticise the world, confront it, scandalise it, not make something of it.

He scandalised it because it was not where he wanted it to be and because it had no place for him within it. He was not, I think, happy on the outside. But nor could he be on the inside. He wanted the world to be different, which was wanting too much. It was always bound to result in unhappiness. Quietly and softly, Morante made the world different in order to re-enter it. In doing so she blended her world and the real world. Pasolini kept them apart, opposed them, contaminated each with the other in perverse, scandalous, monstrous hybrids, contesting reality with his myths of it and refusing reality by means of those myths in order that he might live solely within them, like a character in a fiction. In such circumstances he encountered his death.

Filial relations are at the centre of most of Pasolini's films. The ideal filial relation, no matter from what social class it issued, or to what history or point of history it referred, was one of perfect harmony and love: the child admired the father; the father loved the son, both unconditionally – perfect acceptance and perfect love. It was a sentiment as Utopian and fantastic as Pasolini's idea of a prehistory or his concept of the primitive.

Perhaps we all dream such dreams and never completely let go of them despite all evidence to the contrary in reality. Pasolini, I think, dreamt the dream continually. In his paradise, independently of its other qualities and virtues, the most blessed aspect was the harmony between father and son. It was a harmony he did not have in his life and this caused the pain he expressed in 'E l'Africa?' The only place he could have that harmony was in the Utopian fantasies he wrote. In the poem, what his father denied to Pasolini by the fact of denying Pasolini was metaphorically the paradise which was Africa and the paradisaical pleasure of making the film on Africa, that is the pleasure of poetry, of writing, of being able to evoke paradise. Instead of making the film, Pasolini wrote a poem to what had been denied him, lamenting the loss of paradise and accusing the father(s) who was (were) less than ideal and had sought to deprive him of his ideals (And Africa?).

What were these ideals? They were not simply those of primitivism, Africa, the irrational, noble savages, prelapsarian innocence. They included the myth of the ideal father, the desire for one, perfect filial relation. It was this myth perhaps that is at the centre of all his myths. *Il padre selvaggio*, after all, is a film about fathers and sons, the savage father and the European teacher father from whom Davidson learns to write.

(*Padre selvaggio* was not made partly because of the scandal caused by *La ricotta* and the legal prosecution against it for blasphemy. *La ricotta* evoked the Passion of Christ. It did so by mechanisms of duplication, mirrored analogies and citations characteristic of Pasolini's films. Welles, the film director in *La ricotta*, is making a film about the Passion. In the film that he is making, and on the set, one of the thieves is Stracci. Stracci, outside the fiction being made by Welles, is fictionally a sub-proletarian from the Rome *borgate*, as Accattone and Mamma Roma were.

Stracci is forever hungry. After gorging himself at a Last Supper watched by the film crew and actors, he is nailed to the Cross in the Welles's film. From the Cross he must say to the fictional Christ beside him, 'When you are in the Kingdom of Heaven, remember me to your Father.' Before he can speak the lines, he dies on the Cross of indigestion. He dies within the fiction of the set, thus destroying the fiction inside it, the film of the Passion Welles is making. Stracci is the stand-in Christ, His contemporary analogue. There is a social message: Stracci is the victim of the world which looks on at him, has impoverished him, has made him a non-entity. He is also the victim of the restricted world of cinema and the media which uses and reproduces him. The blasphemy of the film consisted in the accusation against the world in the figure of someone not noticed by it who attains notification only by his death. Welles: 'Poor Stracci, he had to die in order to let us know that he existed.' It is also a blasphemy because in the fiction directed at us, both the film within a film and the film that frames it, Stracci the slob is the analogue of Christ the Saviour.

During Stracci's Last Supper, accompanied by a 'Dies irae', Stracci eats in speeded-up rhythms of the silent cinema, but is looked at by the cast and crew from within their time of the sound cinema. The frames tick by in different seconds, each, literally, from different worlds. The laughter from the epoch of sound is cruel, without compassion. It doesn't know its own prehistory and an earlier, desperate innocence. It is that cinema, by its vulgarity and inability to comprehend, cut off from the past, that kills Stracci, not his hunger and overeating. There is no place for Stracci in the world, only torment and sacrifice.)

In the real world, Pasolini was not accepted (he tried not to be), nor did he accept the reality of the world as it was. He retreated from reality towards impossible worlds where he could write of impossible worlds. He never made these worlds whole or consistent, but only alluded to them by their traces and remains. They were notational, hypothetical, fragmentary, only potential. And, because cited and made of internal analogues and mirrors, they were always collage worlds beckoning to an outside which they came from but could never return to.

In order for these worlds to be completely impossible, they could not completely exist, not even fictionally. Pasolini suggested them, cited them, but never fully created them. His ideal worlds were ideals to evoke in fiction, but not themselves coherent fictional constructions; this is one reason why he referred to them as real, that is as not illusionist. In fact, they were not worlds at all, but figures of worlds, that is, a writing with worlds: 'writing reality with reality'. They were Utopias whose means of realisation were not those of fictional make-believe. He did not ever create a Utopia, he alluded to it and lamented its absence. It was a writing that pointed to myths, but the myths themselves were left unconstructed, unrealised except as fragments cited.

His world was essentially a field of writing striving for a world-not-yet. It is the sense of 'E l'Africa?'. It is also the significance of those works he made as works-yet-to-be-made like *Appunti per un film sull'India*, *Sopralluoghi in Palestina*, *Appunti per un'Orestiade africana*. His finished fiction films were also hypothetical: if-only-this-could-be.

Pasolini constructed his films, certainly from *Edipo re* onwards, as make-believe, that is, marked out as make-believe, hence not to be believed as an illusion of reality. Moreover, this make-believe – and it was one reason why the artifice of them was so evident – was made up of fragments. The structures of the films were composed of fragmented scenes. There was a lack of continuity (and motivation) between them. The fictions were transversed by citations from outside the fiction (as in *La ricotta*) which made them lose their fictional coherence as they attained an intellectual, artistic one. Coherence was not something in the films, nor a fictional quality, but a lost ideal of a coherent other to which the film referred, nostalgically and mournfully.

It recalls for me Edgar Allan Poe's 'The Oval Portrait' which Godard cited in *Vivre sa vie* (1962). As the artist-husband in Poe's story brought colour to his portrait of his wife, she lost her colour in reality in an exactly symmetrical measure. When the artist put the last touch of paint to the portrait, the wife died. In *Vivre sa vie*, Anna Karina dies because of a fictional demand: her death was dictated by the convention that she had to die.

You can't, I think, give life to impossible worlds, because they inevitably carry the mark of their impossibility, doubly the case with Pasolini. His worlds were only cited, like insinuations, not formed. They are never more than a hypothesis, a theorem. For that reason, they are merely signs; to give life to impossible worlds, you have to use them, as Morante did, to accommodate reality. You need to find a way to transform reality, yet recognise it, even accept it.

Morante's manner was not conformity, or a mode of playing things safe, but rather a way to be happy in what was objectively miserable and lonely. Despite Pasolini's obsessive invocations to life, his celebration of the flesh, his fixation on the body, these things are only ideas, not experiences. His intellectuality was such that life, even in his films, or especially in his films, was dead, its flesh pale and pasty, almost revolting. Pasolini's sensuality was in his head, not his prick. It made sex seem, if not obscene or absurd, certainly unpleasant, as in *Salò* and the *Trilogia della vita*. The *Trilogia* was meant to have been a homage to the pleasures of the body, but it was only the idea of pleasure, not its joy.

113

Concepts can be defensive, easier to cope with, since the idea limits the experience. Joy, certainly *jouissance*, can shake you up, make you lose your head. Pasolini's films, literally, never 'come', not because they are waiting for it, in the patient expectation characteristic of the films of Rossellini, Renoir, Antonioni, but because it is impossible, ideal, like masturbating the mannequin in *Salò*.

The potential, hypothetical nature of Pasolini's ideal worlds were often marked by the fact of only being sketched, notations for a-yet-to-be. His ideals, to remain ideals, needed to be unfinished and thus, as well, essentially futile, even preposterous. He identified with what was in these impossible worlds but not in himself (the primitive, the pre-symbolic, not the bourgeois) and he also identified with what was in him, but had been repressed or transmuted. Poetry was his way, as it had been Davidson's, to be like the primitive and yet not be so. The analogy presupposed a distance in order that a conceptual likeness could be formed.

In poetry Pasolini created analogues of primitivism and thereby approached primitivism indirectly and self-consciously in what he called 'free indirect discourse'. [9] In free indirect discourse the author identified with an other, either a character or modes of speech and writing which were not his own and which he reorganised for literature and culture in a hybrid of reason and the irrational, the civilised and the primitive. He said he wanted a primitivism that society had taken from him and now only ran beneath his reason and culture and yet could only be refound now by cultural means. It was less therefore the substance of primitivism than the idea of it, less the experience than the consciousness of it. Primitivism became an effect of writing.

Pasolini could imagine a primitive world and imitate what he imagined. By identifying with this other, he identified with the other in himself which had no place in reality (in the modern world, he said), any more than the primitive or myth, or perhaps even poetry, did. The real world had lost the poetic, he said, because it had lost the primitive, the irrational, out of which poetry came. Pasolini's otherness involved all these elements, but pre-eminently the otherness was constituted by poetry and homosexuality. His otherness was what he was. And it was also everything he identified as ideal, including, perhaps above all, the ideal of the perfect son and perfect father living in perfect harmony. Perhaps, for the Catholic who didn't believe in God, the religious Pasolini for whom there was no divinity, the perfect father was God Himself, that impossible idea which you can never know but only believe in. Had God created a rational universe, there would be no need for Him. Only by creating an absurd one, could God's own absurdity be made manifest, that is as that which makes no sense.

Pasolini exercised his intelligence and passion in order not to be accepted by ordinary society. He outraged, scandalised, puzzled. He wrote in

114

riddles, paradoxes, contraries, analogies, voices that were not his. He imitated others and he assumed a radicalism that was reactionary at its core. He placed himself alongside and in solidarity with entire historical groupings of the excluded and out-of-place: Jews, homosexuals, blacks, primitives, the poor, the downtrodden, the despised, the hungry, the lost, the repudiated, the useless. He situated himself among the unacceptable because with them he felt, relatively at least, if not comfortable, then not alone. He became part of a community of outcasts: in the historical space of the present, and to the end of time and from out of an eternal past as if from the grave.

In these (mythical) societies, among these (non-existent) people, he could have ideal relations, where *he* could make-believe that he was other, and in that other place, in another identity, be accepted and relax: no more disobedience, no more scandal, no more pressures to conform from the father. There, Pasolini could find the ideal father to love him for what he was, not the real father who had rejected him for what he had become and for all that was inside him, his 'difference', his poetry, his homosexuality. The blame, as Pasolini constructed it, was not with himself for being different, but with the father who could not bear difference. From rejection by the real father and his provocation of the father, it was only a step to rejection by the real world and provocation of the real world.

The father, for Pasolini, had taken upon himself the authority of the social law, the symbolic, the state and with these the mechanisms for enforcing an adherence and conformity to the Law. This is the tale told in *Salò*. The fascist libertines create a perverse world in which the essential perversion is reason. It is the symbolic and the Law out of control, gone mad. Who better to have seen it than the Marquis de Sade, from the *ancien régime*, incarcerated by bourgeois order and reason? De Sade viewed reason from within his prison where he wrote its contraries, but contraries governed, no matter how far he went in perverse erotic fancy, by the rules of bourgeois order taken to excess, beyond reason and order but by means of them. It was not the good Marquis who was perverse. Thus, the father, and all he was associated with for Pasolini, would have literally killed him had he been obeyed. The father would have taken from Pasolini his poetry, his Africa, his potential, his love, his soul. 'E l'Africa?'.

So Pasolini invented an ideal place where the father would be kindly and the chief component of a pre-symbolic, primitive universe. How perverted Pasolini was! He was an atheist who wanted God to love him. This father would permit Pasolini to share in the universe of beauty and poetry and Pasolini would be obedient thereby. In *Il padre selvaggio*, Pasolini identifies with Davidson's teacher. He can instruct Davidson because he can recognise Davidson's needs and struggle. But Davidson is also a stand-in for Pasolini, Pasolini-indirect. Pasolini inhabited Davidson. To recognise Davidson's needs fully required that Pasolini be able, as an act of infinite compassion, to identify with Davidson. In that manner, Pasolini could do for himself what his father had refused to do for him. He could love himself, and not simply fictionally. The experience of love was aligned to the task (and pleasure) of growing up (consciousness). It was the subject of his poetry. And it was the reason he asserted, strongly and insistently, that poetry was essentially metalinguistic.

Poetry not only contained what was outside the grasp of the father: it contained a consciousness of that which also belonged to the Father and which Pasolini transmuted into a poetic language. He thus went one better than the prosaic father. Pasolini conformed, and did not conform. In the end, and despite all his scandals, he was an obedient and loving son, as his poetry, and 'E l'Africa?', *Il padre selvaggio* and *Appunti per un'Orestiade africana* demonstrate. These are works about filial love, testifying to it, demanding it, calling out for it, and lamenting its absence. If only ...

Pasolini's *Edipo re* described the attempt by Oedipus, the son, to escape reality in order to maintain a relation with an ideal father – a fictive, adoptive father. Fleeing from that ideal, taking to the road, he encountered his real father. The real father was an awful, nightmare father. Oedipus had to kill him. He was literally in the way, barring his escape from his fictional father. The real father left Oedipus no choice. The real father had wanted to kill him, not once but twice, now on the road and earlier at Oedipus's birth. On the other hand, Oedipus had been provocative.

Chapter 4

Revolution

Only the revolution saves the past.

I

Pasolini was born in 1922, the year the fascists came to power. They remained in power until the Italian surrender to the Anglo-American armies in 1943 and until 1944–5 in all of the German-occupied part of the country. Pasolini grew up under fascism. His first book of poetry, in the dialect of Friuli, *Poesie in Casarsa*, was published when he was twenty, in 1942, during the war and in the last years of the regime. Pasolini had gone to Casarsa, in Friuli, in part to escape the war. Casarsa was his mother's home.

Fascist Italy, of the 30s and 40s, was predominantly rural and agricultural. In the Italian south more than 60 per cent of Italians worked in agriculture. Italian society was localised, regionalised, peasant, economically backward. Italy was among the poorest countries in Europe, particularly so in the south. Most Italians were illiterate and spoke dialect, not Italian.

By the side of this peasant culture was a refined, almost over-refined, literary bourgeois culture. It was a class culture without great national or social depth, unlike the bourgeois cultures of France and England which, though the cultures of a class, were also the national cultures. These more developed societies were culturally more unified than Italy.

There were various motives to fascist policy. One, certainly, was to develop the economy and within it the industrial sector. To that end, and not solely by economic means, the state began to break down the particularism of the countryside, physically and culturally. An aspect of fascist cultural policy was linguistic: to promote literacy and to impose Italian as the national language of communication and hence of culture against the particularism and presumed backwardness of dialect which was consigned to the realm of non-culture.

The rural economy was rationalised under fascism and industrial growth encouraged. A gradual shift began to occur away from agriculture towards the town. For the fascist period overall, there was an internal

117

migration of nearly ten million people from south to north and from countryside to city. Such migration had linguistic consequences, favouring the Italianisation of Italy. Rural groups, from different regions, speaking a variety of dialects, came together in urban areas where Italian became the single means of linguistic exchange. Officially, dialect was discouraged by the state, as if to speak it was to be anti-fascist. In films, a non-accented, uniform, largely artificial bland national Italian was spoken. The same was true for the radio and in part for the theatre.

The countryside was a near and immediate presence for most Italians including the bourgeoisie. Pasolini, bourgeois and educated, had rural origins on his mother's side. There is an image of that in the modern framing sequence of *Edipo re*. Pasolini fell in love with the Friulian peasantry and peasant life at Casarsa. When he went there, his only language was Italian. He learned the local, essentially peasant dialects of Friuli and Veneto and began to write in them. In doing so he was acting against the fascist Italianisation policy of linguistic uniformity. Rather than losing dialect as the state encouraged, Pasolini acquired it.

Pasolini had various motives for learning dialect and writing poetry in it. Some of them were literary and decadent and had little to do with a political populism or love of the peasantry. Friulian was chosen simply because it was dialect and therefore restricted. Outside Friuli it was incomprehensible. Friulian was more purely a language of sound than Italian because the sense of it could not be widely conveyed. This made it more serviceable to poetic expression than prosaic communication. Pasolini assigned Italian to the prosaic.

In Pasolini's aesthetic, Friulian was a purer language than Italian because it came from the peasantry, hence more archaic, and also because, in the context of the modern world, it was meaningless if for no other reason than its limited geographical range. And state policy was for the imposition of Italian nationally against the local particularism and regionalism of dialect.

> I was seventeen. I wrote these early Friulian poems in the heyday of hermeticism, the main figure of which was Ungaretti. At the margins there was a certain provincial symbolism; Montale committed himself to poets like Eliot and Pound; to sum it up, all the hermetic poets lived with the idea that poetic language was an absolute language. From there, it was only a small step to close oneself off in a language reserved for poetry precluding any intrusion by prose.
>
> I adopted the idea of being incomprehensible rather naively and chose to that end to write in Friulian dialect. For me it was the highest point of hermeticism, of obscurity, of a refusal to communicate. Instead, something happened that I didn't expect. The use of this dialect gave it a flavour of life and of realism.[1]

Dialect as Pasolini used it was the reverse of a political language, even if support for dialect under fascism could be construed as a political act because dialect was not Italian and thus not in accord with state policy. On the other hand, the obscurity of dialect rendered it politically impotent in its substance. To whom could it be addressed? Pasolini's dialect poetry did not engage with politics or history, even in the formal presence of dialect in his work independently of what it said. It was rather a retreat from these areas of social reality.

His poetry belonged to an Italian hermeticist tradition. By that fact it could be argued that it was un-Italian with regard to the way fascism had defined Italianness, and therefore was anti-fascist. But if so, it was an anti-fascism distant from the experience of ordinary people even if it reproduced ordinary dialect speech. His poetry may have used their language, but it did so to speak a class language of the literary, not a popular language of the peasantry. Pasolini had poeticised and hermeticised it.

Fascism, like Italian communism, presumed to speak in the name of the people. Like communism, fascism was ideologically populist even though it pursued policies not in the popular interest. As under the current social democracy, there was under fascism a tendency to conflate the people with the nation. Such conflation can sanction anti-popular, even anti-democratic measures in the name of a future national good, for example measures like wage restraint or anti-trade union laws. To the extent that fascism was populist, it was culturally critical of narrowly class, experimental, decadent writing and as much opposed to the avant-garde as the Communist Party was after the war. Such writing necessarily was not for the people or representative of them. In that sense it could be considered to be against the people by the fact of being non-popular. Similar views to these were expressed by socialist realists in the 30s in the Soviet Union. They were reiterated as part of popular front ideology in the 40s and 50s by the Italian Communist Party.

Pasolini's dialect poetry written during and immediately after fascism in fact had little political weight. When, later, he assigned it such weight, he did so retrospectively, in the early 50s.

Pasolini maintained that despite the urbanisation of Italy in the 30s as a direct consequence of fascist policies and the increasing number of workers and sub-proletarians being established in the cities, working class culture continued to be essentially a peasant culture in language, gesture and values. Thus, he argued, though Italy was becoming more urban and uniform, a popular class culture was able to maintain itself and that culture, peasant in origin, was the culture of most Italians.

Accattone and *Mamma Roma* were offered up in evidence of this. The Rome *borgate* were formed by two social components: peasants who had come to Rome from the south, and established Roman communities whose homes and neighbourhoods had been destroyed by the grandiose imperial urban renewal schemes of Mussolini.

The fascists rased the area around the Roman Forum and Colosseum to build the vast avenue, the Via Foro Imperiali, that runs from the Colosseum to the Piazza Venezia and the monument to Vittorio Emanuele. They did the same around the popular *borghi* between St Peter's and the Vittorio Emanuele bridge to build the Via di Conciliazione. The avenue destroyed Bernini's careful, considered organisation of the space of St Peter's Square as it related to the surrounding narrow streets. The Via di Conciliazione was built to commemorate the Lateran pact between the Fascist state and the Vatican, both formerly hostile to each other. The people who lived in the Vatican City between the river and the basilica paid dearly to celebrate the peace between fascism and the church.

In Pasolini's two *borgate* films, the *borgate* and their language were depicted as distinct from the Italian and bourgeois culture at the centre of the Rome of church and state. The culture of the *borgate*, like the culture of Friuli, was constructed by the films as pure, with laws and gestures all their own, sealed off from the centre. Inevitably, and it is the parable related in these films, purity is contaminated by values from that centre. Alien, bourgeois Italian values, then, are made to be forces corrupting an original, prelapsarian purity. The gestures of purity and innocence, though now in the city, were, for him, by the fact of their primitivism, ancient and peasant. He referred to urbanisation in Rome in the 30s:

> All that did not injure the past, did not lacerate its models or its values. Urbanism was still peasant. The world of the worker was physically a peasant world; and its recent anthropological tradition was not violated. The countryside could still tolerate these new forms of life (*bidonvilles*, shacks, tenements) because its spirit was identical to that of the villages and the farms. And for that reason the revolutionary worker has this 'spirit'.[2]

The historical accuracy of these assertions is less important than the fact that Pasolini believed them to be accurate and that he used them creatively and polemically. What mattered to him was that if it could be said that the Italian working class was potentially a revolutionary, anti-bourgeois class from a Marxist perspective, this was so for Pasolini because the working class was linked to the countryside and to a preindustrial, agricultural society, not because of its industrial character. That is, the revolutionary nature of the working class did not reside for him in its relation to modern capitalism, but rather to a pre-capitalist archaic, peasant world. It was revolutionary by the fact that it was still peasant.

This view had odd consequences. If it could be argued that the working class was revolutionary insofar as it was predominantly peasant and non-modern, the more it retained its peasant origins and remained in the past, the more revolutionary it would then be, as if the less the working class was working-class the more revolutionary it would be in modern capitalism. Politically, this was nonsense and did not even correspond to Marxism. It has an idealist and Utopian character. The working class so conceived was an ideal posed against a reality, like a cavalry with lances sent to do battle against tanks.

There are no worker heroes in Pasolini's three first films. The films were made in the Rome *borgate*. He said they belonged to his 'national-popular Gramscian' phase. They centred on the Rome lumpenproletariat. Its characters, like Accattone, are part of Pasolini's 'aristocracy of labour', *because they do not work*. They refuse to be integrated into the productive process. They are pimps, thieves, layabouts, whores, the unemployed. Their elitist position is not as skilled workers in a Marxist heaven, the true aristocracy of labour, but as unemployed parasites in a Pasolinian Utopia. They are useless. It is for that fact of uselessness for a capitalism where use and function are everything that they are ideals. In that sense they are analogies of poets and what they do is as poetic as what poets do.

Revolution, in a Marxist view, could only come from contradictions between classes, principally the working class and the capitalist class, formed by a contradictory relation in production. The working class was the key to revolution because it was central to production. The lumpenproletariat had no revolutionary potential because it had no economic strength, in contrast to workers who had revolutionary potential because they had economic strength.

The trap for revolution is social democracy. Workers, once given a stake in the existing society, are reluctant to dismantle it and tend instead to accept its terms; this leads not to class opposition but class compromise, eventually class complicity. Reality, or rather actuality as Pasolini called it, was the actuality of a consumerism that destroyed class boundaries and ideological positions, making the whole world one in consumerism. It was a homogenisation of class and individuals, or, in other terms, their bourgeoisification.

Revolution, given the political, economic and social realities of Europe and Italy, was not a possibility. Certainly it was not a possibility from the point of view of the policies and positions taken by European communism and the European working class. Both the class and the party had adjusted to capitalism. Pasolini shifted the revolution from a realm of reality to one of ideals, to an ideal reality, that is to the realm of the impossible. There, as impossible, it could function as critical ideal against actual reality. It was its uselessness, the fact that it could not be realised, that made it an absolute and unassailable revolutionary proposition. If it was truly impossible there was no need to compromise with reality.

Pasolini was well aware that the pre-capitalism he identified as having once been at the heart of the Italian working class which had so recently emerged from the peasantry was not in fact a state that could be restored.

The world was not going to move backwards economically nor was it going to recycle its social-cultural past. The pre-capitalism Pasolini idealised, and the urban lumpenproletariat and rural peasantry he associated with pre-capitalism, were not temporal states or social groups that would endure; indeed, either they did not exist or they would soon cease to exist. Their role was only critical, an accusation against what was and witness to the fact that it was no longer.

Pasolini's revolutionary ideal was beautiful, not practicable, and in that lay most of its beauty. It was like an elegiac poem. His political commitment was to art. Art was his impractical politics and as such had political force. It was an art of the ideal which functioned as a criticism of the real. But based as it was on ideals of poetry, it was also a poetics. Pasolini's artistic practice was a critical practice and therefore an art of (political) commitment. Both his politics and his art were potential, and for that reason revolutionary. To maintain the power of his ideals politically, he needed to keep them as far away as possible from the realities of politics. He converted the ideals instead into a fictional reality of language and texts of language and into a theory of that conversion, a poetics. His theory of art was also its practice, an art theorising itself. In that sense his artistic language was the self-consciousness of that language, that is its celebration and criticism.

Pasolini said his poetry was metalinguistic, which was why it sometimes seemed passionate but not sensuous. The passion was a theoretical passion, avoiding itself in a self-consciousness which lamented and longed for the sensuality it was not but whose loss ensured the need and form of his lament, and more importantly, the perpetuation of it. Like revolution, sensuality and the body were maintained at a distance from any reality. It was that which gave them their force, a force of desire and attraction for that other part of themselves, their ideal mirror in the other.

Pasolini's ideal Utopia was like the medieval parodies of the Passion found in Rabelais's banquets discussed by Bakhtin, Ginzburg and Argan. Pasolini staged such banquets in the Last Suppers in *Accattone*, *Mamma Roma*, *La ricotta*, *Il Vangelo*, *Il fiore delle Mille e una notte*, and in the eating of Julian by the pigs in *Porcile*, and the banquet of shit in *Salò*. At these banquets everything was reversed. The sacred was not found in a celestial heaven, but in terrestrial shit. Pasolini reversed the conventional order of the sacred and in so doing offered a criticism of the existing order, and of order itself, especially that of the authorities, of power. He countered power with shit and in a language often composed of it.

Such disordering may have been ineffective politically, but it could be aesthetically productive and in a political manner. Pasolini's criticism of existing conventions and the disorder he thereby created in them opened the way for the new and Pasolini's artistic practices were new. These conventions were not simply linguistic, or formal, but also social and cultural.

Pasolini outraged not only language, but representation (*Salò*): for example, the analogy he made between the closed primitive world of the lumpenproletariat and the hermetic use of dialect, or the analogy suggested between dialect as a primitive speech and a poetry which imitated that primitivism by returning to something before sense and the symbol.

The fact that Pasolini was interested in formal-linguistic contaminations, those contaminations formed by often surprising juxtapositions of high art and low life, the sacred and the terrestrial, literary speech and gutter slang, was a means for bringing together formal structures and representation, form and substance. The elements in these monstrous hybrids made differences felt in the grating and similarities seen in the reflections. It could create considerable formal beauty even when the content of the representation was vulgar or even repulsive. Pasolini was one of the major stylists of Italian letters, but the effects he created always included a critical effect. Even as one part of him fled from commitment because it risked compromising beauty, the other part of him embraced it. Commitment was always present mixed in with the beauty and tempering it.

It is not by chance that Pasolini made a Franciscan film, *Uccellacci e uccellini* (with Totò), within which he cited Rossellini's Franciscan films, *Francesco, giullare di Dio* (1950) and *Dov'è la libertà?* (1952–4) (with Totò). Rossellini's *Europa '51* (1952) is also Franciscan in inspiration. There are Franciscan elements in Pasolini's other Totò films: *Che cosa sono le nuvole?*, which cites the puppet sequence in Rossellini's *Paisà*, and *La terra vista dalla luna*. St Francis was a carnivalesque figure. Pasolini's Utopia is in part within that tradition: the reversals, the discovery of the sacred in shit, the bringing of the high low, the linguistic mix, the irony and the bodily outbursts.

Pasolini's lumpenproletarians are partly Franciscan innocents and belong wholly within the carnivalesque when they are framed as saints: Accattone, Stracci, Zumurrud, Ninetto. They are not modern but ancient and with an ancient purity to stand against a contemporary corruption. In effect, they are innocents in a corrupt world. Their actual social positions as economically useless and unproductive gives them an ideal status as critical emblems opposed to a society from which they are excluded.

Their otherworldliness, essentially their uselessness, made of them revolutionaries in *this* world. Not in the world, they did not compromise with it; instead, in an innocent aggressiveness, they refused it and reality as it was. They were faithful to another, alternative reality which capitalism was destroying or already had destroyed, the rural society from which they came (or from which Pasolini said they came) and the past of that society to which they related (or to which Pasolini said they related).

Their revolutionary character was doubly otherworldly because it was situated outside the modern and because it was situated primarily within fictive worlds and fictive languages. Its revolutionary character hinged on its aesthetic character. Pasolini honoured these figures with a sacred halo, as if they were sanctified angels. He made them into Masaccio saints,

Caravaggio apostles, a Mantegna Christ, a Piero della Francesca Madonna, the Christs of Pontormo and Rosso Fiorentino. In this manner bourgeois salon and lumpenproletarian gutter were conjoined. The poet who wrote hermetic verses in Friulian and novels in *borgate* Roman slang was one with the lumpenproletariat by promoting uselessness as a scandalous revolutionary value. His work returned to a past misunderstood in the present, as their gestures related to that past, making them similarly damned.

The Pasolinian lumpenproletariat which had dislodged a Marxist working class was similar to his use of dialect and regionalism to dislodge Italian and a socially uniform idea of the nation. Basically, these were aesthetic signs, part of a decadent-hermetic tradition and not Marxist categories from a socialist one. Pasolini's political stands were always reconverted into artistic signs for artistic ends. However modern his aesthetic was, the politics which circulated within it looked back to the past. As an art it was new. As a politics it was retrograde.

Pasolini's peasant-based working class, refashioned as the lumpen-proletariat, was revolutionary not because it represented the people and was anti-bourgeois, but because it was peasant and anachronistic. His people were not, as in populist ideology, the heart of the nation. His people instead formed a disappearing ideal entity, a non-existent and complete other. It was everything the actual people of the real nation were not.

Unrealistic and politically irrelevant as this position may appear to be, it nevertheless emerged from within an Italian populist tradition to which the culture of the Italian Resistance, and hence of the Communist Party just after the war, belonged. In this perspective the people were not divided into classes as workers and peasants, but united into the single entity of the people by the fact of their peasant origins. The people, therefore, distinct from the (un-national) Italian bourgeoisie, were truly national. Their status as representative of the nation related to their cultural-social coherence as peasantry and their opposition, real and symbolic, to bourgeois class culture and reality, including bourgeois linguistic reality, that is Italian. Italian, thus, was not the national language, but rather a class language imposed on the nation. The national language was made up of all the diverse languages of the nation, that is dialects. The nation was not the fascist nation of uniformity, but the democratic socialist one of diversity, and necessarily so because of the social reality of a predominantly rural, peasant Italy.

Fascist cultural policy exactly reversed this idea of a popular or, it could be argued, Italian culture as the Italian left had conceived of it. Italian, for the left, was synonymous with the people, hence with dialect, the regions, the particularisms of local cultures that fascism, in the name of modernisation, sought to eradicate, and which the Italian bourgeoisie after fascism did eradicate, as Pasolini tirelessly complained.

Pasolini's populism is consistent with political thinking over a wide spectrum at the end of the war. But he carried it on long after, when the world to which it related was already gone.

Immediately after the fall of fascism and the end of the war, the sign of the nation in Italian films became the dialect and regions of the people, not the uniform Italian which fascism had promoted and the (petite) bourgeoisie of the cities on the movie screen spoke. The linguistic image of a uniform proper Italian had dominated the Italian cinema of the 1930s. After the war, the universal came to be represented in the particular and the mundane. It was a different view of the nation and a different view of the people who constituted it.

The view which identified culture with the people and not with the bourgeoisie led to cultural positions by the PCI and by some Italian left intellectuals which vaccinated Italian intellectual life against experiments in European culture, especially French culture. It was a cultural position absolutely opposed to an avant-garde, because the avant-garde was bourgeois and divorced from the people and for that reason politically suspect.

This was essentially a problem for writers and intellectuals of political commitment in their writing to ordinary Italians. They hovered between a politics of culture and a politics of politics which they tried to align. Pasolini was caught within this problem. He was a modern artist and also an artist committed to the people. He shared with the left some of its political positions, but artist that he was, he had to find a way out of its cultural ones. A return to the past was a key. Rather than distancing himself from the populism of the party, he took it to an excess beyond any political reality, making the peasantry truly ideal. Pasolini could be, as he stated in his reflections on his dialect-hermetic poetry, avant-garde in his hermeticism and populist in the dialect language in which it was written. The two positions, literary and popular, bourgeois and revolutionary, were reconciled by the commonality of their anachronicity: the art, because it could not be fully comprehended and was experimental; the politics, because it looked to the past. The two were one in being analogous ideals.

The cultural politics of the left had a damaging effect on Italian culture generally, evident particularly in the culture of the Resistance, in part exemplified by Italian neo-realism. It was true that the experience of fascism and the overly literary culture of the Italian bourgeoisie in the past made it seem that Italian bourgeois culture and the national culture were different, and even opposed, and that the culture of the bourgeoisie and the culture of fascism were either the same, or if not at least not the culture of the people. But this was a confusion. It was partly the result of the fascist experience and of the left in the fascist period. Bourgeois culture was not merely a class culture, nor was it necessarily anti-popular, even when it was not populist. The politicisation of culture within this cultural frame could only do the culture harm.

Neo-realism in the cinema, and literature, were not quite as uniform ideologically or stylistically as it might seem I am suggesting nor were they necessarily anti-experimental and conventional. There are the stunning examples to the contrary in the works of Rossellini, De Sica–Zavattini, Calvino, Morante and Pasolini. The problem, nevertheless, was there: how not to be merely a class artist, yet avoid the provincialism and conventionality – often no more than an old naturalism – associated with realism and the people.

Much of the writing and films in post-war Italy, at least until the early 1970s, was a response to this problem. The Tavianis, I think, are interesting in this regard. In films like *Fiorile* (1993), hope and revolution are defined as impossible, naive and destructive. While this is the subject of their films, they also enunciate a manifesto for burying a Resistance-socialist past which was artistically harmful precisely because of its populist fervour. The end of revolutionary hope is the subject of the Tavianis' films and the pretext for their existing at all. Only by ending those hopes could an experimental narrative cinema like theirs become possible.

One of Pasolini's most important achievements was the way he addressed the problem of commitment and writing, and redefined it. He attempted to be a modern committed writer without compromising his writing or renouncing his political faith. He brushed along the edge of the avant-garde. At the same time he avoided a political commitment which would be mere obedience to the party. He was not alone. Pasolini, Franco Fortini, Roberto Roversi, Alberto Moravia and Italo Calvino were involved in the literary journal *L'Officina*, founded in the 1950s. The editorial policy of *L'Officina* was to find a literary path through the confines of party commitment on the one hand and the obscurity and apoliticism of the avant-garde on the other without compromising politics by ignoring it (as the avant-garde had) or art by conventionalising it (as the party desired). In the 60s, the Gruppo '63, in which Umberto Eco was involved, had a similar concern. Gruppo '63 and the writers who supported *L'Officina* chose language, poetry and a poetics as the terrains on which to carry on a fight, which was political because it was aesthetic and linguistic.

For the left, the overlap, and confusion, between political positions, social class and cultural work was particularly harmful to Italian culture in the 40s and early 50s. In 1947, for example, the Communist Party, after having sponsored Elio Vittorini's literary journal *Il Politecnico*, closed it down on the grounds of its openness to American literature and literary experiment. The Cold War began a couple of years after the end of the world war. *Il Politecnico* wanted literature to be thought of as autonomous from politics, certainly not subject to party management and dictation. If Pasolini leaned politically towards populism, his literary work did not, even if, or especially if, written in dialect, a gesture correctly read by the party as modernist and elitist, having nothing to do with the culture or needs of ordinary people. The party had no illusions about Pasolini's populism and communist positions.

Pasolini had been a Communist Party branch secretary in Friuli. The party expelled him in 1949 and he fled Casarsa for Rome. Pasolini was accused of molesting schoolboys at a school picnic (the charge was never proved). In addition to his alleged sexual behaviour the party had problems with his literary behaviour. *L'Unità*, the PCI daily, commented:

> The incidents which have provoked grave disciplinary action against the poet Pasolini provide us with the opportunity to denounce once again the harmful influences of certain ideological and philosophical currents represented by figures like Gide, Sartre and other poets and decadent men of letters who give themselves airs of being progressist, but who, in reality, represent the very worst aspects of bourgeois degeneration.[3]

The party linked decadent poetry and decadent manners, literary experiment and perverse sexuality. The 1948 Italian elections had dissolved an uneasy popular front coalition government formed after the war which had included the Christian Democrats, the socialists and the communists. The PCI was caught between a Cold War politics and Italian electoral politics. It needed simultaneously to display its responsibility and respectability and its cultural traditionalism, the latter expressed in a culturally retrograde populism.

The entire range of Pasolinian potentials and ideals, whether in literature, film or social structures, were ideals from the past that had been eliminated in the historical march forward of modern capitalism or repressed by capitalist, rationalist progress. The need to reassert these ideals as a cornerstone of Revolution – the reassertion of the past in the present – was a social-historical liberation and a psychological-existential one. The two spheres met in writing and culture, the areas simultaneously of the self and of the social. For Pasolini, then, the centre of revolutionary activity was poetry in the widest sense and an irrational, archaic primitivism to which it connected. Poetry for him promised a liberation from present repression in all its forms. Poetry was an uncompromising other to social processes and the absolute criticism of them.

For Pasolini, the communists as well as the fascists, the Communist Party as well as the Christian Democrats, were complicit in having promoted a consumerist capitalist society which he regarded as a threat to the values of the past of mankind and to the soul of humanity. So he resisted the contemporary and its politics with the force of an ideal past and an ideal writing, with beauty and poetry. That past which he invoked and largely invented to pose against the present was constructed of thoroughly modern means.

The very impossibility and unrealisability of such potentials, their quality as ideals, gave them their strength. They were always outside the grasp of consumption, commercialisation, commodification. As ideals they could resist any blandishments. And because they were not yet in fact, but always at the border of realisation, there was nothing there in substance to get hold of and use. Uselessness, for him, was a revolutionary, or at least radical-critical virtue. Though Pasolini participated in the modern mass media and at all levels, he refused to deliver to it an accommodating product. His ideal, by its nature, was contradictory and paradoxical: it was also formally upsetting, what he called 'scandalous'. The scandal of his work was a guarantee of its unconsumability and unpossessability. Of necessity, his work was difficult and not as a byproduct of other intentions, but as part of its specific design, like the recourse to an ideal language of dialect which was not comprehensible, but pure language, pure sound. The difficulty of his work resided both in its codical breaks and in its return to a lost sacredness and irrational beauty. It was these qualities that sustained the social world, he felt, and in order for them to continue to give sustenance, they had to be just beyond the reach of the world they sustained. They had to remain untouched, sacred and ideal and, at the same time, matters brought to consciousness to include a consciousness of their unpossessability.

In the 60s Pasolini was a regular writer for *Vie Nuove*, a weekly magazine on the political left. In it he responded to readers' queries on a broad range of social and cultural matters. The form of his column was a dialogue, but the practice of it was monologic. Pasolini spoke to himself as if he were speaking to another or in his own tongue even as he adopted the dialects and gestures of others. In the issue of 25 June 1960, Pasolini responded to a reader inquiring about the generality of sexual intolerance in Italian society and especially an intolerance on the left.

There is some *prudery* in the Italian Communist press: sometimes, some articles seem to have been written with the prohibitionist anxieties of a maiden aunt. ... But it isn't difficult to explain: at the heart of the choice of Marxism by a bourgeois (and there are many bourgeois by origin, naturally enough, among Communist Party leaders) there is an irrational, moral impulse. This morality, which is often indignant – of sacrosanct indignation – informs all of their behaviour. The problem of sexuality – which you indicate – is not, obviously, a moral problem: but since the Catholic petité bourgeoisie is accustomed, hypocritically, to consider it to be, the average Communist Party leader also thinks the same, out of inertia. In fact the matter has never been clearly stated given that it is only a secondary question. There are other more important questions to pose and resolve. Despite the fact that an *irrational operation* would be desirable for Marxists, they, in fact, by identifying irrationality with the irrationality of decadence, ignore it. But irrationality (in which the problem of sexuality is involved) is a category of the human spirit: thus it is a problem which is always current and urgent.[4]

II

Pasolini's historical reflection on the presence of the irrational and the archaic within the Italian working class was also a global and universal reflection. It characterised the Italian people before and just after the war through to the economic boom and consumerism of the mid-50s and 60s (which effectively destroyed, he said, the archaic peasant past), and also the peoples of the Third World only just experiencing industrialisation post-war. By extension, historically, it included peoples everywhere.

The peasant, primitive past which everyone had shared and was part of all histories for Pasolini was at the centre of his Third World notational films on India, Africa and the Middle East and his feature fiction films like *Il Vangelo, Edipo re, Medea, Porcile, Teorema*. It was also important for his films which address the idea of revolution, *La rabbia* and *La sequenza del fiore di carta* (1969). In *Teorema*, for example, the rural maid working for the Milan bourgeois family, who is still in touch with the sacred, can perform miracles. She levitates, calls up springs from the earth and it is to the earth that she returns.

Pasolini's interest in the peasant past of all histories was a common preoccupation in the post-war world which was rapidly becoming consumerist and industrial. It was an important element in modern social anthropology, notably that of Claude Lévi-Strauss. Lévi-Strauss's and Pasolini's work belong to a history of the literature of Western imperialism and the meeting imperialism effected between a developed West and an undeveloped non-West, 'nous et les autres'.[5] The non-Western societies encountered by the West were often tribal, primitive, savage, certainly exotic. Social anthropology presumed that these societies were signs of a past that had been the past of all humanity. This was Pasolini's thesis in his *Orestiade* and the basis on which his analogies between contemporary Africa and ancient Greece were formed. It was also in part the subject of Lévi-Strauss's *Tristes tropiques*, and was involved in Rousseau's invention of *le bon sauvage*, with which he criticised contemporary Europe. Pasolini invented a primitive past for similar ends. A core of primitivism figured in the racist theories of Gobineau, Renan and later Nazi writers. The nostalgic regret in Pasolini's work at the loss of primitivism and of a genetic-cultural-social variety he associated with it was similarly expressed in the writings of Loti and Segalen. There was an undercurrent of these sentiments in the novels of Marguerite Duras set in the Far East. It was more than an undercurrent in the writings of Gustave Flaubert and D. H. Lawrence for whom primitivism and exoticism were sexually charged, anti-bourgeois and anti-progessist, much as they were to Pasolini.

Prior to European imperialism, the contrast between the primitivism of the people and a civility that threatened it from above, whether bourgeois or aristocratic, had been a permanent feature of European cultural history.

It was present in the supposed clash of Greek civility and Roman barbarism, later of Roman civility and European barbarism. It was also central to the history of Christianity which conceived itself as a civilising force against paganism. Similar ideas were set out in Gibbon's history of the Roman Empire. And it was the subject of Aeschylus's *Oresteia* and Euripides's *Medea*, both works cited by Pasolini in his films. Thus structures which shaped European thought about other peoples in the 19th and 20th centuries were part of a historical tradition.

In such histories and literature the meeting of civilised and savage was at the expense of one or the other of the two terms: a noble civility threatened or a noble savagery destroyed. In Pasolini's work, the purity and innocence of primitivism were the victims of a modernity that had forgotten its primitive past, hence its soul. It was the near relative, but reverse, of an aggressive positivism, sometimes racist, which regarded the spread of European civility beyond Europe to the barbaric world as a positive good which could serve as a justification for the the most rapacious imperialisms.

There are traces of Rousseau's idealism and Enlightenment idealism in the work of Lévi-Strauss. His social anthropology involved a contrast between 'authentic' and 'inauthentic' societies. The authentic was primitive, archaic, traditional, oral. It lived in myth and magic. The inauthentic was modern, capitalist, artificial; it lived in history and science. Anthropology was the meeting ground of these two cultures and the means to mediate them. It was a scientific discourse encountering a mythic, sacred world. It seems like very familiar Pasolini territory.

The authentic was not a descriptive term, but a term of value. In Lévi-Strauss's anthropology the authentic was that which he explained, preserved, articulated, even as it disappeared before his eyes under the sway of the inauthentic. His anthropology, though a product of inauthentic worlds, was the consciousness of the authentic, as Pasolini's writing was. Lévi-Strauss lived in one world from which he gazed nostalgically at another just beyond him.

Lévi-Strauss's science was rationalist and scientific. But the theoretical operation of that science consisted in an attempt to imitate primitive thought, to find, as Pasolini tried to find, an analogy of it in his language. The analogy functioned as the metalinguistic knowledge of the other, without seeking to dominate it or know it from the outside in the positivist fashion of an older, more conventional science. Lévi-Strauss's science, like Pasolini's art, took into account its subjective entry into the object. Because the object was primitive, and Lévi-Strauss traced the path of that primitivism, his science was modern by reason of its regressive gesture, of its return to myth not only as the object of his enquiry, but as the means for it. Lévi-Strauss took the side of the primitive object by approaching it mimetically and analogically. He defended the authenticity of the primitive less by explanation than by duplication. The mythological manner of his understanding constituted the primary aspect of his defence of the object he sought to comprehend. Lévi-Strauss's social anthropology might have been a metalanguage of primitive myth and culture but it was so by sharing a mythical aspect with primitive thought. Lévi-Strauss simultaneously imitated the myth he regarded and stood at a distance from it. He used metalanguage as a type of second-order myth.

> By seeking to imitate the spontaneous movement of mythic thought, our enterprise … needs to bend itself to its needs and respect its rhythm. Thus, this book on myth is, in its way, a myth. … If the ultimate aim of anthropology is to contribute to a better understanding of the thought as objectified and of its mechanisms, that comes down to what occurs in this book as the thought of the native South Americans takes form under the work of my thought, and mine under the work of theirs. What is important is that the human spirit, without regard for the identity of its chance messages, manifests here a structure which becomes more and more intelligible in proportion to the progress of a move doubly reflexive consisting of two thoughts, each acting on the other, and thus, one or the other can be the match or spark of connection which will blaze forth in a common illumination.[6]

This way of thinking is like Pasolini's: the plurilinguism, linguistic contaminations, citations from the primitive, analogies with the sacred. The structure is dialogic with the past and the other. It does not surrender to the other but is alert to its presence within oneself. The attentiveness is a means to know oneself.

Lévi-Strauss's study of primitive myth found in his rationalist language an analogous one to the language of the primitive, a myth of myth, a metalanguage of myth which was necessarily mythological – how else could myth be grasped? – composed of fragments of the mythological languages and narratives he sought to explicate. The encounter with the primitive shifted his science, made it come to terms with its own mythological foundations. Lévi-Strauss explained not from a position on the outside, but from within, by a kind of tracing which duplicated the original object but took its distance from it by pointing to the mimetic trace. His activity constituted both a consciousness of the primitive and a consciousness of oneself as preconditions for knowing the other.

To understand the 'authentic', defined as belonging to myth, Lévi-Strauss used artificial means to mirror it: a myth of myth. Analogy was central to his theoretical discourse and also its central conclusion: nature was not natural but cultural, something appropriated by culture and named by it; nature was revealed by the stories and myths of it; the primitive constructed himself in narrative myths like the fictions of moderns. Was this not Pasolini's conclusion too? Nothing was more unnatural than nature and nothing was less real than reality. Such conclusions revealed the object and justified the means of revelation whether they were anthropological or aesthetic, scientific or poetic.

Freud's analytic language was on the outside of the object analysed. His psychoanalysis was a means to uncover the rationality within the irrational without substantially upsetting the positivism of the analytic language. Lévi-Strauss (and Pasolini) entered into the object, not analytically, but by miming it. The Lévi-Strauss analytic experience was more subjective. He had not been cleansed of his subjectivity by a prior analysis to guarantee objectivity, nor had he been cured of unreason. On the contrary he sought it out.

The Lévi-Strauss method was more akin to the experience of the analytic patient who duplicates in analysis and with the analyst experiences of the past, real and symbolic, and by that act of mimesis and by an artificial re-living of the past begins to understand. With Lévi-Strauss (and Pasolini), the language of knowing was placed at risk by the method of understanding, since the method included the object and the subjectivity which sought it out.

In part the aim of his work was to find the irrational core of it, the other language within it, his own primitivism, hence a common humanity. It was the aim of his work and the means of it. There was no objective language to his enquiry which could exist outside and beyond the act of enquiring. Lévi-Strauss (and Pasolini) employed poetic rather than scientific means to delineate the object, or more precisely, to constitute it. It was an object not only to understand but to love, an object of desire, hence subjective. Primitivism and irrationality were not maladies whose cure Lévi-Strauss sought, but positive values which he wanted to share and possess. Neither he nor Pasolini was an exorcist of the irrational, but instead they sought to recover it, in a way one might recover through psychoanalysis a past repressed, that which they believed modern society threatened to make us all lose, our souls. Their work was intended to be a liberation from (modern) repression, by a joyful acceptance of what had been repressed, not the curing of it. Their embrace of the irrational was open and passionate and reasonable. It bore a resemblance to the story of Orestes and the institution of the Eumenides.

They lamented what had been lost in reality in the modern world and as a consequence of modernity and progress, but they also celebrated having regained paradise lost, having brought it back to the heart of consciousness in texts, fictionally, mythically, anthropologically and poetically, for which reason and symbolic language were prerequisites. It was an affirmation of what had been lost and a carnival of its reinstitution, of paradise regained.

Lévi-Strauss, like Pasolini, regarded the destruction of primitive societies by modern ones as a curse. In the end, he concluded, backwardness was a lesser evil than cultural destruction. Better to be poor but spiritually whole than economically developed but spiritually empty. Pasolini said the same thing. Capitalist society, for him, had initiated a cultural genocide as horrible and massive as that of the Nazis against the Jews. It had destroyed differences, all people and things that did not conform to its laws and conventions. The poor and the backward had begun to accept the rationales for development and the ideology of capitalism which ended by turning them against themselves. They became vile to themselves, hating themselves for not conforming, for being on the outside, for being poor or primitive. They began to agree that the worst evil was poverty and that nothing was more shameful than their backwardness. At that moment, by accepting a history that was not theirs, Pasolini said, they lost their paradise. They became the victims of an alien myth of progress which denied them. It made them sorrowful to be who they were.

Pasolini said consumerism had levelled classes and ideology, made everyone bourgeois and everything bourgeois, including history itself. There came to be no other history than bourgeois history, no other story than the story of bourgeois triumph. The cultural-ideological genocide of the other made actual genocide, like the slaughter of Jews and gypsies, possible, indeed necessary. Left and right, communist and fascist, workers and clerks, peasants and youth began to speak alike and dress alike and even physically look alike. The different had become the same even to their gestures. And ideas, like dress, were dictated by fashion as so many marketable commodities.

Lévi-Strauss had said similar things. He said that fascism, communism, liberal democracy were only variations of totalitarianism, part of the global movement of Westernisation-modernisation characteristic of the new phase of capitalism post-war. In the Middle East and in Africa Pasolini encountered the Chinese who were helping the Third World to develop, but it was a development which only degraded. The consequences of Chinese assistance seemed to him no different from those wrought by the Americans. In Pasolini's *Orestiade,* the bookshop at the University in Dar es Salaam was built by the Chinese and sold books written by Americans. Together, America and China were partners in global destruction.

In the 50s and 60s, it seemed to many in Europe that the social classes from which, in a socialist perspective, revolution and change might have come were being lured by consumer capitalism to accept, not oppose, society and to work within its political-economic structures rather than seeking to change them. Revolution was no longer on a socialist or communist agenda.

The PCI, during the Resistance and until after the Italian elections of 1948, maintained a popular front policy which, in the name of national unity, postponed social and socialist reform to a 'second time', until after the defeat of fascism, and until the party had established its political-national legitimacy within the democratic structures of the new Italian state. By the mid-60s, the PCI had become another social democratic party within a social democratic state structure, certainly not a party of revolution.

The *rapprochement* of left and right in Europe in the mid-60s resulted in centre-left, social democratic governments, including the centre-left government of Italy. The PCI never formed part of the Italian centre-left. Nationally, it was always in opposition. When it formed local and regional coalitions, these were with the socialists, not with the church and the Christian Democrats. Parties on the left, including European communist parties, moved closer to bourgeois democratic principles while parties of the right were willing to accept the need for social reform and economic equality, that is social democracy.

Such policies also characterised the social reformist and liberal democratic politics of America under Kennedy in the 60s. The Kennedy administration was anti-communist, as was the European centre-left. Anti-communism was one of the reasons for the existence of the centre-left, an anti-communist but reformist political bloc to keep the communists out of government. The Kennedy administration expressed its anti-communism by demonstrating its social conscience, that is the social conscience of liberal capitalism. The main feature of the Cold War was not so much hostility to the socialist bloc of countries as it was a resistance internal to capitalist states to policies of social and economic equity which the socialist bloc in theory represented. Socialism was conceived of as an internal threat to capitalism. It was in this context that the witchhunt of subversives within capitalism was staged. Subversives were those who recommended social reform. They were enemies of the nation, un-American, pro-Russian, Reds, who risked the security of the West and its way of life.

The Kennedy administration cleared some of the paranoia of the Cold War years. It claimed to be the heir of Roosevelt's New Deal and countered the Cold War perception of an opposition between economic development and social reform. The Americans began to see the two spheres as complementary and necessary to each other, social harmony being the precondition for economic progress and economic progress the key to social harmony. In this situation social-liberal reform returned to Western politics. The ideological shift represented by Kennedy was in part engendered by shifts in the structures of world capitalism. The American government no longer adopted the position that economic progress presupposed social exploitation, still less that social reform represented a threat to free enterprise, individual initiative, in short to the survival of the capitalist system.

The Kennedy administration had a practical political and economic interest in serving the poor, the underprivileged, the disadvantaged and racial minorities. Liberal American policy was extended by Kennedy abroad and particularly to Europe where the Americans impressed on European governments the need for social reform. The European right which had been backed by Eisenhower and Nixon, no longer had such support. The Kennedy administration was also openly anti-colonial and it gave its blessing (sometimes qualified) to independence movements in the Third World, especially if these were seen to be nationalist, not socialist. The Kennedy presidency began to dismantle the policies and institutions of the Cold War and substituted for them new ideals of social justice and reform, the New Frontier.

The Vatican also changed its policies, with considerable consequence for Italian politics, and for the politics of the entire Catholic world, particularly in Latin America and the Catholic countries of Eastern Europe, like Poland, and some parts of the Soviet Union like the Ukraine. The papacy of John XXIII redefined the role of the church as caring for the poor, as a church committed to social and economic justice. It renounced, as the Kennedy administration had and the centre-left European governments were doing, its Cold War policies of militant anti-communism, hostility to social reform and support for parties of the right.

In Italy, the Vatican shift signified the end of its uncritical support for the Christian Democrats. It now gave qualified support instead for the broad social policies of the Italian centre-left. The opposition between communism and Catholicism, atheism and religiosity, rationality and sacredness, which had been central to Vatican ideology during the fascist period and for nearly two decades after the war was bridged by a concern for social justice and betterment which it could now share with the communists.

Social democratic policies of the 60s were centrist. The right, like the Italian Christian Democrat Party (DC), under pressure from its liberal wing, adopted programmes of social reform, which had been part of Italian socialist policies and also communist policies for decades. The parties of the left softened their socialist demands and tended to redefine socialist ideals in bourgeois democratic terms. The Socialist Party (PSI) formed a centre-left coalition government with the DC while the PCI used the PSI as a bridge to the centre-left and, in parallel, the Catholic workers movement as a bridge to the church and the Christian Democrats.

The move towards a centrist politics, which blurred distinctions on the left and right, was indicative of social-economic changes which had made social class, certainly social class struggle, seem less important than it once had been and more complicated than it appeared in Marxist formulations. Prosperity and economic development had led to class integration and cooperation. Calls for class struggle and class interest seemed less relevant. Pasolini complained that society had become completely bourgeoisified.

In the climate of political compromise and consequently of ideological compromise, the cultural-political role of committed artists and intellectuals as it had been conceived in the 1930s under the threat of fascism and in the 40s during the Resistance was equally compromised. Less and less did the social world appear as one of divided, opposed classes and ideologies. The notion of commitment and the place of intellectuals as at one with the interests of the revolutionary classes now seemed a less tenable proposition.

The social and ideological oppositions on which intellectual left commitment had been formed and flourished were changing. One dramatic sign of that change was the detente between the United States (and its European clients) on the one hand and the Soviet Union (and its European clients) on the other. The change seemed to many like Pasolini to have made any political commitment impossible. Commitment had presupposed divisions now being blurred. The social-cultural institutions to which these divisions related and in which intellectuals had worked and struggled were altering absolutely.

Pasolini's *Uccellacci e uccellini* is a film about the end of ideology and the end of commitment. It is movingly expressed in documentary footage of the funeral of the PCI leader, Palmiro Togliatti. The death of Togliatti is a sign in the film of the end of the ideological-political dominance of Italian communism, the end of ideology, and the consequent crisis of political commitment for Italian intellectuals. The lesson of the film, and of Pasolini's subsequent films, was that consumerism and economic prosperity had effaced a world in which socialist ideals and revolutionary change were possible, hence, where intellectuals were possible and had a national, social and popular role. Intellectuals no longer could claim, as they once had, a political role by virtue of the fact that they identified with revolutionary classes like workers and peasants and their struggles. The bourgeois intellectual had had a political option to escape from a class heritage in socialism and its revolutionary or at least radical perspectives. The social other of worker and peasant could be served and led by the bourgeois intellectual. Thus, the intellectual would be saved from his or her class, to become at one with revolutionary classes and the revolution. Much of the energy and optimism in the Italian Resistance and in the ideology of Italian neo-realism after the war was based on this assumption of class identification and of a national role for an Italian bourgeoisie which previously had been confined within an elitist, literary, class culture.

Pasolini said that the films he made before *Uccellacci e uccellini* (*Accattone, Mamma Roma, La ricotta, Il Vangelo secondo Matteo*) had belonged to his Gramscian, national-popular phase. They were films that were popular in style, addressed ordinary people, and at the same time seemed to suggest the possibility of social-political change. The films belonged in part at least to an older, more traditional role of commitment. For this reason, at the time, films like *Accattone* and *Mamma Roma* were regarded as neo-realist. The mechanism of this commitment in Pasolini's work, as he explained it, was the 'free indirect subjective', a device by which the artist found a means to identify with a protagonist who was other than himself, and usually proletarian, or, in the case of Pasolini's novels and Gramscian films, lumpenproletarian.

Pasolini marked out this mechanism as characteristic of the work of neo-realism. Bourgeois writers became, by an act of literary identification, the class revolutionary protagonists of their novels or films, having been able to enter into this world of the other. Pasolini, nevertheless, also criticised neo-realism for structuring its identifications more at the level of content than of style. That is, the identification was from the outside, external to the world of the other and therefore incomplete. The writer remained bourgeois, no matter what may have been his or her political intentions. Pasolini instead adopted the language of the other and thereby subsumed his subjectivity in the other. At the same time he also made that language of the other literary. Linguistically, he was no longer bourgeois, but the lumpenproletariat he had adopted and imitated was no longer lumpenproletarian either, but within literature and speaking a hybrid literary speech. It was this difficult task he said he had accomplished in *Ragazzi di vita* and *Una vita violenta*.

From *Uccellacci e uccellini* onwards Pasolini's films became less popular, more stylistically difficult and obscure. Rather than the films defining a social position with political consequences, they tended to be parables set in an antique past whose principal lesson was the impossibility of political action. The politics of these films shifted away from a representational reality, for example the world of the Rome *borgate*, to the linguistic-stylistic form of the film. This form violated, he said, existing stylistic codes and hence conventional (bourgeois?) forms of expression, for example the plurality of their languages, the lack of plot or even story, and the emergence of a representational text which seemed primarily textual and linguistic, and only minimally narrative and representational.

Because the other no longer seemed to exist in reality or did so only tenuously – which seemed not to have been the case in the early 60s when Accattone and the poor of Calabria corresponded to real social instances and hence had been taken from reality – the other now had to be invented in fictional parables like *Uccellacci e uccellini* or myths imitating the antique like *Medea* and *Edipo re*. The Gramscian lesson of Pasolini's films of the early 60s supposed a match between an otherness stylistically conceived and an otherness which was real. With *Uccellacci* otherness was no more than a textual trace. It had lost its reality to become a textual lament for the loss. The only real was a massive funeral for the end of commitment signified in Togliatti's funeral. And that real was absorbed into a parable fairy tale which included the story of a Totò-St Francis talking to birds and a crow talking to humans. The voice of the crow is Pasolini's. He reads out Marxist lessons with no apparent relevance and of no interest to the ordinary people, Totò and Ninetto, until, irritated beyond measure, they kill the crow'and eat it. Only a few bones remain.

The politics of the post-*Uccellacci* films resided in their obscurity and the stylistic innovations which made them obscure. Pasolini had never completely abandoned his early hermeticism. It resurfaced with *Uccellacci* and along with it ideas of the purity of art, an absolute, uncompromising refusal of the actual, and an opposition between a pure art and an impure world. The renewed hermetic insistence in Pasolini's work and its antipolitics were presented by him as a more radical and absolute politics. He had never renounced commitment or abandoned a social role for himself. His new position had been dictated, he said, by the depoliticisation of the world lured by consumer mass capitalism. Hence, there was all the more reason for an absolute and uncompromising politics. Necessarily, this was a politics of art which he asserted as the only effective politics precisely because it was outside real politics. It contested a political real by being other to it, its complete ideal alterity.

Pasolini's hermeticism gathered within it three strands of European post-war culture, especially evident from the late 50s. This was a period of economic boom, social levelling and political centrism, all the things Pasolini said he hated most with a hatred that was instinctive, visceral and passionate. He summed them up as 'consumerism'.

One strand, evident among left intellectuals, was a nostalgia for a working class and working-class culture which began to disappear in reality as it made its appearance for almost the first time in historical writing. The working class, dying as a class, was being reborn in history (fiction). This was the time of labour history and working-class studies. It brought the working class to the centre of social history at the moment when this class was being pushed to the edges of social oblivion.

These histories, written by bourgeois intellectuals, were filled with nostalgia not only for the working classes who had been neglected in bourgeois histories but also for the intellectuals themselves whose political role had been linked to the working class and defined by a Marxism which had given the working classes *and* intellectuals a central revolutionary and ethical role. This history was a dirge, in part for oneself, for one's own past including the past of Marxism. Labour history was a way to become relevant again.

These histories, like E. P. Thompson's *The Making of the English Working Class*, tended to be populist in ideology. They may have given workers their historical due, but they asserted a social-political place for the working class and for themselves on the basis of that history which in fact was no longer possible. Some of the arguments between the new and the old left in Europe and America in the 60s concerned such issues. The new left in Britain, for example, argued against the populist, romantic, sentimental view of the working class in labour history, certainly against the idea of the continued central political importance of the working class within current forms of capitalism.

The new left was more superstructural in its outlook than the old. It saw revolutionary change at levels of culture, language, philosophy, science, theory, the legal system. The new left reweighted and revised Marxist schema away from an interest in direct productive forces and towards more indirect but no less crucial aspects of society. By distancing itself from a declining working class and from theoretical structures which had given that class a privileged political role, the new left assumed a greater role for theory and intellectual work and thus an enhanced political role for itself. It emphasised the importance of Marxist superstructural

138

factors for social action as well as, and sometimes instead of, the traditional structural features of the economy and class.

Another strand in Pasolini's work was represented by figures like Lévi-Strauss. Like labour history, Lévi-Strauss's anthropology was nostalgic for a lost reality. But it was also more existential and universalist than labour history and more theoretical. It centred not on the modern world but the primitive one and the most ideal, theoretical aspects of primitivism, its myths and thought systems. Lévi-Strauss was more interested, for example, in the terminological features of kinship relations as an explicative framework of kinship than he was in actual kinship arrangements. Lévi-Strauss's anthropology and the structural anthropology which he helped to develop sought to discover not the exigencies of a class within history, but the fundamentals of humanity beyond history, somewhat before history even, trans-historically and structurally. Time was not the central feature of this anthropology. It was structure.

Much of labour history was about the heroic struggles of the oppressed. It criticised bourgeois history for its biased, ideological positions and condemned capitalism for its inhuman acts and for that reason tended to concentrate on the early history of industrial capitalism when it was at its most brutal and working-class sufferings the most extreme. The anthropology of figures like Lévi-Strauss was in fact more absolute, philosophical and total in its criticisms of modern society than labour history was. It was at the same time less directly political than labour history because it was less tied to contemporary political realities; in fact the very basis of such anthropology was implicated in a criticism-rejection of the contemporary.

Anthropology was also, however, by the fact of that rejection, more political. Its criticisms and claims were universalist. By being, in a sense, outside reality, structural anthropology, in the names of truth and humanity, could more totally condemn the actualities of the contemporary world. 'It is far better', Pasolini wrote, in an echo of Lévi-Strauss, 'to be the enemy of the people than to be the enemy of the truth.'[7]

The third strand in Pasolini's thought was represented by the new left. As has been sketched, the new left had shifted the political-revolutionary role of intellectuals and of the revolution away from the working class and the economic base of Marxist theory, towards a revised Marxism in which superstructural features were given increased importance. Part of that superstructure embraced the work of theorising, including the theorisation of the superstructure, a theory which could also reflect on itself ('theoretical practice'). Intellectual work was thus seen not as tied to class interests or economic ones, still less to party, trade union or class struggle, but as something autonomous from these with political consequences and a political importance all its own. It was no longer

139

subordinate. Certainly, the party was less in a position to demand that intellectuals be, as they once were, party intellectuals. The entire culture of commitment had shifted ground.

Many on the new left argued that the socialist political cause was best served by work on the superstructure including areas of culture – cinema, language, painting, theatre, literature, television – that is the mechanisms which formed consciousness and perhaps did so even more effectively and truly than economic structures did. In any case, it was no longer acceptable to argue a subordinate political role for cultural work, or to argue that culture and ideology were mere reflections of economic forces. Theory, in the widest sense, became a political activity in its own right and began to incorporate within itself interests outside a traditional Marxist framework, embracing some which could be argued to be hostile to Marxism: semiotics, structuralism, linguistics, psychoanalysis.

If it could be said, for example, that codes of representation and composition manifested the ideology of a society, then to challenge those codes, disrupt and re-form them, or, as Pasolini said, 'scandalise' them, would constitute a political action of consequence. Indeed, it could be said that it was politically more effective to break these codes and hence affect ways of thinking and perception than it was to take traditional militant class action, like going out on strike. It was not by intellectuals identifying themselves with the working class that revolution would become more possible therefore, but rather by distancing themselves from the working class and the tradition in which it was the central political protagonist. Instead, intellectuals should take an autonomous critical-revolutionary role independent of a class politics.

The society which left intellectuals sought to criticise had compromised the revolutionary potential of the social classes with whom they had once identified. Part of Pasolini's criticism of post-war consumer capitalism was that it had destroyed the revolutionary social classes, hence had destroyed the possibility of revolution itself. He assumed a committed role despite these changes, but most of that role consisted in criticising the society for having altered as it did with the attendant consequences for writers and intellectuals like himself. In fact, however, the old commitment, had it really been possible, would have been the least comfortable position for someone like Pasolini. He preferred to regret its loss in the present more than he would ever have enjoyed its existence in the past. Even in 1947–8 when Resistance populist culture was at its height, Pasolini's identification with the peasantry was through dialect and sentiments which had about them a funereal quality as if already lamenting the passing of a present he identified with into a past he could mourn.

In terms rather like Pasolini's, Umberto Eco recalled the militant Gruppo '63, to which he had belonged. But unlike Pasolini, his reflection was not a lament. It looked forward to future terms of action, not backwards in attitudes of longing and regret. Gruppo '63 was composed mainly of writers and poets on the Italian left. Eco:

Since we had grown up in a field of exclusively cultural possibilities, there was no way we could affect root structures. ...

Only one path was open to us: we had to call into question the grand system by means of a critique of the superstructural dimension which directly concerned us. ... Hence, we decided to set up a debate about language. We became convinced ... that to renew forms of communication and destroy established methods would be an effective and far-reaching platform for criticising – that is, overtaking – everything these cultural forms expressed.

We had one clear idea: if one was moving towards a point of total rupture at the level of literature, art, and philosophy ... it was absolutely no use to 'communicate' our plans by way of known and tested *media*; on the contrary, we had to smash the very *media* of communication. This was the 'poetics' of the Gruppo '63.[8]

The nature of the speech of structural anthropology severely limited the group to whom it could speak. If the ideals it argued for were indeed gone, then so too was an audience who might appreciate the argument. To what humanity might one lament a lost humanity and lost ideals? The conclusion of Lévi-Strauss's work, like Pasolini's, was that the new world left few to whom Lévi-Strauss could speak. Among the things he and Pasolini mourned were their isolation and irrelevance.

The older socialist left, still wedded to a class politics, had tried to create a constituency which the new left exposed as vanishing, regressive or simply non-existent. By the 60s, it certainly was difficult to continue to maintain that the working class was progressive, still less revolutionary. On the other hand, recourse to the theoretical, to linguistic analyses, to codical scandal had its limits. It may very well have been that a new art and new theory, by placing languages into crisis, the language of naturalism, for example, or that of classical representation, might challenge the old intellectual culture and its political assumptions, but the social relevance or political effectiveness of such positions was in fact doubtful.

The nature of these positions cut them off from the workers and from ordinary people, even from the wider bourgeoisie. The languages of intellectuals became more specialised, elitist, less engaged than ever before. Pasolini's hermeticism had become common enough. The languages of intellectual discourse, especially critical and theoretical languages, became most obscure and least available when they addressed themselves to popular expressions like cinema, rock music or television. The languages and theories of film and television studies, and more widely of communication studies, have become largely recondite and inaccessible. They speak about what everyone experiences daily in a language that no one experiencing these things can understand. Speaking to no one has become a feature of intellectual life.

The death of Gruppo '63 was a death attendant on the dilemma of how to speak, to whom and in what language, which the events of May 1968

helped to dramatise. It was a dilemma about the social relevance of intellectuals and the nature of a commitment centring on language and art.
Umberto Eco:

> Our whole attempt to extricate the structures of language was suddenly
> unmasked for what it was: an experimental study of *class* language. We
> were brought face to face with the real language of factory workers and
> angry students. The French avant-garde had posed Lacan's question,
> 'Who is to speak?' whereas the problem of the contemporary literary
> avant-garde in Italy had suddenly become: 'Who is one speaking to?
> How is one to do it? Why? Should one go on speaking (i.e writing) at
> all?' Some of the group even began refusing to write at this point.[9]

In the post-war, post-fascist period, and linked to the loss of political
power by the European working class and the loss of position by European
intellectuals, anti-colonial and anti-imperialist events in the Third World
assumed increasing importance for the European left. The struggles of
Third World peoples for national independence (Africa), sometimes with
socialist forms (Vietnam, Cuba, Algeria, Ghana), came to be associated
with a general pattern of revolutionary requests. These were connected to
Marxism, the European working classes and the familiar issues of commitment. Associations between the Third World and the working class of
Europe, associations which historically had been racist and reactionary,
assumed a progressive, even revolutionary aspect. Pasolini entered into
this terrain, but he did so primarily idealistically, that is from a position
relatively divorced from the actuality of anti-colonial independence movements, or only linked to them by ideas and ideals which predated them and
were regressive in relation to them. He welcomed these movements, but
with little understanding of what constituted them.

The connection between the exotic savage and the domestic peasant, later
to be the domestic (domesticated) worker, was common in European conservative thought and racist theories. The connection came out of a
progressist, positivist ideology in the 19th century which had made European civilisation the absolute ideal and the bourgeoisie of Europe, particularly of northern Europe, the principal embodiment of that ideal. At the top
of the tree of superiority were the northern European bourgeois and at
the bottom primitive savages. Close to them were European peasants and
workers since, if northern Europe was at the top of the tree of humanity, its
peasants and workers were conceived to be at the bottom; in class terms,
they constituted a Third World within the First – just as Pasolini claimed.
Somewhere in the middle were Italians and Turks. Such connections served
European imperialism and domestic repression of peasants and industrial
workers. All of these groups were equally inferior, and equally and therefore
justifiably exploited for the benefit of the civilised and civilisation.

The north/south division in Italy, a matter of cultural and economic
questions, also included a division between civility (north) and primitiv-

ism (south), which corresponded to a more comprehensive division between a civilised northern Europe and an uncivilised southern Europe. In popular and erudite literature, certainly in ordinary exchanges, the Italian south was linked to Arab Africa, while the Italian north was linked to Europe. The north belonged to civility, culture. The south was sunk in barbarism and superstition. An emissary of Cavour on a mission to Naples wrote to the chief minister in Turin: 'But, my dear friend, what kind of places are these. Molise is the Land of Work! What barbarisms! This is not Italy! This is Africa: the Bedouins, compared to these bumpkins, are the very flower of civil virtue.'[10]

The connection Pasolini made between southern Italy, in particular a peasant southern Italy, and Africa was a familiar one. It belonged to imperialist thinking by northern Italians towards the south within Italy and by Italy towards the Third World, as the newly unified Italian state assumed its share of the white man's burden in East Africa in the late 19th century and upheld it until the colonial adventures of fascism. Pasolini made the same connection, however, not within a progressist myth which had justified imperialism, but within a regressive one that criticised it. The south in Pasolini's universe, Italian or Third World, belonged to an order which reversed the values of progressism. He constructed the primitive as morally and culturally superior to the civilised by the fact of being in touch with the irrational which was for him the source of poetry and beauty.

What made Pasolini's idea of revolution new was not his reversal of the conservative-racist formula but his insistence that revolutionary forces were peasant and primitive, that is those least able to make the revolution. Such an impractical thought enabled him to have his political commitment which was populist and revolutionary without compromising his artistic commitment which was hermetic and elitist. He argued that the despised and wretched of the earth were in themselves, in an existentialist and symbolic way, the embodiment of an irrationality and sublimity central to his poetry and to all poetry. To defend the primitive and the peasant as revolutionary forces was a defence of poetry at another level. He shifted his writing to a social politics and his social politics was turned into a poetics. It was the irrational poetic substance of the primitive that made him revolutionary. Those despised and rejected were as much codical breaks to the structures of society as his writing was to the structures of literature and film. His languages were hermetic and by that token revolutionary, just as the primitive in his glorious uselessness was poetic and therefore revolutionary. The primitive indeed was a sign, but a real one, a sign of himself. This 'writing reality with reality' was a way to escape reality altogether.

When Pasolini looked at national anti-colonial movements in the Third World, what he saw was the reassertion of a traditional peasant culture. When he looked at the traditional European/Italian revolutionary classes, he saw in them, insofar as they were revolutionary, their peasant origins. When he began to say that these classes no longer had revolutionary potential and he turned from them towards myth, it was because, he said,

143

they had lost their link with a peasant past. And when he turned his attention to the Soviet Union and Eastern Europe, he found the peasantry there as well. And when he contemplated his own social exclusion and marginality, he relocated himself amid all these excluded others. He longed to be them as a way truly to be himself. But he could never quite possess either himself or the other. Both were ideals which presupposed one another, including the impossibility of reaching or possessing them. It was that ideal that incited his writing as a writing which sought to have what it could never have but which was the precondition for writing at all, hence the lament in the writing, and the joy of it.

III

Pasolini's story of an irrational primitivism repressed by civilisation had been a West European story for some time. Freud, who was positivist and optimistic, told the story in his extra-psychoanalytic writings, *Totem and Taboo* and *Civilisation and its Discontents*. The repression was presented by Freud as ambiguous. It was a necessary price for civilisation, but the price could be exorbitant in individual unhappiness and neuroses.

The appearance within left discourses, from the late 50s, of Freud and structural anthropology gave Marxist theory a new colouring. The capitalist system became not only exploitative in economic-social terms, but repressive in existential and psychoanalytic ones. It limited happiness, compromised pleasure, destroyed the soul, alienated feelings, buried our deepest sentiments.

Primitivism came to figure as a political critique of capitalism, as a sign of a repressed nature, like *le bon sauvage* in the writings of Rousseau. It became part – and not only in Pasolini's case – of writings and expressions which criticised contemporary society for what it had caused us to lose for the sake of economic development and political order. The criticism of capitalism was primarily in superstructural terms. It was made by discourses which addressed themselves not to economics, but to the soul.

When Pasolini went to America, he contacted Allen Ginsberg, part of the beat generation of American poets. He found a kinship between his work and the poetry of the beats in a grouping which included Whitman and Pound. With the beat poets, a rough, hypnotic, rhythmic, musical, popular, street language was critically juxtaposed to conventional speech and manners. Beat poetry was a form of protest poetry, protesting against repressive conventions of writing by asserting raw feelings, primitive energy, explosive sentiments which, it was implied, established literary writing could not express or contain.

Primitivism, the irrational, the bodily, the unconventional, sex, scandalous language, dirt, shit, pressed against the conventional. It did so by asserting that its anti-conventionality and new language were at the very source of the imaginative and the creative. It asserted that its poetry was

144

not only the sign of the imaginative, but in being so it was a social protest against all that would kill the imagination. The imagination then belonged to a primitive and existential repressed.

In roughly the same period, Mikhail Bakhtin in the Soviet Union wrote his study of Rabelais and the carnivalesque.[11] In Italy, Carlo Ginzburg published work on magic, religion and folklore from early Christianity up to the European Renaissance.[12] Ginzburg argued, like Bakhtin, that the carnivalesque represented an incompletely repressed popular spirit and belief system in the medieval period.

Within the high established art of the late Renaissance, however, these same archaic elements which had made their presence felt within the framework of the church and its rituals (and in part against this framework) in the medieval period, re-emerged again in the early 16th century in Italian Mannerism: Michelangelo, Pontormo, Rosso Fiorentino.

Ginzburg argued that the anti-classicism of Mannerism, its use of archaisms, its artificiality, asymmetry, its overturning of the balanced order of classical painting were evidence of a new religiosity, an attempt to express something magical and sacred beneath the secularised calm of early Renaissance art, something which the logical order of Renaissance painting had suppressed. The unity of Renaissance space, the rational temporality of its compositions, the fact that everything had an assigned place in a geometric and essentially historical perspective, including the space of the viewing subject, was disrupted by Mannerism. The appearance of a new religiosity, of feelings not accounted for within the logical spaces of classicism, not only disordered that space, but disordered the place of the subject within it and the historical framework in which the subject was constructed.

> The deliberately archaic, medieval elements in one of the masterpieces of early Florentine Mannerism, the *Deposizione* painted by Rosso (Fiorentino) in 1521 for a secular brotherhood controlled by the Franciscans ... was succeeded by a style of 'impasto' compounds. ... Also, in the same period, the emergence of a disturbed, agitated, anti-classicist painter like Pontormo can probably be explained in the light of the needs of a new religious piety and not by merely formal requirements.[13]

Pasolini called himself a Mannerist. He has been named a Mannerist by critics. His citations of paintings in his films were primarily of Mannerists. The fact of citation and of citation from a past, Mannerist (Rosso Fiorentino, Pontormo, Leonardo, Michelangelo), also medieval and archaic, and not simply citations as icons or duplicate works, but as language, linked him to the stylistic gestures of the early Florentine 16th century. But there was also in Pasolini's mannerism, and it accords with the logic in Ginzburg's conclusions, a strong element of the medieval carnivalesque.

Ginzburg said that the early church, especially during the Carolingian years, was a missionary church intent on Christianising a rural, pagan Europe, in much the same way as Europe later tried to Christianise the heathen savages of Africa, Asia and Latin America – a process whose dramatic beginnings date from the voyages of discovery in the late 15th century. Such Christianisation was never complete. Pagan and popular cults and beliefs went underground or were given a Christian symbolic gloss by the church without, however, losing their pagan substance: attachment to agriculture, to fertility, to the seasons.

These popular elements were essentially rural and peasant. The Renaissance, certainly the *Quattrocento*, had an urban, secular, historical ideal. Argan and Fagiolo:

> It did not matter that the themes and recurrent motifs were religious ... Italian art of the 15th century and after is 'secular' insofar as it ceased to be an instrument of religious or political power and became the expression of the religion and politics of a society, and, naturally enough, of an urban society, because the rural population was considered to be non-social. It seems perfectly legitimate therefore to see in the city, in its typical spatiality or structure, the underlying unity of Italian art, thus linking the identity of city-history with art-history.
>
> Beyond the walls of the city there was not history, but nature. The idea of acting historically and thus within an urban space conditions the entire morphology of 'humanistic' art ... rural areas, the countryside, wild nature are, in their 'naturalness', the exact contrary of the city.[14]

The medieval church contained within itself two languages, two distinct ideas of the sacred. One idea was spiritual, separated from the body, civilised, hierarchical, logical, and it looked to heaven. The other was terrestrial, linked to the body, vulgar, popular, and it looked to the earth. The tension between these two languages was not simply formal, but also social and cultural-economic. Christianisation was part of a process whereby feudal power and control were extended over the land and the peasantry, also a certain religiosity. By the *Quattrocento* this seems to have been ideologically achieved.

The tension between these two languages, in effect two views, two worlds, two opposed notions of the sacred, burst out in uncontrolled violence in the medieval period (peasant revolt), and in controlled, more governable ways in carnival, where the body and the folk were allowed, for a period of days or weeks, to come to the surface, to give vent to desires and impulses normally repressed and kept down: the sacred was overturned, hierarchy brought low, the holy smeared in shit, in the sexual, in the orgy, in an excess of food and bodily pleasures. The whole of the conventional world was derided, parodied, imitated, ridiculed. In effect, the holy was brought to earth, agriculturalised, repaganised, if only for an instant.

The parody of the sacred in the medieval carnival by play, ritual inversion, licence, was not a marginal aspect of medieval culture. On the contrary. Ginzburg insisted that the juxtaposition of the sacred and its comic parody was not an opposition of sacred to profane, but the expression of alternative, yet complementary notions of sacrality. Carnival, because it gave scope to a popular alternative, also kept that popular within bounds and thus preserved, through religious means, a social-political equilibrium.

Ginzburg's writings, and more so Bakhtin's, gave a populist interpretation to carnival. Carnival was the voice of the people (overwhelmingly peasant). The derision of the sacred was thus a form of popular articulation. And, insofar as the sacred was the conventional, the people, by means of carnival, challenged conventionality and the conventions of the social order, including its languages.

It is at the junction of language and the social, and the idea of carnival as the embodiment of opposed languages and worlds, that Bakhtin argued the potentially radical aspect of carnival especially at the level of language. As with most populisms, but in Bakhtin's case it was given a semiotic, even avant-garde or at least experimental gloss, the people, by their earthiness and peasant primitivism, are depicted as not only threatening to overturn the ordinary social, but promising a revolution in language, expression and art. The vulgar, for Bakhtin, was a source of energy, scandal, above all invention and creativity. It is the idea of the people as cultural innovators, as an avant-garde. And Bakhtin cited the stunning example of Rabelais, simultaneously carnivalesque and artistically radical, outrageous.

It can be said of *belles lettres*, and especially of the modern novel, that they were born on the boundaries of two languages. Literary and linguistic life was concentrated on these confines. An intense interorientation, interaction, and mutual clarification of languages took place during that period. The two languages frankly and intensely peered into each other's faces, and each became aware of itself, of its potentialities and limitations, in the light of the other. This line drawn between the languages was seen in relation to each object, each concept and point of view. For the two languages represent two philosophies.

The line of demarcation between two cultures – the official and the popular – was drawn along the line dividing Latin from the vernacular. The vernacular invaded all the spheres of ideology and expelled Latin. It brought new forms of thought (ambivalence) and new evaluations; this was the language of life, of material work and mores, of the 'lowly', most humorous genres ... the free speech of the marketplace. ... On the other hand, Latin was the medium of the official medieval world. Popular culture was but feebly reflected in it and was distorted, especially in the Latin branch of grotesque realism. But the picture was not limited to the vernacular and medieval Latin. Other languages were intersected at this point, and linguistic interorientation was complex and manifold.

Languages are philosophies – not abstract but concrete, social phi-losophies, penetrated by a system of values inseparable from living practice and class struggle. That is why every object, every concept, every point of view, as well as every intonation found their place at this intersection of linguistic philosophies and was drawn into an intense ideological struggle.

Such an active plurality of languages and the ability to see one's own media from the outside, that is through the eyes of other idioms, led to exceptional linguistic freedom. Even formal grammatical construction became extremely plastic. The artistic and ideological plane demanded first of all an unwonted freedom of images and of their combination, a freedom from all speech norms.

It is possible to place oneself outside one's own language only when an essential historic change of language occurs.[15]

I doubt if there were direct connections between Bakhtin and Ginzburg, still less between these scholars and Pasolini, or between Pasolini and the experiences of medieval carnival or the Mannerist 16th century. But the indirect connections are startling. At times, Bakhtin and Ginzburg seem to be writing a direct interpretative gloss on Pasolini and the asso-ciations Mannerism-Pasolini, carnival-Pasolini appear exact. What is true, I think, is that these three shared with other European intellectuals post-war, and anthropologists and historians, a populist sensibility which functioned as a rearguard critique of contemporary society. The criticism was made at the moment when the reality of Western capital-ism was changing the social composition of Europe and of the entire globe. Much of these writings, then, especially when denied the cover of objective historical studies or scientific anthropology, have beneath them a nostalgia and lament for a lost and irrecoverable way of life. On the other hand, these studies, whether by Lévi-Strauss or Bakhtin, re-member, quite literally recompose, the fragments of these lost worlds in their texts. The texts, like those written by Pasolini, constitute new theoretical openings in literary studies, linguistic studies, history, an-thropology and poetry, and precisely in an analogous manner to what they value and resurrect from the past: worlds of linguistic clash, of challenges to established convention, of the earthy and repressed against the hierarchical and repressive. That is, they have made of these ele-ments of the past an experimental writing and have even created out of them entirely new discursive formations. Their work doubly attests to the power of a popular culture, albeit of the past, to renew and even revolutionise the present.

Yet, in the present, these writers loathed and retreated from the popular culture. That culture, contemporary culture, as they regarded it, seemed to them debased and homogenised, depoeticised and devalued by the capital-ist, modern societies they were criticising from the position of a distant, often archaic past. These were modern writers using the past, even arguing

148

it as an ideal, but in ways that were thoroughly new even as they sought analogies for their work in the archaic they were reviving. At their best, certainly at Pasolini's best, they were trying to hang on to what the left, and particularly left writers and intellectuals, always had trouble reconciling, a political commitment to ordinary people and a commitment to the very best of writing.

It was evident, certainly by the late 50s, that a populist faith in the present could not endure. The present had destroyed the very classes and people in whom such faith might be placed. The past offered these writers a new present in which their idealism, located in the displacement of a current reality by a past reality while relocating that past in a present-day text, could contest reality with writing, oppose it with recollections of past beauty or past radicalisms, and with the present of that writing – texts, forms of poetry, imagination.

Rabelais or Pontormo may have been radicals in their time, but it is Bakhtin and Pasolini, with their splendid writings and creations, who offered hope for a current radicalism. Oddly, they benefited from the displacement of traditional Marxist culture from the base to the superstructure, from economics to culture, and contributed to the fact of it. In effect, they reconfirmed an old role of commitment for intellectuals by defining in their work new intellectual locations.

IV

La ricotta is the Pasolini film closest to Bakhtin's notions of the carnivalesque. It contains all the elements of carnival: derision, orgy, excess, blasphemy, reversal of the normal, parody, the sacred paradox. Into the conventions of the proper, as narrative subject and as codes of representation, *La ricotta* intrudes the earthy, the vulgar body, a sensuality out of control, the scandalous, and these disrupt, overturn the holy and the respectable. *La ricotta* paid homage to the Gospels by a comic reversal of them which seemed to have gone too far and the film was condemned and sequestered for being blasphemous. The holy had been dragged into the muck.

La ricotta was, like other films of Pasolini, a collage and pastiche of languages set at the edge of each other: languages of film and painting, writing and image, the popular and decadent, silent film and sound. In that respect it had elements of carnival. And its excesses, as in carnival, by overturning the conventional, constituted something formally new and stylistically radical. To have banned *La ricotta*, then, was to have banned not merely a subject, but a form of writing. It was not the fact simply that an analogy of Christ was found in a gluttonous, lower-class slob, but that the slob was part of a writing system, the terms of which included the analogy and the scandalous imitation, and it was this system of writing that was disruptive. The writing was joyous and comic, inventive, new, creative, and, by returning to the forms of carnival and reforming these forms, it posed both the antique and the popular against the apparently modern and narrowly proper. And at the same time it offered another practice of the popular against the popular culture of the present.

The legal ban on the film was instructive. The language of *La ricotta* was indeed a political language and Pasolini's poetry was thus committed and radical. The film went beyond the experiments of an avant-garde and became, as a result of a language which at the time was the very embodiment of what was modern, an actual scandal and more than society could bear. By going beyond the socially acceptable and in apparently useless forms that touched all at once on the antique, the rural popular, the decadent, the hermetic, he had found a form of a criticism within language that became an absolute form of criticism of the social.

The two positions of the social and the literary, the political and the stylistic, often opposed and always a problem for intellectuals and artists concerned with social commitment to reconcile, found in *La ricotta* a temporary, unstable, but nevertheless strong fusion. In part, the scandal of *La ricotta* was constituted precisely by this hybrid fusion and its originality. It had taken the stakes of art and commitment very far indeed.

In the languages *La ricotta* used and cited of medieval carnival, late Renaissance Mannerism, silent film comedies, and the ancient appeared to be socially uncontainable in the present. Literally, he used the past against the present, but in radical forms more present-day than most contemporary forms, certainly in the cinema. It was a practical demonstration of Pasolini's assertion that revolution guaranteed the past, that it saved the past while the past, in the manner in which he presented it, became absolutely modern and absolutely radical. The scandal of *La ricotta* had forced the repressions of society to show themselves and in extreme forms. Pasolini had not only overturned forms, but he made that action socially and politically instructive. The scandal his work created throughout his life was not something consequent on the work of which he was innocent, or not culpable, nor was scandal a contingent fact of his work. Scandal was its central, crucial feature as it was in the carnivalesque. Scandal was the intention of his work and its political lesson. It embodied his commitment. He worked to scandalise as he made himself a scandal, to be like his films, a blasphemous presence in the contemporary.

Pasolini believed that in consumerist capitalist society everything would be absorbed by the social, made part of it. Even liberal social tolerance was a means to invade all aspects of privacy, especially the privacy of the body, sex, sentiments, to find for all these appropriate signs, an order, an acceptable place socially, symbolically and linguistically. To contest society one had to find what it could not accept, digest, would not consume or stomach, which went beyond the limits. In the beyond-the-social, for Pasolini, was a self that society had not possessed and hence was the place of freedom, above all the freedom to write and to scandalise as a means to preserve that freedom. Persecution did not endanger him, it was his stimulus. It inebriated him. He represented the beyond-the-social as a previously existent present which he cited and textualised to form into a desirable ideal which was unassailable. The past was a challenge to the present. In the past were all ideals, hence the need to reinstitute them as ideals and only where they could be, as an artistic practice. The ideal was not only what was not, but it was what could never be in reality, and for that reason it was an uncompromising, absolute, unnegotiable criticism in language of present reality and all that is.

As a result of the blasphemy case against *La ricotta*, *Il padre selvaggio* was never made. In 'E l'Africa?', Pasolini implicated his father by associating him with Bini in the case brought against *La ricotta* and the consequent impossibility of making a film of *Il padre selvaggio*. The father was made into a censor. He was, by analogy, Bini, the magistrate, society itself, the one who prevented the film-poem from existing. He had cancelled out a past. That past was the entire social past, and also Pasolini's past and the past which included the father. That past, in all its radical intentions, had been the subject of *La ricotta* and a past reconciled in the poetry and subject of *La ricotta*.

Davidson in *Il padre selvaggio* was able to follow his father, even to a savage hell. There he refound and reasserted his primitivism, not merely by action, by taking part in a tribal slaughter, but by making his past conscious, remembering and memorialising it, and using it as a source for poetry. The past was poeticised and there it remained, analogous to the Eumenides who tamed the primitive Furies. Africa was the source of Davidson's creativity which he could transfer to the civilised world, to the other, and also challenge that civility, radicalise it within a poetry which returned to the past in subject and in its forms.

In 'E l'Africa?' Pasolini's father denied the poet his poetry. In the poem his father demanded he pay the price of his creativity for the sake of conformity and as a sign of obedience to his authority. It was a demand for the end of poetry and for the spiritual death of the poet. The f(F)ather presented Pasolini with a dilemma: disobey and lose love and be rejected, or obey and lose poetry and oneself. But poetry was his absolute. He had no choice, but it was painful.

> I am forced to identify with the paternal image all of the symbols of authority and order, of fascism, of the bourgeoisie. ... I nourish a visceral, deep, irreducible hatred for the bourgeoisie, its self-importance, its vulgarity; it is an ancient hatred, or if you like, a religious one.[16]

The dilemma posed by the f(F)ather was a dilemma posed by the social. To be a poet in *this* society was to be an outcast. But to be a poet, in diversity, in a refusal to be integrated, to touch an irrational by means of poetry, the poet became a revolutionary and a disobedient son. Poetry had to be asserted against the f(F)ather who had left him no choice. He had to choose disobedience and risk paternal love. He was not so lucky as Davidson.

Revolution and poetry were lonely pursuits. At one time, 'Once upon a time ... ', it seemed that the places from which they issued and which inspired them could be identified in actuality: the poor, the south, the lumpenproletariat, Calabria, India, Naples, the savage, primitivism. By the late 60s, Pasolini no longer believed that the actuality any longer existed, and even doubted if it ever had existed. He began to think that his earlier beliefs in an existent primitive popular reality expressed in his Gramscian national-popular phase were invented. The people whom he invoked then did not exist. They were his dream, not a reality, as mythical as the myths of an Edenic, primitive past he now self-consciously created. At one time he mythologised reality, but he believed in the reality. Now he began to see it as the myth it was and thus could now create myths as myths, as always having been so, and thus a dream, an artifice to confront reality in all its forms and even from the beginning of the world.

Either the people had been corrupted long ago, or his desires had deluded him and the people never were as he imagined them. In any case, there was no longer a people or places which he could identify as an Other in reality and which he could use to practise his 'subjective indirect discourse' upon, and through which he might enter a world of outcasts. Fellini was perhaps more honest, or more clear-sighted, certainly more joyous than Pasolini. He knew right from the start that the past was what he invented and that he was also his own invention, as much a fiction as his Rimini was, and that he was never anywhere, never actually present except in the invention of the past and the invention of himself. He was always elsewhere to his self-image. He was Fellini the fiction. Pasolini, instead, became in his mind a total real outcast, unloved. This was the subject and source of his mourning. Being an outcast was the price he paid for being a scandal as a poet and as a homosexual: '... a love beyond compromise ... a scandalous love, a love that destroys, that changes the idea the bourgeoisie has of itself ...'.[17] It was the theorem of *Teorema*, of an impossible, unrequited love, which isolated him not unlike his figure of Christ.

A way forward for Pasolini from his existential dilemma was to reproduce that dilemma textually. But the restatement of it because it was poetic only made his dilemma all the more confining and difficult to resolve. His ideal was in the past. Indeed, it was the past. In the past, sons obeyed the father. The revolution by guaranteeing the past and restoring it would restore both a social ideal and an existential one, a time of filial obedience *and* paternal love. In it, the popular and the decadent, the primitive and the civilised, the symbolic and the pre-symbolic would be reconciled and father and son happy to eternity. The problem of commitment which had been so difficult for the European and the Italian left and for Pasolini for so long would be solved. The trouble was that ideal was a myth. It possibly never existed in a real past nor could it be established in an actual present. The very nature of the present as

Pasolini thought of it made the realisation of the ideal impossible. Poetry was only an apparent domain where the ideal and the real could be reconciled. It was the act of writing itself that made the ideal he expressed an impossibility. To be effective politically, he needed to keep his writing in the realm of the ideal. But to keep it there was also to condemn it to being permanently ineffectual.

Pasolini was isolated by constructing a realm of pure potential but without any actuality. The truths he told were mythical truths which he knew to be false, but whose force required that they remain artificial and in a potential that could never be. It was their potentiality that was radical and critical and it was that status he needed to maintain.

> One has to have the force for a total criticism, for refusal, for desperate and *useless* denunciation [italics added].
>
> I don't believe you can do anything politically. ... I don't believe in a work which is *a priori* social, worldly, organised. Although I don't believe in these things, I continue to act and to behave socially, as if I did believe in them. ... And while one is young, or until one is old, one can continue to believe and it is right that one does so. It would be foolish of me if I said I still believed but behaved as if I didn't. From disappointment to disappointment one ends by seeing reality as a horrible, intolerable thing, a perfidious joke played by some creator god who is like the devil, or as a game.[18]

V

The policies of the Vatican from 1945, under Pius XII, until the accession of Pope John XXIII in 1959 were socially and politically anti-communist and reactionary. In Italy, the Vatican supported the Christian Democrats against the Communist Party and globally, in the context of the Cold War, it took far-right, anti-Soviet positions. It urged the Italian DC not to accommodate with social reformist policies or co-operate with political parties to its left. It used its enormous power in Italian society to influence Italian politics in a conservative, sometimes reactionary direction for more than a decade. The papacy of John XXIII resulted in a major shift in Vatican policy. John XXIII's political positions were in line with a political-social liberalisation taking place elsewhere in the world. In Italy, his pontificate became a major force for liberalisation in contrast to the conservative policies of the Vatican in the past. The importance of the new Vatican liberalism for the future direction of social reform in Italy was as important as the Kennedy presidency was for Italy, perhaps more so.

John XXIII's most significant act was the publication of the encyclical, *Pacem in Terris* (*Peace on Earth*). In it he redefined the work of the church as primarily spiritual and pastoral, not political. Ideals of charity, generosity, love were stressed instead of political values or even confessional-religious ones. The social needs of people were to be respected independently of political beliefs or social ideologies. It was a programme of peace, love, social equality, humanity, not the class hatred, social divisiveness and ideological struggle characteristic of the Vatican during the Cold War of the 40s and 50s.

Central to the anti-communism of the Vatican in the past, and irrespective of the politics of the Cold War and the social egalitarianism of communism, was the identification by the Vatican of atheism with communism. The ideological differences between communism and the church went to the heart of Catholicism and therefore to the heart of Italy, a Catholic country but with the largest communist party in the West. Many Italian communists and socialists were Catholics. If, in theory, there was a conflict between politics and faith, in practice, except when exacerbated by the church, for many there was no conflict. The contraries were simply lived as if they were not contrary.

Except for a brief period in 1946–7 Pasolini did not belong to the Communist Party. Nevertheless, he called himself a Marxist and communist. He also said he was an atheist, but one with a sense of the sacred and the religious. And though he was anti-clerical, he thought of himself as a Catholic insofar as he, and all Italians, had behind him and within them nearly two millennia of Catholic history and culture.

Italian Catholics and communists, to varying degrees, lived the contrast between religious and secular faith. Pasolini bore the split less easily than most. The split in part formed him and it also contained for him the divisions he constantly invoked between sacredness and reason, primitivism and civility.

Pasolini's social thinking did not go much beyond a populist and simplistic schema of masters and servants, bourgeois and people. For him, because the people embodied a peasant-irrationalist culture, revolution on behalf of the people and with the people as its protagonists would restore a cultural past threatened with erasure by new forms of capitalism and the mass society which he equated with social genocide. For him, this quality of a popular and primitive culture from the past, which also contained a sense of the sacred, predated not only urbanism and capitalism, but also Christianity, and even history itself. It was pre-history and the pre-symbolic.

Thus, the Pasolinian revolution, by restoring the people to history, would restore an archaic mythic past within the present. This past had a religiosity distinct from the institutionalisation of religion by the church and an irrationalist core independent of any social-political order promised by Marxism or a communist revolution. There always had been a place in his thinking for the reconciliation of Marxism and Catholicism. It would occur in his mythic Utopia of the irrational-sacred which stood as a living criticism of existing society.

The traditional irreconcilability of the church and communism, Catholicism and Marxism was founded on the ideological difference the Vatican had stressed in the period of the Cold War. *Pacem in Terris* swept away much of this ideological rancour. The encyclical took a position which recalled the popular frontism of the 30s and the Resistance of the 40s, though with significant changes. Programmes of social-economic equality and justice argued by socialists in the 30s and by Italian socialists and communists after 1943 appeared or were made to appear socially divisive, as a call in the name of social justice to class struggle because society as it existed was neither egalitarian nor just. The task of the popular front was not social reform but anti-fascism which, to succeed, necessarily had to be interclassist. The language of class struggle would have compromised the battle against fascism which required bourgeois support and the support of all social groups and parties. Moreover, on the whole, the Resistance was confined to north and central Italy. From Rome south and indeed from Florence south, the Resistance had been limited or non-existent. Only north of Florence was the Resistance a sustained and popular struggle. The popular front, particularly after the end of the war, spoke about humanity, goodness, civilised values without giving these a sharp social edge. They were values all could agree on and though they were inflected by social concerns they were not dominated by them.

The struggle against fascism was expressed as between civilised values and barbarism more than as a struggle for social justice against exploitation, still less of socialism against capitalism. The popular front disengaged a critique of capitalist society from the attack on fascism and it made fascism less the product of capitalism than an exception to it. This was very marked in liberal and Crocean thinking which regarded fascism as an aberrant interlude in the essentially liberal tenor of Italian society. The Italian Resistance, for example, with which Italian neo-realist culture was identified, made its appeals on the basis of universal and liberal values more than on the basis of social or economic reform except insofar as such reform was regarded as necessary for the reinstitution of a liberal-democratic Italy.

By the late 50s, the anti-fascism of the popular front and the Cold War division between a right-wing anti-communism and a left-wing anti-capitalism had lost most of its reason to exist and hence its force. Calls for social reform were no longer thought of as calls to revolution or social disruption or as economically destructive of capitalist production. They became rather a part of the social conscience of capitalism and one of its means for maintaining social order and economic prosperity within the capitalist system. In Kennedy's social ideology expressed in his New Frontier, social justice ceased to be antithetical to capitalism or a threat to its operation, but its very essence. Indeed, capitalism came to be characterised in its liberalism as more capable than an authoritarian communism of delivering social equality and economic well-being.

Despite analogies that can be made between the shift in Vatican policy and global social reformism within capitalism, *Pacem in Terris* was a document all on its own and of considerable political and social moment. It united peoples by their common humanity rather than dividing them by issues of class. Common humanity was not defined, as it had been during the popular front, in terms of vague humanist ideals, or by bourgeois democratic libertarian ones (*liberté*, *égalité*, *fraternité*), but by terms which were predominantly social and economic. The encyclical talked about the social needs and rights of the people and condemned any denial of those rights by political-economic systems of whatever ideological persuasion.

It certainly contributed to the formation of the Italian centre-left and to a dialogue encouraged by the church, between socialists and communists on the one hand and Catholics on the other. It established common ground for a dialogue between the church and the Italian Communist Party and, by that fact, a dialogue between the PCI and political parties to its right, including the left wing of the Christian Democrats.

Pasolini was enthusiastic about Pope John XXIII and *Pacem in Terris*. He wrote about the irrational core of Marxism and the rational core of Christianity and bore witness within that schema to his sentimental, sacred love for the people, a love, he said, that had moved him to identify with the Friulian peasantry. Later, with the peasant agitations of 1948 in Italy and PCI support for the peasantry, his sentimental attachment became, he said, political, Marxist, rational, without ever surrendering its irrational origins. His sacrality became thereby social and political. At the same time he glimpsed within the social of the peasantry and the political of the PCI a sacred essence.

These formulations reverberated in his 'free indirect subjective', that is in an identification based on love and on the desire to identify with the beloved other, to lose oneself within it, and by means of a literary and symbolic mechanism to express this identification and bring it to a plane of beauty and poetry and, at the same time, of consciousness.

Pasolini's reworking of Marxism with his sense of the sacred and his reformulation of Catholicism by his sense of social commitment was a theme in all his work: the languages of the rational and the irrational, the symbolic and the sacred, the civilised and the primitive, and their mutual contamination. Marxism and Christianity became for him not opposed but analogous. The secular-rationality of the one contained the sacred, and the sacred-irrationality of the other glowed with a social conscience. For a moment, in the social illumination of John XXIII's papacy, it might have seemed that heaven had come to earth.

The Father, the Pope, the Church, Authority, Society, all the things Pasolini loathed – loathed, he said, in his very being, with a visceral uncontrolled loathing – seemed, for the first time, not only benign but positive. These odious spectres were a succession of analogous Pasolini fathers, real and imaginary, including the ghastly, monstrous, amoebic, physically repulsive father in 'E l'Africa?'. These fathers also included, however, on the edge of his loathing and at the other side of it, ideal fathers, the ones he loved and longed for, who were never far away, the fathers who would not have condemned *La ricotta* for blasphemy as the magistrate did, who would not have made the realisation of *Il padre selvaggio* an impossible dream, and all savage fathers merely mythical. The ideal father had become roly-poly John XXIII.

La rabbia is a film in part about revolution. The images in it all came from existing documentary footage, mostly newsreel footage. The voice-over was spoken by the novelist, Giorgio Bassani, and the painter, Renato Guttuso. They speak in alternate voices of poetry and prose. The film is like a poem, not explicative, but expressive and exemplary. The voice-over counterpoints and punctuates the images, colours them, rather than informs. Most of the film centres on the revolutions of Third World national independence movements in Africa and Latin America. But the revolution featured as central in the film is the Soviet Revolution. To this revolution are added other, related, sequences. One is the death and funeral of Pope Pius XII and the election of John XXIII.

The papal sequence begins with crowds filing past the bier of Pius XII on display in St Peter's basilica. It closes with John XXIII's election, shots of the jubilant crowd in St Peter's Square, and John's address to them.

A pope from a distinguished family is dead – great landowners in Lazio. His world was a world of peasants: but during his careful life innovations in the world began to make of fields of grain and vines an ancient world.

Ah, none of these dignitaries in tears shall know or will ever want to know the necessities and the reasons why Christianity became the religion of the king, bourgeois religion. The bourgeoisie now follow, along with their subproletarian brothers, the bier of the agrarian pope, to St Peter's, as if it were in the square of a great and funereal country.

Nothing has changed of the sixteenth-century fixed ideas of the church: nothing, except the industrial revolution in the cities. ... But when will the countryside have entered into this implacable circle? When will the sweet peasant world be as far away as the world of the Bible? Who will come to the funerals of the future popes? Sons of captains of industry or of workers?

Dark Roman shopkeepers, pale Italian bureaucrats, plebeians with the epileptic look of gypsies, priests from the north whose modesty prevents them from showing any life. ... It is the crowd from the 1960s, the sea of our century, which still desperately needs religion in order to give some sense to its panic, its guilt, its hopes.

The new pope is also a peasant. Nothing ought to seem different except that his smile is that of a son of small landholders who have become in their old age the equals of moralistic fathers or miserly grandfathers. And it will be this way – the smile of the pope – for years to come yet: because there are one thousand million subproletarians on earth.

The scene shifts to the puffs of white smoke from the Sistine Chapel which announce the election of a new pope.

There will be white smoke for pope sons of peasants from Ghana or Uganda, pope sons of Indian farm labourers dead of disease on the Ganges and for pope sons of yellow fishermen dying of cold on Tierra del Fuego.

The slow death of the peasant world that still survives populating continents – beside thousands of fjords, on coasts crawling with sharks, islands carbonised by volcanoes – breathing in this white smoke the slow archaism of its existence. Into a future of decades and centuries.

The equal to the devious father and to the grandfather drinker of prize wines, a figure unknown to the subproletariat of the earth, but also the cultivator of the earth – the new pope with his sweet, mysterious, tortoise-like smile, seems to have understood that he must be the Pastor of the Wretched, fisher of sharks, pastor of hyenas, hunter of vultures, sower of weeds, because their world is the Ancient World and it is they who will take him through the centuries with the story of our greatness.

Smile Father Heathen: and Renzo and Lucia will happily be married in front of your eyes: even now the baroque arches are theirs, and the golden salons of Don Rodrigo, and the great cathedrals, and the little churches hidden in hillsides without destiny – the History of the Grand Styles is theirs.

They alone live amidst the monuments constructed over the centuries by the powerful, and with them, are adrift in a changing history.

'The Spirit is the inheritance of the peasant world, and you are the Pastor of the ancient world and in that spirit there is life': are these the words which the angel whispered into the ear of the sweet pope with the mysterious big head of a tortoise?

The Pope John XXIII depicted in *La rabbia* is a peasant pope from an agricultural past, heathen, pagan, who smiles an African smile illuminating the present with the beauty of the past. For that reason he is a revolutionary pope as Pasolini is a revolutionary poet. 'I am a voice from the past.' 'Only the Revolution saves the Past.'

There are two worlds in *La rabbia*. One is a developed First World in which the past is being obliterated. The other is the developing Third World, where the past in its purity is still alive. In the film it is in the Third World that revolution is being made: a catalogue of anti-colonial nationalist wars and suffering, the past from the Third World crying out, reasserting itself.

There is only the barest historical reality to this vision even if it is made to seem true by the documentary images in *La rabbia*. It was the projection of Pasolini's schizophrenic interior outside him to the historical world, dividing it into the contraries which divided him against himself. On the other hand, his interior division was historically generated by a social and economic reality that was changing and by the sexual and existential differences these changes pressed on. It involved his negative revulsion for his father and all that was legal and symbolic and social that he loaded on to the f(F)ather, and his positive attachment to his mother and all the beauty and irrationality he endowed the m(M)other with. It was with her that he could claim his homosexuality but against the father he needed to assert it not only in self-protection but in protecting his mother and all that she was personally and historically for him. Sometimes it is difficult to know with Pasolini what was inside and what was out, where he ended and where the world began. His indirect subjective was an artistic instrument for imaginary identification. It was also a trap for self-delusion and schizoid projections.

The images in *La rabbia* tell a parable or offer a theorem in much the same way as *Teorema* did. It is the parable that he always told and was so personal a story: the loss of sacredness and authenticity in the world. The theorem in both films is the 'what if', the hypothetical what if the sacred returned to earth, what would happen to the bourgeois world which thought it had conquered it within itself and its own soul and outside itself in actions which it described as progress and development and the end of poverty. The theorem then relates to the ideal world of potentials, the theory of the potential, the ideal which castigates the reality.

In *Teorema*, a sacred visitor arrives in a bourgeois Milan family and every member of the family in turn disintegrates into madness and despair. Each finds the knowledge of the authenticity they have lost and of the impossibility of refinding it and hence refinding their lost souls. Only the maid, Emilia, for whom the rural past is still alive, can return to a past which is barred to the bourgeois family. She returns to her village, to sacred magic. She levitates, eats nettles, makes the waters spring from the earth, cures disease as Christ cured the lepers. The theorem, the 'what if', like that of 'what if Christ now came to earth?', destroys the present world for the sake of the past world. It is revolution in action.

This theorem is also that of *Il Vangelo secondo Matteo*. What the sacred visitor in *Teorema* does, and also what Stracci does by implication in *La ricotta*, and the national anti-colonial revolutions do in *La rabbia*, is to overturn a present which has lost its spiritual way by representing it with the evidence of that loss in action. And this is not only what happens in Pasolini's films, it is what the films are meant to provoke and what Pasolini in his being and body meant to provoke, a revolution of the spirit. That revolution was at best productive of wonderful poetry in all its forms, including in film, but at its worst it produced a moralism and a political face which was not only turned backwards but sometimes was reactionary and hateful, as prophets of doom restoring the people to lost values often are.

In *La ricotta*, Stracci, the lumpenproletarian, inhabits an authentic cultural world associated with a rural poor, a world lost to the troupe who taunt him and to the film director making the film within the film, played by Orson Welles. Stracci is made to live literally in a different time, that of the silent cinema, at eighteen frames a second. He is caught, however, within the time of the modern world of the 'talkies' at twenty-four frames a second. This makes him ridiculous because it speeds up his actions, and probably more than one-third, as if Pasolini had widened the time gap between the two speeds even more. It makes the world that causes this acceleration cruel because it is that world that brings Stracci to his death. He eats at their speed, too quickly, in order to eat enough to keep alive in their world and it kills him. It is a joke which goes too far. The joke crucifies him just as the world crucified Christ. 'What if a Stracci came into the world?' 'He would be killed?'

'And what if a Pasolini came into the world?'

At Stracci's Last Supper where he gobbles his food as if at a Rabelaisian banquet, the time of eating is eighteen frames a second, though the time of regarding him and containing him is twenty-four frames. The same is the case with his comic run at eighteen frames to buy ricotta. His actions are unreal because of the two diverse times. There is the odd fact too that the slower the speed at which the film strip goes through the projector, the faster the projected action and vice versa. For other reasons Emilia's levitation and the miracles she performs in *Teorema* are made to appear false. They are as representationally false as the miracles of Christ in *Il Vangelo*, or the special effects in the films of the *Trilogia di vita* of demons who fly, a monkey who talks. They seem unreal because they come from another world, therefore Pasolini made no attempt to cover the falsity, to find a special effect to make the unreal believable. He wanted to make it unbelievable in order to emphasise a difference in perception. It is an oddness in perspective. Stracci, Christ, Emilia all lived in a reality that could not be comprehended from outside, the outside where the others were and where we are. From the outside the reality of the Straccis seemed absurd and if they insisted upon it too much, or if Pasolini insisted upon too much, they risked, as Christ did, a martyred death on behalf of an unacceptable reality, yet one which Pasolini knew was the 'real' thing, real reality which appeared to be different and perverse for those who lived in a false reality. The lesson is not simply in the film, but it is by the film, in its structures placed against the structures of perception which view it. It is a provocation and a scandal to the spectator. In part the provocation is an insult.

The unreality of these events emphasised their otherworldliness. They were literally unavailable in a world of twenty-four frames. The peasants in *Teorema* can believe Emilia because they come from her universe. This belief is not possible for the bourgeoisie who come from another universe, hence their despair in realising a truth they cannot fully reach or even completely comprehend. The gap of the frames is too great. The lepers who are made well by Christ, the blind who are made to see, the multitude who are fed with the fish and loaves that Christ multiplies, are persons and miracles from another world, a magical one, which can only be fully believed from within it. Not even an indirect subjective and a non-illusionist identification with the other can make it possible.

Pope John XXIII in *La rabbia* is the same as the sacred visitor from *Teorema*. He is an 'as if', a 'what if' the sacred came to earth. In a structure of analogous relations in *La rabbia* revolution from the old world seems to be everywhere in the new world in imaginary juxtapositions that only mathematical theorems and films are capable of creating, both equally at home in the ideal abstract.

Pasolini dedicated *Il Vangelo secondo Matteo* to the memory of John XXIII. *Il Vangelo* is Pasolini's *Pacem in Terris* film. His Christ is a social reformer within a magical, sacred world, the world that produced the Gospels. The film is set in present-day Calabria, but a Calabria that belongs completely to a past which resembles the Palestine of the Bible but is no longer actual in modern Palestine. Monuments to the biblical past remained in Palestine but the past itself was gone. In Calabria it was still alive. Calabria was an archaic left-over, a trace of antiquity like John XXIII. The social reformist zeal and anger in Pasolini's Christ came from an indignation with the present. Christ, like Pasolini, was an anti-modern. He was the peasant, obedient son of John XXIII.

Pasolini's *Sopralluoghi in Palestina* is the record of his journey to Israel in search of locations for *Il Vangelo*. He was accompanied by Don Andrea, a Catholic priest of Pro Civitate Cristiana in Assisi, where St Francis taught and where there is the cathedral that bears his name. In *Sopralluoghi* Don Andrea is given the role of the Catholic priest with a social heart, filled with reason and historical knowledge. Pasolini assumes, as his companion, the role of the Marxist but alight with the fire of the sacred. They are themselves internally divided and each is the reverse of the other. They form a hybrid combination of communist and Catholic making their way to Bethlehem where Christ was born.

The couple composed of contraries, schizoid like the sphinx and the centaur and the monkey man, unbearable paradoxes, are everywhere in Pasolini's films. It was the component of the relation between Pasolini and Moravia in Pasolini's *L'odore dell'India*. Moravia is reason and the father. Pasolini is the excitable, passionate son. He shivered with excitement as he approached Bethlehem, just as he had on the streets of Bombay.

Pro Civitate Cristiana was founded in 1939. It did not proselytise but, like St Francis, it gave witness to the Catholic faith. It did not criticise the church or seek converts. It exhibited its faith by its simplicity, social works, commitment to the needy, inspired by a sense of the sacred as self-sufficient. The social message of the church and the sacredness of the faith were the same for Pro Civitate as for St Francis and Pasolini's John XXIII, hence sacredness became in its expression a social and not merely religious state.

St Francis was not a figure of simple piety for Pasolini. He was also a figure of the burlesque, of a sacredness that was popular, belonging to carnival, hence socially disruptive and radical. Ginzburg on St Francis:

His style of life is typically carnivalesque. Carnivalesque is the exhortation Francis made to his own body: 'Enjoy yourself, brother body.' Carnivalesque is his insistence on joyfulness. ... Carnivalesque is his behaviour which a near-contemporary chronicle attributed to Francis during an audience with Innocent III, when the Pope exclaimed to him: 'You look more like a pig than a man: go therefore and preach your rules to the pigs.' Francis went and rolled himself in a pigsty and returned to the Pope all besmirched and said: 'Now you must listen to me'. Sublimely carnivalesque is the kiss Francis gave the lepers. The originality of the religious genius of Francis consists exactly in this fact: in his attempt to identify the carnivalesque paradox with the Christian paradox. By his presence alone, he gave witness to the falsity of commonly accepted values.[19]

During the pontificate of John XXIII Pro Civitate sent out an invitation to artists and film-makers to come to Assisi and talk to them about Jesus. Pasolini took up the invitation in 1962 and subsequently involved Pro Civitate in *Il Vangelo*. The jury of the Ufficio Cattolico Internazionale del Cinema awarded a prize to the film. The jury statement testified to the spirit of *Pacem in Terris*, an important sign to Pasolini after the condemnation of *La ricotta* by church and state. The prize suggested a new relation for Pasolini with Catholicism and through it with all the fathers he had implicated in the ban on *La ricotta* and the difficulty it created for filming *Il padre selvaggio*. He could follow the Father now, be the obedient son, not the outrageous, scandalous, blaspheming one who had made *La ricotta*. He was the good son who made *Il Vangelo*. Current fathers like John XXIII and Don Andrea had recalled the past, allowed him to write, appreciated him, welcomed him home, given him awards, kissed him on both cheeks. 'Mio caro figliuolo.' The statement of the jury:

The author, without giving up his own ideology, has faithfully translated, with simplicity and piety, often very movingly, the social message of the Gospel, in particular love for the poor and the oppressed, while sufficiently respecting the divine aspect of Christ. ... For the simplicity of its style and thanks to the humility with which the director presents the various characters, this work is far superior to earlier, commercial films, on the life of Christ. It shows the real grandeur of his teaching stripped of any artificial and sentimental effect. ... Though the director has given the impression of interpreting the Gospel within a historical human dimension, the Jury was sincerely moved by the strong representation of the social teaching of Christ which is of particular relevance today.[20]

Sopralluoghi in Palestina, like Pasolini's other *Appunti* films, sought an authenticity assumed to be in the antique, in this case in ancient Palestine, an evangelical place, and at the time of the Gospels. He hoped to

translate the authenticity he would find by re-evoking the actual existent reality of the past as context and citation in *Il Vangelo*. But Palestine
disappointed him as India and Africa had. It had lost its antiquity to the
modern:

> At this point the Arab world is very close. And here in fact this scene is
> absolutely typical of the archaic world of the Arabs. This sun, this
> straw, as you see, are perfect elements for the figuration of ... of an
> evangelical parable. Here one would not have to change anything: that
> tent, this pile of grain, the movement of this old peasant.
>
> It was at this moment that my hopes were still intact: I thought in
> fact that Israel, its very places, that is those where Christ preached,
> could be the perfect scenes for my film, without the least change. How-
> ever, already at this point, I began to have the suspicion that there was
> something too modern, too industrial in the countryside. Very shortly,
> in fact, you will see ... a countryside ... contaminated by modernity.

The Africa and India films were notes for films-to-be-made and thus what
was not made yet: the potential and hypothetical film was the ideal subject
of the actual film which pointed to the potential. The problem with
Sopralluoghi in Palestina was that while it too was a film in notes for another film to be made, the notes taken were completely unusable. Pasolini
had found faces, bodies, places, smiles, odours in India and Africa of the
present to enable him to imagine an analogy with a lost past. But in Palestine all traces of the past had been erased. There was only the modern. But,
perhaps, as a result, in this case, and without notes taken, Pasolini made a
real film, *Il Vangelo*. Perhaps the absence of the past in Palestine forced
him to find it elsewhere, as he did in the poorer regions of the Italian south
of Basilicata, Calabria, Molise and Sicily, and, in a way, it was better so,
since these places provided a better analogy being further away from a
historical biblical reality. In the Italian south Pasolini found his Arabs and
his Jews and in Spain he found his Christ. Because Palestine in fact lacked
its past, nothing was there with which he could form a comparative. The
present was present insofar as it had erased the possibility of an analogy.
What could a present which had lost its past – hence all reality for Pasolini
– be analogous to? 'Small white houses of workers, some factories. ...
Look, here are Israeli houses that you would be able to see in the countryside around Rome, or even in Switzerland.'

Pasolini was not an illusionist. He would not consent to recreate the past.
He had to find it. And he needed to find it because his central impulse was
critical and political. It was to demonstrate, and by documentary means, by
means of an existent reality, as he had done in *La rabbia*, the loss of the past
and the obliteration of the Ideal. He needed to show the gap. He could resort
to make-believe, for example that Calabria was Palestine, but he needed to
reveal that the make-believe was analogic and thus Calabria was not Palestine. Artifice exhibited was the means to a hidden truth.

Analogy and imitation, then, were political tools as well as aesthetic techniques. It was commitment and beauty brought together and used to expose and criticise the present *and* decry the loss within it of the beautiful. The beautiful was what he refound in the films and re-enacted in them. He reproduced an ancient purity by the analogy, which always presupposed a gap, and which was a tool of beauty and an instrument of politics. It made the two spheres of politics and aesthetics alike without compromising either. It was an accomplishment that neither the avant-garde nor the politically committed had been able to realise.

The main constituents of the Pasolinian analogy were time and history. Pasolini re-established the past in the present by selecting a present whose past was its principal component. 'Calabria now is like Palestine was.' But by that fact another proposition inevitably formed, namely, 'Palestine now is what Calabria will become', hence the funereal aspect within the celebration of a present-past, that hybrid tense in which almost all Pasolini films seem to operate. 'Calabria now contains the sacred of the Gospel which the modern had obliterated in Palestine and would obliterate again in Calabria.' The film thus re-posed the question of revolution to save the past since only a radical transformation of the contemporary could enable it to think of contemporaneity in other terms, in the tense, for example, of the present-past.

Those who had crucified Christ were the Pharisees, Philistines, the state, authority, fathers. In what did Christ's sacredness consist for Pasolini? He didn't believe in God, still less in the Ascension. But he did believe in, and could identify imaginatively with, the belief of the people who believed in the Ascension and in Christ. It was this belief that created the magical event of Christ rising to heaven since life as it was then was a sacred one in which miracles were believed to have occurred. Christ was not crucified once but repeatedly. The message of his sacrifice and resurrection was embedded in a popular world. That world, and Christ, had been and were being eliminated by the other world that had crucified Christ, hence the repetitiveness of the Crucifixion. The fathers who killed Christ had killed Oedipus, had tried to kill Pasolini's poetry. Christ crucified therefore was a revolutionary sign of the sacred against the profane of authority. It was the idea made fact and made flesh. The ancient sacred and the need for revolution were thus summed up in the paradox of the Crucifixion. Was it the father who had killed the son? Or was it the son who willingly sacrificed himself in an act of supreme filial obedience to shame the father and save the world for the sacred?

Pasolini's analogy embraced language and reality, art and politics, a formal signifier and the substance of a signified. The analogy activated the past in the present within language which was the means of that activation and the site of it. Pasolini thus made language, as he constantly insisted language was or ought to be, both aesthetic and political, formal and meaningful, by deploying the form of the analogy which housed that difference.

Il Vangelo ends as Matthew's Gospel does, with the Crucifixion, Deposition and Ascension. Pasolini's other films end similarly. A death and closure in the story told become the beginning of the consciousness of what had once been living, hence what had been lost, and hence what motivated the telling of the story. The telling is to memorialise what had once been and now is again in the story of its absence. At the end of the story what is born from within it are story and language. His tales are parables about the birth of language and art. Because Christ died, we knew him as we know Stracci. 'Poor Stracci, he had to die to make us aware that he ever existed.'

Pasolini's stories turn back on themselves in a circle. They end in death and consciousness which are the beginnings of the reason for the story and hence the beginning of language to tell it. In the beginning there is nothing, an insignificance out of which the significant is born. The signifier predates any signification. It is to that pre-signifying void that Pasolini's stories point. The interest of the stories is not in the dissolution of meaning but in the moment of meaning's birth, when meaning is only a trace and not-yet. His stories literally give life to the word, to the pre-existing unrepresented ideal as in Poe's 'The Oval Portrait'. Film and writing do not follow reality but form reality, and do so by example, that is by the analogy which mirrors and contains it.

Sopralluoghi ends at a small Romanesque church in Israel which records the Ascension. 'The most sublime moment in the entire Gospel story: the moment when Christ leaves us alone to search for him.' As in other Pasolini films, the search for authenticity ends at a place of death which becomes the place from which consciousness and story begin. The motive which requires the story to be told is the conventional one of parables and tales, that something has been lost, a harmony and symmetry disturbed. But in Pasolini's parables what has been lost is the past and what the parables do, and it is the sense of them, is to restore the lost balance, the obliterated past, the forgotten sacredness. The loss of Christ and of authenticity are disturbances of this kind. If Christ had not died and had not risen, there would have been no cause to search Him out. He was called to Heaven to become an unrealisable, unpossessable ideal. The ideal is the motive for Pasolinian writing, to possess the sublime and the ineffable, not by seizing it and bringing it to earth, but by duplicating it, reproducing it in language. It is a paradox of reality but alive only where paradox can be in language which forms it and which for Pasolini is at the heart of the formation of language.

Some moments before the end of *Sopralluoghi* at the Romanesque church recalling the Past, Don Andrea remembers a message of St Paul's, the saint Pasolini memorialised in a script for a film he would have called

'San Paolo' but which he never made. His 'San Paolo' was to be about St Paul as revolutionary. Some scenes in the script take place in present-day Rome, Paris, New York, and London. The ancient revolutionary is remembered in hypothetical contemporary situations. It is the 'what if' theorem of the sacred visitor again. Don Andrea's quote from St Paul concerns a paradox which is pure Pasolini.

> That which is deemed ignorant by the world has been chosen by God to confound the knowing. And that which is deemed weak by the world has been chosen by God to confound the strong. He has chosen what has neither nobility nor value for the world, which does not exist, in order to reduce to nothing that which exists.

VI

Pasolini's historical-political picture of the world and his Marxism were simplistic. I want to assume his picture and to some extent his voice, nevertheless, in order to see its complicated yield.

Let us assume that the class struggle is a struggle between capital and labour, between those who own the means of production and those who produce. The struggle is between those with everything material and those who own nothing but their labour: '... so long as man exploits man, so long as humanity is divided between masters and slaves, so long will there be neither normality nor peace.'[21] Capital belongs to the bourgeoisie, labour to the labouring classes. Each of the opposed classes has its own history, social gestures, culture and also ideologies which are the expression of these differences. Bourgeois intellectuals, though belonging to the class of capital, can, nevertheless, imaginatively identify with the labouring class and take its part ideologically and politically. The political mechanism for that identification is the Communist Party, and through it, Marxism, a theory and ideology which can comprehend the class struggle.

The Russian Revolution of 1917 was a revolution of the people against the bourgeoisie and capital. The revolution displaced one class by another, one history by another, one ideology by another. It was the triumph of the labouring class against the class of capital. In the revolution, peasant and proletarian fathers struggled to give their sons what had been denied peasant and proletarian fathers and sons historically by the bourgeoisie.

The division of the world into classes guaranteed to the labouring class, kept down in an eternity of exploitation and backwardness, the maintenance of their popular culture, one of whose features was the continuation of traditions by which fathers handed on their world and culture to their sons. Class, then, guaranteed filial obedience and loyalty on the one hand, and paternal compassion and strength on the other. It may have been an imperfect, even harsh world, without riches or comfort for those who laboured and were exploited, but it did have the wealth of its culture intact and to underpin it and sustain it a paternal-filial closeness which guaranteed a cultural coherence and endurance over centuries.

The Russian Revolution brought the popular past into the present and future by giving the popular classes a dominant social-political position within the state. Thus, a popular and populist revolution, by establishing the people in power, established the past of the people, that is their culture, simplicity, irrationality and reality, and assured that these would be maintained. The revolution was the guarantee of the past. It also guaranteed therefore one of the salient features of the past, the obedience of sons to fathers, the son who followed in the footsteps of the father and, symbolically at least, emulated the past.

The central sequences of *La rabbia* are about the Russian Revolution. I want to quote the voice-over in these sequences spoken by Guttuso, the voice of prose. In particular, I want to quote those words that concern the relation of fathers to sons.

A nation that began its history all over again gave first of all to men the modesty of innocently duplicating its fathers.

There is a greatness in tradition which can be expressed in a gesture. Thousands of fathers saw it, and, through them over the centuries, it became as pure as the flight of a bird, as basic as the movement of a wave. But only the Revolution saves the Past.

Blessed are the children whose fathers were servants of the glebe; blessed are the children who can say: 'My father laughed heartily in his village where the boss and the bureaucrats of the tsar caused him to die of hunger for thousands of years. The puritan violence with which I laugh, the theatrical ingenuity with which I enjoy myself, in my village, in my factory, he gave to me!'

Blessed are the children whose fathers were heroes. ... 'My father fought against the tsar and against capital, and the freedom I have, he gave to me. The earth that I plant and the factory which I work he gave to me, and I can be proud that I resemble him and believe that I shall resemble him always.'

'I want to carefully enjoy life, doing things that have been denied me for centuries, and that the young people from the provinces who were richer than me had done for centuries. I want some dance, some society, some theatre: everything that ideal fathers had, but certainly not flesh and blood fathers. And I am proud to clothe myself once again in my poor worker's clothes: the morning, under the harsh sun of my province, of my village.'

'Everything that ideal fathers had – and my father of flesh and blood did not have but so wanted – I want to have it.'

'I want to take possession of the traditional culture: I want to possess what is beautiful and noble and has been denied me for centuries.'

'I want to teach myself with the spirit of a generous father, to read like a young father, to understand with the heart of a religious father.

With obedience, because I am the first educated son of a generation which had nothing, except calluses on its hands, and bullets from capital in its breast. And, now I can, for the first time in the history of my nation, I, a young man of the people, want to hear the voice of culture, of science, of art.'

As long as there is a class struggle, there is an ideological struggle and a struggle between opposed class histories. And so long as there is a class struggle, the possibility exists that the popular classes, in that struggle and in a hoped-for victory, will gain the power to sustain their class culture and the social obedience at its heart. In the revolution, sons will follow their fathers.

In the West, the class struggle for the most part has been won, not by the people, but by the bourgeoisie. The victory of the bourgeoisie has resulted in the world becoming bourgeois. The popular classes have become bourgeois at heart and have lost their culture for the reward of prosperity and the ability to buy and consume. There are no longer bourgeois and proletarian, but only bourgeois. Hence, there are no longer bourgeois fathers and proletarian fathers, and bourgeois sons and proletarian sons, but only bourgeois fathers and bourgeois sons.

History was *their* history. The people, as far as we are concerned, have their own history apart, archaic, in which sons, simply, as the anthropology of ancient cultures teaches, reincarnated and repeated the fathers.

Today, everything is different: when we speak of fathers and sons, if by fathers we continue to mean *bourgeois* fathers, by sons we mean both *bourgeois* sons and *proletarian* sons. The apocalyptic picture which I have sketched of sons now includes sons of the bourgeois and of the people.

The two histories have become one: it is the first time that has happened in the history of man.

There is a key idea held in common by everyone, sincerely or not: the idea that the worst evil in the world is poverty and that therefore the culture of the poorest classes must be replaced with the culture of the dominant class. In other words, our guilt as fathers is constituted by this fact: *believing that history is nothing other and can be nothing other than bourgeois history.*

In the period of the class struggle, a bourgeois son could become a disobedient son and a revolutionary son by joining the revolution and identifying with the class he was not of, by becoming a son not of his father but of the people. He would join the class struggle on behalf of the working class and oppose thereby his (bourgeois) father and, through the father, society, the entirety of the established world and the institutions of social power. This is what Pasolini said he sought to do with his artistic machines: the indirect free subjective, analogy, imitation, the literarisation of popular speech. It was what he meant by commitment in an old-fashioned sense.

Even if the class struggle had been lost in the West, and irrevocably lost, it had not been lost in the non-West. The non-West was still under-developed and therefore not yet bourgeoisified. Its societies were not yet mass consumer societies. There still was a people. The imaginative move beyond the borders of the West by European intellectuals like Pasolini towards an identification with the Third World was a move to refind a lost people and thus an old commitment. It was to be disobedi-ent once again (in the populism of anti-fascism, in the Resistance, in Marxism) by aligning oneself once more with the obedient sons of the people, now predominantly black, like Davidson. This commitment and its disobedient consequences from the subject of 'E l'Africa?'.

> In Africa there is no conflict between generations, the fatal and biologi-cal clash between fathers and sons. Black sons seem to want nothing more than to be obedient sons.
>
> One feels that sons, all sons, are obedient sons.
>
> Fathers and sons have the same cheerful and sweet eyes, which smile spontaneously with a smile that is fundamentally kindly, ingenuous, but never shallow; it is a smile veined by a warm sense of humour; the humour is peasant, the ancient matrix of bourgeois humour.
>
> In this aspect of black life, we can see fragments of a peasant life that slowly was eroded in Europe; a dialect and regional life – in effect, a feudal life.
>
> Not even in the 'poor' areas of Europe, southern Italy for example, up until only just yesterday, was there a generational conflict.[22]

The association of the lower orders in European society with a lower order of humanity in the savage areas of the world belonged to a racist tradition. It helped to form racial hierarchies of superiority: northern Europeans, then southern Europeans, then Asians, Africans and the primitive peoples of Oceania. The European working class and peasantry were thought to be like the Africans. Race and class were thus confounded in theory, and often confounded in practice by imperialisms abroad and class exploita-tion at home.

It was inevitable that the capitalism which had bourgeoisified the West by an outstanding economic development would in turn bourgeoisify the world, including the Third World where Pasolini's commitment had fled by the late 60s. The possibilities of identification with the other had a life only so long as the other in fact continued to exist. This existence was being threatened by a capitalism without limits. The whole of the world's peoples and cultures would be absorbed by it.

A politics of commitment required a real focus. Without it, a practical politics was not possible.

The aesthetic politics of Pasolini were contained within a structure bounded by the terms of the same and the diverse, the same and the other. His aesthetic formulation of the 'indirect free subjective' was a device by which the intellectual-writer entered into the other linguistically, and turned that otherness against the same to scandalise it and expose it.

There was another set of terms related to the Same and the Other. These were primarily bodily and nutritional: Absorption and Egestion (*Salò*), Nutrition and the Inedible (the cannibal in *Porcile*), Digestion and Indigestion (Stracci in *La ricotta*). Eating in his films was often a deadly activity. Food was sometimes inedible (snakes, butterflies, humans, shit), or lethal (poisoned, with razor blades, causing cramps, diarrhoea), or it became food that consumed you (in *Porcile* humans are eaten by pigs, dogs). The outer limit of otherness was that which could not be absorbed or stomached. The political problem posed by the same and the other was the threat that the other might become the same (bourgeoisified, a consumer) and the resistance by the other to sameness (revolution, scandal, an insistence on diversity), its refusal to be absorbed, taken over, sold out, compromised.

Thus, when there was nothing left in fact, when the other as a social-political reality in the First World and indeed in the Third was absorbed or in the process of being absorbed, there could nevertheless be a resistance in theory to the same, an ideal resistance which resisted being absorbed by being absolutely other, that is unconsumable, by the fact of remaining outside and apart from actuality, by continuing to remain ideal.

This inconsumability was that which could not be used, that is an absolute scandal, the disgusting, utter meaninglessness. It was either what you would not want to possess, or that which you could not possess. What you would want to possess, but could not, was the ideal and that ideal was beauty. Beauty was that which you could neither have nor know. In Pasolini's work all that was irrational, unknown, primitive, that is other in every way, including other-than-possessable, other-than-established, and other-than-normal, was what was beautiful. The beautiful was more than was necessary and more than could be contained, beyond reach individually and beyond the reach of the social. It was what you could not comprehend, like God, and like God it was sublime and sacred. The sacredness of beauty made it revolutionary. No matter what else could be absorbed and digested, the sacred, by definition, was always out of reach and by that fact it retained its power.

It is hard to escape the conclusion that the past which the revolution would ideally save would be a past that the revolution could never *in fact* save, because all revolution was bound to be compromised. The past saved by the revolution would have to be the idea of revolution and the idea of the past. It would have to maintain itself beyond current reality in order to contest it. The central features of the past included an ideal filial relation of love and obedience and the ideals of the sacred and the beautiful. The past was that which contained the sacred, or, in other terms, that which contained the ideal. The ideal was always an ideal by being other, diverse, primitive. The Pasolinian past, fundamentally, was a sacred, religious past, like manna from heaven, and, like it, poetic; and the poetic, by that fact, was revolutionary.

It is not by chance that conformists and dissenters are equally deaf to poetry ... unless it is technicised, in the products of the avant-garde *which says nothing of their existence as producers*. If, thus, I can hope for the 'restoration' of a true revolutionary spirit, extremist but not fanatical, rigorous but not moralistic, I welcome as a positive sign the appearance of a neo-existentialist poetry, *which instead speaks a great deal about the existence of its authors*: who are necessarily *diverse*, and thus a scandal for the conformists and ridiculousness for the dissenters; a crack in the 'industrial puritanism' which the directors of Fiat and the young outside-of-parliament communists share in common.[23]

VII

Pasolini's idea of revolution was of a revolution to be made against the same which he associated with the authority of the father and the authority of the state. Thus revolution was both an individual, personal act of obedience and a social, political act of obedience. His identification with the other, however, was an identification with an ideal which included the ideal of filial obedience and paternal acceptance and love. Revolution was to be an act performed to restore the ideal state of a love Pasolini felt had been denied him in reality by the accidents of his birth and class, by a father who rejected him and on grounds which were part class-historical (fascism, the army, paternalistic structures) and part existential.

But his disobedience to the father was also an ideal act of love aimed at restoring a situation of filial love and paternal acceptance that he dreamt had once been, an ideal possibility in an impossible world, almost before his birth, certainly before his painful entry into language and the symbolic universe where his father was and the social law prevailed.

Pasolini turned for love to those who like him were the excluded and the peripheral, the unrecognised, all that was socially other: the savage, peasants, blacks, Jews, homosexuals, the irrational, the magical. He identified this other as himself, objectifying his existential exclusion in a global and historical one for which there were innumerable instances at hand. He located his self in his otherness and in the others who were other historically. Otherness was what Pasolini was and, I suspect, to feel other than what one is as what one truly is, to be so internally split, was not always a happy state. It was his otherness that his father had denied to him. To find within himself that love denied by an imaginary identification with the other was a precondition for his survival, certainly the precondition for what he survived on, his poetry. In hating the bourgeoisie as he did, so viscerally, it was as if he was hating his own body and soul. But in loving the other as he did, it was a way to love that body and soul by inhabiting and sometimes torturing other souls. Everything he loved he hated, and everything he hated he loved. His

171

loathing for the young as he later expressed it was to provoke them in order that they might be lovable again.

By identifying with the other and loving it he could love himself. After all, perhaps in the end, and in order to grow up, we have to accept that we must displace our parents as the source of love and begin to depend on ourselves for love. The otherness which Pasolini cycled was partly a way to do that, but because it was exteriorised, it could never succeed and he could never quite grow up, hence the scandals, the constant requests, the exhibition of pain, the will to martyrdom, like threatening to leave home.

The desire for the restoration of a past in Pasolini's work, so caught up in revoution and scandalous disobedience, had behind it an enormous charge of emotion and nostalgic feelings that were personal and dated from infancy, but were also social and mythical and came from the beginning of time. His Revolution was not aimed to kill the father, but to reinstate him as an ideal. Real fathers were as awful as ideal ones were not. The idyllic image of son following father was the most touching, and most mythical, aspect of Pasolini's revolutionary myth.

The same had a double edge. It was the same of consumer capitalism and the bourgeoisification of the world, and it was the same of the institutionalisation of the ideal when there would be nothing but the ideal. The full establishment of either condition was the enemy of poetry, since poetry was that which existed in the gap and opposition between same and diversity. Poetry required that the other remain permanently so as to be a precondition for writing. Pasolini, necessarily, in order to be able to write had to be equally uncomfortable in an ideal he could never attain and a reality he could not bear. Had he reached the heaven he desired, he would have lost the desire to attain it for which his writing was the means and his pleasure, and his pain.

The Russian Revolution section of *La rabbia* also contained Bassani's voice of poetry. In one sequence, a teacher shows young Soviet students around an art gallery of socialist realist paintings idealising the revolution. The students are addressed by him in the literary, other voice of poetry spoken by Bassani. It is mimicry poeticised, much as Pasolini mimicked the lumpenproletariat of the Rome *borgate*. It is clear from the words of the poem that the class struggle, like desire, and like the unpossessable revolutionary ideal, has to be kept alive against the certainty of idealisations, especially the smugness of idealisations in socialist realism. Only then could real beauty and genuine revolution survive as ideals, that is by not being realised, or at least not in the emptiness of socialist realism, empty because it lacked its other, its negativity. Without the negation of the ideal and only with the ideal, there could no revolution, for revolution was permanent, constantly in search of beauty and poetry and constantly invoked by those means. It was the other that Pasolini craved, even more than the ideal.

Young comrades ...
I am here in the name of our Committee
and ... and ... to you so full of the desire to know
I must teach you about the glories of Soviet painting
And I will do it. ... As in the Stalin years
I will continue to do my job as guide ...
I will say to you: look how well done
are these comrades miners,
these comrades from the collective farms. ...
This I will say to you. ... Nevertheless something else weighs
on my heart
of a functionary who does his duty as he did during the days
of Stalin!
It is a terrible weight young comrades, because
it is the weight of truth, which is,
even if it is not said. ... These paintings,
oh! certainly, are full of our genius,
of our fraternal feelings,
that make life beautiful and friendly. ... But
– I sweat and blush to tell you this,
like a comic character of Chekhov's ... like
a boy who speaks with his father for the first time
of matters of love – in these paintings there is an
error.
We must remove them from these walls!
Put them in storage, say goodbye to them
as to an entire epoch of our life. ...
We must begin again from the beginning, from where
there is no certainty, and the sign is desperate,
and the colour strident, and the figures
writhe like the cremated at Buchenwald,
and a red flag has the tremor
of a victory that must not be the last.
Because the class struggle is not over,
and we are not Russians, we who fight:
we are Spanish, Italian workers,
French intellectuals, Algerian partisans,
we are not in Moscow or Leningrad,
but in the factories where we fight the class struggle,
and in the deserts of the colonies where we fight for
liberty.

VIII

Perhaps in every revolutionary there is a secret wish that the revolution
will never come. It would mean the end of the revolutionary ideal, and

result in a Robespierrian, or Stalinist, or Maoist terror to maintain the idea in the face of reality, which can be a fanatical and murderous path. Pasolini's revolutionary ideals could only be maintained by having no possibility of being realised. He wanted a revolution to restore an ideal past, a lost, impossible world, what-could-never-be, the desire for which sustained the idea of it and the desire for it. The sign of desire was writing, a writing that guaranteed what it sought would only exist in the writing which sought it. The revolution was in writing, not in reality. It was always other and always unattainable since writing could do no more than evoke it. The revolutionary ideal was sustained by writing the desire for it. Revolution as idea kept desire alive, hence it kept writing alive. Pasolini refused reality in order to maintain the absolute ideal of it. It brought him to positions of total renunciation of all that might have been practically possible and absolute hope in what was impossible except in an ideal realm. Reality was not real for him while the not-real was his only reality. It was the justification and motive of his work.

Chapter 5

Gennariello

What is required is total criticism, refusal, desperate and useless denunciation.

Anti-Theory

The distinction cinema and film in Christian Metz's cinema semiotics was derived from the *langue/parole*, language/speech, distinction in structural Saussurian linguistics. The Saussurian distinction was essentially formal. Language was a system, a code, a set of conventions which governed speech acts and made them comprehensible. The system was not exactly hypothetical, but neither was it actual. Language needed to be deduced from an analysis of concrete instances of speech. The language system was metalinguistically constructed.

Metz spent much of his work enquiring into a possible equivalent language system for the cinema. Films are creative acts somewhat different from speech acts. Films tend only in part to issue from a code or set of conventions. They are their own systems. They invent codes and thus break with, rather than confirm, general conventions. Because film is not primarily an instrument of communication, but an artistic one of expression, the system of cinema does not have the permanence of the system of language. The cinema is less useful and less necessary.

Pasolini did not seek to find an objective set of rules and so define, with scientific precision, the structure of cinema as the system of cinema. Instead, Pasolini's idea of cinema was a critical one. He thought of film not in terms of the way it conformed to or departed from a set of conventions (cinema as a semiotic *langue*), but rather in its distance from a potential ideal. The ideal he called Cinema.

Pasolini's cinema was not the sum of the operations of film derived from an analysis of individual films – so many particular speech acts which presupposed the existence of a language system behind it – but rather cinema for him was simply the analogue of reality as infinite and whole as reality itself, indicated perhaps by the major theoretical figure or mechanism in his theory of cinema, 'the infinite shot-sequence'. He defined Cinema in part as this infinite shot-sequence coextensive with reality itself. Cinema was not, as it was for Metz, an articulated system, or one whose articulation he sought, nor was it a system from which analytic tools could be derived for understanding films. Instead it was an ideal, a Utopian measure of the actual.

Cinema, for Pasolini, even if it could be called a language, was a language in a special way. It was the analogue/imitation of reality. It spoke not with the signs of reality in a representational way, but with reality in a mimetic way: with the reality of reality, with real objects and in the time and space of reality. It was absolute duplication:

> While for a writer things are destined to become words, that is symbols, in the expression of a film-maker things remain as things: the 'signs' of the verbal system are therefore symbolic and conventional, while the 'signs' of the cinema system are to the contrary things themselves in their materiality and in their reality. They become, admittedly, 'signs', but they are signs, one needs to say, that are living signs of themselves.[1]

It was as if reality had found a language which could duplicate it: 'reality spoke with reality'. His cinema almost became an exact equivalent of this reality-speech. It 'wrote reality with reality'. Reality spoke and cinema wrote. Cinema, thus, was a language, but not a symbolic one. It wrote reality, exactly as reality did, with objects, not signs. The language of cinema then was, for Pasolini, like reality, pre-symbolic: it was a language which, monstrously and impossibly, came before language.

But how could that be? Could there be a language without signs? And could there be a language before language? This language was not even an Edenic language. It was an impossible one. Or, in other terms, an ideal and critical one.

The social world is a world of signs. The Pasolinian idea of reality pre-existed the sign. It was pre-symbolic and, fundamentally, pre-social. Just as there was for him a pre-language language, there was a pre-social social, society before society.

Social reality is composed of social signs, conventions distinct from and apart from reality. So too is film. Film is a linguistic-stylistic system of social exchange separate from reality and representing it. Film, in Pasolini's cinema theory, was the opposite of his idea of cinema. The opposition was different from that suggested by Metz and the literature of cinema semiotics. Film, for Pasolini, was not a concrete instance of an abstract system, but an evocation of an ideal system. Cinema was 'that-which-was-not film', and which film evoked as its absence.

The absent cinema was not a hypothetical language system as it was or might have been in a semiotics, but a hypothetical ideal reality, lost to film, and only refound by it as the consciousness of what had been lost in reality. It was the price every sign system must pay to remind us of the loss of that which it represents and symbolises. At the centre of the Pasolinian relation, Cinema/Reality, was the idea of a potential, ideal cinema, never realised and, more importantly, never-to-be-realised.

Non-realisation functioned critically. Cinema was a critical concept which, by indicating a lost reality – the pre-symbolic – indicated that which ran beneath not only film, but language and society as well: the irrational, the uncoded, the unsocialised. These elements, for Pasolini, were the very stuff of society, indeed they were society's lost ideals. Reality pre-existed language and the social. It was irrational and sacred, almost at the edge of the Creation. Cinema called attention to the operation of film (and language) in having instituted the loss of reality as the precondition for its own existence: the code, the social, language. Cinema, then, could not only not be realised, it could not be expressed. Like Pasolini's other concepts of ideals, it indicated an unpossessable desirable beyond, an ideal substance whose ideality made it sacred and mythological.

If you try to apply Pasolini's theory of cinema and seek to bring it to earth or realise it, it escapes your grasp. His cinema belongs to a theory of a cinema whose primary feature is that of having no possibility of being actualised. It needs to remain ideal, that is exclusively and absolutely theoretical and by that fact uncompromisingly critical.

His theory is a theory about what film is not, but once might have been. It is the myth and dream of cinema. Its potential and conditionality needed to remain always potential. Anything more concrete would have made it lose its critical power. The potentiality of cinema issues from a past which is essentially mythological: beyond the social and beyond the historical in a past perfect even before time.

Pasolini's idea of cinema was impossible as an existing fact and useless as a referential system for comprehending film. It is a theory without application, without theoretical yield. It produces nothing. It is instead a permanent ideal other, a total alterity to what is. This theoretical otherness was also true for his poetics, his idea of beauty, his notion of the sacred.

Pasolini's theory of cinema is unlike semiotic theory whose goal was to understand language systems. His theory attended to that which was beyond the borders of understanding, an anti-semiotics dressed up as a semiotics, and very close to faith. It indicated a field beyond which reason needed to halt, not a field to enter into in order to understand. Understanding and knowledge were the last things he desired.

Pasolini's social and political theories were as ideal as his theory of cinema. He proposed an anti-politics, an impractical politics, an anti-social Utopian social. And just as he despaired (or made-believe that he despaired) that the ideal cinema of a lost reality would ever be realised (it was the source of his criticism of the present, indeed the very motive of his criticism), so he despaired that the ideal society and values of the past, as he presented them, would ever be realised. The ideal could only endure as ideal, as a theoretical concept. Even his ideal language, or perhaps especially that language, was so ideal that it could not ever be reached, only pointed to.

Until late into the 60s, Pasolini believed that there were still remnants existing of the antique world in the contemporary one: sub-proletarians in the cities, an abject rural backward peasant poor in the countryside, whole peoples only barely grazed by capitalism. Hence, while he criticised the present, he could still refer to the existence within the present of his ideal past of the other. At the very least then, his criticism was protective: the revolution, to be made on behalf of ideals, was a revolution to sustain the past (the only place where ideals could be situated). After 1968, as he looked around him, he saw not only the past disappearing before the on-slaught of consumer capitalism, but also the possibility of revolution dis-appearing. Who would make it? And in the name of what? And what would it consist of? Global social structures were changing, and abso-lutely. The peasantry, the Third World, the sacred, beauty as he under-stood it, poetry, and he, the poet, who had identified with these, seemed no longer real forces. They had become useless, fading-out anachronisms, only ideals. It was the crisis of a humanist culture.

After 1968, Pasolini's writing seemed a writing addressed to no one: the other was no more. And in the writing, he often complained no one could hear. Yet, he continued to write. But why? To whom? And how? His writ-ing seems especially poignant after 1968 because it was addressed to the youth, those traditionally the hope of the future. But it was a youth he said he hated and with all the loathing he had previously heaped on his own father, on all fathers, on *the* Father. He wrote to the youth, but they could not understand. He spoke to them, but they could not hear. They could not even hear his hatred, or if they did they were indifferent to it. He provoked them, but they ignored him.

They were like Ninetto in *Fiore di carta*, whom God, in multiple voices, tries to reach. In the end, not being heard, God kills Ninetto, just as Christ blighted the innocent fig tree. The youth were the sons and Pasolini had become a father. Between them there was an abyss of incomprehension.

In Pasolini's myth of the present, the old father, the father who had instituted the social and the Law, had bred sons who were obedient and accepted what the father had made. They were the children of consumer society and the bourgeoisie, or if not bourgeois, they yearned to be. Even as some young people challenged their fathers in 1968, they had, in this Pasolini myth, accepted that the only values and the only history were bourgeois. Thus any opposition they formed to their fathers was at best a squabble in the family, even civil war, but it was not a revolu-tion. It was not an attempt to change values or transform the father's Law in terms of another law and other values. They had inherited and accepted the inheritance which suppressed all that was other to them-selves. It was the erasure of the other which their fathers had instituted. This acceptance prevailed even when sons seemed to be revolutionaries. In fact they were the obedient sons of obedient fathers. And, for Pasolini, they were therefore all the same: not only had class distinctions been dissolved, but also political ones and beyond all physical traces of differences. There was now no telling a communist from a fascist, a worker from a bourgeois.

Insofar as Pasolini was the disobedient Son who opposed the old father and the bourgeoisie, the prevailing Law, and harked back to a past of a different father and a different history, now he, Pasolini, a father because a teacher and a writer, opposed, like Davidson's teacher, the sons begotten by the fathers whom Pasolini loathed. He was now a father hating his sons, killing them as Oedipus's father tried to kill Oedipus in order to protect the old world and the past: but Oedipus was saved and there was plague, pestilence and death. In the name of the ideal, it seemed Pasolini had shifted from the position of Oedipus (patricide) to that of the father he murdered (filicide), a step backward indeed. As Pasolini murdered young people with his words ('Il Pci ai giovani'), and his images (*Salò*), he continued to address them (*Gennariello*). Then one day a young adolescent thug from the Rome *borgate* murdered him, as if to prove his fantasy to be real, but it was he, the father, who had been devoured by his adored, lumpenproletarian sons who had strayed: ' ... we are two strangers, whom nothing can bring together.'

Workshop

Officina was a journal of poetry and literature which Pasolini helped to found in the late 50s with Franco Fortini, Alberto Moravia and Roberto Roversi. They wanted to promote a literature that would be politically committed, popular, or at least accessible, and at the same time modern and experimental. They wanted to avoid the contentism and obedience to party ideology which had vitiated with its populism some Italian literature post-war, and in which neo-realism was sometimes implicated, and also to avoid the narrowly stylistic and linguistic experiments of the avant-garde which, it seemed to them, had turned away from politics and the popular altogether.

The position was an important one. It is possible to see, I think, and especially in film-makers like Fellini, Pasolini, Visconti, an unhappiness with contemporary culture in three regards: as avant-garde culture, as committed political culture of the party, and most of all, as mass culture which they connected with what was worst and most vulgar in the contemporary. Television, but the mass media generally, certainly for Fellini and Pasolini, was the most cheap and degraded aspect of present cultural expression. In different ways but with, I think, not dissimilar impulses, these film-makers of a generation which grew up during fascism sought out popular forms which predated consumer capitalism like the circus (Fellini), carnival (Pasolini), melodrama (Visconti), and refashioned them within a high bourgeois and humanist culture which they experienced as being threatened and which predated fascism and the economic boom and transformation of Italy post-war. In the work of these three film-makers in particular it is possible to see an attempt to reconcile an old popular culture and an old bourgeois culture against the popular of the present. It seemed sometimes that this traditional popular, which contained elements, very strong in Pasolini, of the rural and the peasant (dialect, the body, natural functions), was being exploited to preserve one's own class culture whose elements included a political commitment to that which was other than bourgeois.

Officina can be translated as workshop. The connotations of the noun are artisanal. *Officina* was meant to suggest a time prior to consumer capitalism, the capitalism which had spawned a vulgar mass culture and a precious avant-garde one which Pasolini and *Officina* called the neo avant-garde. *Officina* was opposed to both these cultural manifestations. According to *Officina* the opposition to mass culture by the neo avant-garde was founded on literary experimentation seemingly devoid of social commitment even if its proponents asserted that by changing linguistic forms, they were altering perceptions, and thus by offering the possibility of a different vision, they offered the possibility of a different society.

Pasolini and the other members of the editorial group, the majority of whom were poets, therefore sensitive to style and language, thought of *Officina* less as a journal for a defined literary product than as a workshop for a new means of literary production. The editorial group was composed of writers committed in the first instance to writing, not to subjects, contents or a defined politics: nevertheless they wanted to produce a committed writing.

Pasolini's means of literary production were connected to a conceptualisation of poetic language as popular in a traditional sense and therefore in touch with the real. For these reasons it enabled him to believe that he was enjoying the cake of reality (and commitment) with the eating of experimentation (and high art). It was a way to resolve a split which *Officina* addressed between a commitment to ordinary people and a radical politics on the one hand, and a commitment to literature and a radical art on the other. In Pasolini's case he deployed what he regarded as elements of an ancient popular against a restricted bourgeois culture to upset and reinvigorate the latter while, to an extent and in the way poetry functioned in *Il padre selvaggio*, taming the popular and the primitive, by instituting the *Eumenides* in a medieval Italian *officina* manned by poets fashioning their every word with artisanal care.

Gennariello

During 1974–5, Pasolini regularly contributed articles to the daily, *Corriere della Sera*. Though *Corriere* is a national paper, it is also a Milanese, north Italian paper. It is relatively establishment in its positions though not by that token illiberal or always conservative, especially on cultural issues. Pasolini's contributions to *Corriere* were controversial and included a series of articles in which he argued against abortion at the time of the referendum on its legalisation.

From March to June 1975, less than six months before he was murdered, Pasolini contributed a series of fourteen articles to *Corriere* under the general title 'Gennariello'. Though the articles were part of a series, each was self-sufficient. They were later collected and published by Einaudi in an anthology of Pasolini's late writings as *Lettere luterane* (1976). Almost all the *Lettere* were written for *Corriere* in 1975, virtually up to the day of Pasolini's death early in November. The last one is dated 29 October: 'Le mie proposte su scuola e Tv' ('My Proposals for School and TV'). 'Gennariello' is the heart of the *Lettere* though all the contributions are part of a criticism of contemporary Italy and of the young.

'Gennariello' is in the form of a primer. It consists of didactic letters written to a young man as a guide to life in contemporary Italy. The letters are also partly love letters. They are paternal, affectionate, from the older man to the young boy, like the relationship of the European teacher to Davidson in *Il padre selvaggio*. The letters instruct and seduce. They speak of politics to the young boy with intimacy. Pasolini assumed the role of teacher, making Gennariello conscious of himself and of the world around him, but also conscious of the father who was teaching, and of his care. But consciousness was often a dangerous instrument for Pasolini, necessary, but potentially lethal.

Gennariello is an affectionate Neapolitan name, like the name 'Ninetto' (Davoli), the sweet, joyful, innocent Calabrian. Pasolini's love for his invention 'Gennariello' is attached to the fact that Gennariello is a Neapolitanism, hence natural, lively, of the people, therefore real.

> Neapolitans as a type strike me by their being down to earth, and, what is more, ideologically congenial. In these last few years in fact – and, to be precise, during this decade – they have not altered much. They have remained the same Neapolitans for centuries. ... With Neapolitans, I have no physical reserve, because they, in their innocence, have none with me. With Neapolitans I can presume to teach something because they know that their attentiveness is a favour they give to me. The exchange of knowledge is thus absolutely natural. With Neapolitans I can simply say what I know, because I am full of an almost mythical respect for their knowledge, which is also full of joy and natural affection.
>
> Someone might think that a boy like you whom I am describing is a miracle. In fact you can be bourgeois, that is to say a student of the first or second level of high school. I would be prepared to admit that you would be a miracle if you had been a Milanese, a Florentine or even a Roman. But the fact that you are a Neapolitan does not prevent you from being internally sweet, even if externally you are bourgeois. Naples is still the last popular metropolis, the last great village (and with cultural traditions that are not strictly speaking Italian): this general and historical fact physically and intellectually levels social classes. Vitality is always a source of affection and candour. In Naples, both the boys who are poor and the boys who are bourgeois are full of vitality.[2]

Pasolini presumed to a double knowledge. He knew the Neapolitan (the not-bourgeois) whom he addressed and he also knew the not-Neapolitan (the bourgeois) from which his address came. The latter had brought him, with sympathy, to the former, from the civilised to the primitive pure, from reason to innocence. By the imaginative act of writing he could, as he did in all his work, invent an other, call it real, and then inhabit it, body and soul, not as real but as text. In *Fiore di carta*, he invented an innocent Ninetto, but had to destroy him because Ninetto's innocence was obdurate to any teaching. He wanted to save Gennariello and so invented him, as he had Davidson, in order that he might learn.

What could Pasolini teach Gennariello? Essentially he had two lessons to confer: he could teach Gennariello to be conscious of his precious Neapolitanism *and* to be aware of all that was outside it and threatened it, the bourgeois world and the capitalist consumer world.

The ability to learn about your innocence and the gracious gift it is entails the acquisition of the knowledge which would put an end to the innocence the knowledge was acquired to protect. But consciousness was less a threat than a necessary defence of an irrational severely threatened by a capitalism which would obliterate all otherness including the preciousness of Gennariello's Neapolitanism. Reason was a means for rescuing the irrational and while it required the acceptance of its loss in the actual shape of the world, it retained it in thinking and memorialised it by re-expressing its forms in texts, essentially poetic texts which mimeticised and memorialised a reality lost in order that it might be re-experienced, albeit at another and more distant level. Writing then, and poetry in all its forms, was an existential and even revolutionary necessity. It was a way to save your soul, as Davidson was saved ('E l'Africa?').

As Pasolini addressed Gennariello, he realised that Gennariello was already dying, as he was being addressed. Pasolini's writing had created Gennariello and was also destroying him by forming him, as the artist in Poe's 'The Oval Portrait' does, erasing the life of his wife as he traces her portrait on canvas. Gennariello, the innocent Other, is finally no more than a textual example of what no longer is, to be killed off in order that his lesson might live, as Stracci was killed, and Ettore, and Christ, all martyrs needed to exhibit what they were and what the world had lost in not knowing what they were, and to such a degree that the world murdered them. They are sacrificial lambs reminding us of what we once were and still could become or at least not lose. Like 'E l'Africa?', these deaths remember a lost ideal that is also a critical one because it criticises what is and because not to heed it will be our death.

Pasolini may have hated the bourgeoisie, but he did not hate bourgeois culture. It was the means he employed to be critical, even to hate. With knowledge and culture one could possess the world. These he juxtaposed against innocence and against the destructive arrogance of consumerism.

The new mass society had forgotten old values and the old values were inadequate to deal with the horrors of the present. Pasolini reminded the present of the past and reminded the past that it was in the present. What was missing from either term or position and what Pasolini furnished was not innocence (for the consumer) or sophistication (for the primitive), but the cultural gift of writing and reason, able to know and with that knowledge preserve an irrational being denied and a humanist culture being ignored.

Bourgeois, literary, humanist, committed culture was on the wane and along with it, primitive culture, in exact proportion to the waxing of capitalist consumerism. The bourgeois culture he belonged to and which he used to defend the primitive were both cultures of the past and irrevocably tied to one another and mutually dependent. Defending the primitive was an act of (bourgeois) cultural self-defence as much as was the invention by Rousseau of the critical term 'le bon sauvage'.

Pasolini's work was more a passionate regret for a lost humanism than it was a lament for a lost primitivism. It was the former that had invented the latter. He wrote from within the suppositions and traditions of an Italian bourgeois culture which included his decadent, romantic nostalgia and regret for a lost irrational past of primitivism and the sacred, a projected Other which was his own self. It was not Pasolini alone who was schizoid, the culture was.

Central to Pasolini's idea of an irrational was less the primitive than the poetic, beauty and writing. And these notions had within them an inspiration that was Crocean and idealist. It was these that had no place in contemporary society, hence society seemed to have had no place for him, or so at least he experienced it. He may have been defending the world from vulgarity and its suicidal cultural, social self-destruction, but essentially he was trying to save himself. He said to Gennariello:

My culture (with its aestheticism) places me in a critical position with respect to 'things' modern, understood as linguistic signs. Your culture, on the contrary, causes you to accept things modern as natural, and to heed their teaching as absolute.[3]

Sana'a

In one of his letters to Gennariello, Pasolini related his trip to Sana'a in South Yemen where Pasolini had gone in 1971 to look for locations for *Il fiore delle Mille e una notte*. The letter was in the form of a political, social and cultural lesson. It addressed itself to discussing pedagogical language and aesthetic language, matters of beauty and the means of artistic production. At the beginning of the lesson, Pasolini discussed the the difference between the cinematic sign which was his anti-sign of reality and the pre-symbolic, and the literary sign, the sign proper, of artifice and the symbolic.

Sana'a, like all of the Third World for Pasolini, was two things, an intact, sublimely beautiful medieval Arab city of the past, and a corrupted, degraded city being developed in the present. The old, exquisite Sana'a was being threatened with destruction by a new, coarse Sana'a taking shape within it. In 1974, Pasolini made a film in the form of a plea to UNESCO to save Sana'a from the destruction of modernisation, *Le mura di Sana'a (The Walls of Sana'a)* (1971). In the film he represented the co-existence of the two languages of the city, its two semantic worlds, its two contradictory times, not unlike Stracci in a world of eighteen frames a second caught in a world of twenty-four frames a second

He said to Gennariello that as a writer he might have gone to Sana'a and only chosen to see its antique beauty – the literary sign was never natural. But as a film-maker, he was bound to see everything – the cinematic sign imitated reality. And this was the case even if later the film might edit reality out and represent only selected things, turning them into signs in the way literature does. The presence, however, of reality remained if only as a pressure on representation as the absence representation had caused to be repressed. The non-symbolic and immediate nature of Cinema necessarily insisted on the presence of all there was in Sana'a, the beautiful as well as the base, the sublime and the ridiculous vile. Pasolini's literary culture had pointed the camera in a particular direction which literally exposed reality, even though one debased. Thus Cinema, which he defined by its ideal relation to the real and hence to the past, became an instrument for exposing the present. It was a practical demonstration of the force of the past, materially concrete in old Sana'a and concrete in the means of Cinema. The film celebrated the past by its own modern means of film which included a past encased in an ideal Cinema: hence the film became a metalinguistic reflection on itself and on Cinema generally. What was not there was the double real of a suppressed Sana'a and the suppressed reality of Cinema.

The modern means of film encased the values of Pasolini's literary culture. If the literary culture criticised the present, it was film that enabled him to re-express it. The two semantic universes in *Sana'a* were cited by a film language which was the evidence of the semantic corruption the film was witness to in the actuality of Sana'a. And cinema, because it was 'the written language of reality', did not simply re-express reality, but permitted it to be re-experienced. Cinema was a means to relive reality:

> If I had gone to the Yemen as a man of letters, I would have returned with an idea of the Yemen completely different from having been there as a director. I don't know which one would have been more true. As a man of letters I would have returned with the idea – exalted and static – of a country crystallised in a medieval historical context: with high and narrow red houses worked with white friezes as by a rough gold-smith, bunched up in a smoking desert, so limpid as to scratch the cornea: and here and there valleys with villages which exactly reproduce

the architectural form of the city, amidst sparse terraced gardens of grain, of barley, of small vines.

As a film director I saw instead, amidst all this, the horrible, 'expressive' presence of modernity: a leprous stain of lamp posts placed chaotically – huts of cement and corrugated iron built without any cognisance of the presence of the walls of the city – ghastly public buildings in a nineteenth-century Arab style, etc. And, of course, my eyes *of necessity* saw other things, smaller or downright mean: plastic objects, tin cans, shoes and manufactured goods of the cheapest cotton, tinned pears (coming from China), transistor radios.

In short, I saw the coexistence of two semantically different worlds, brought together in a single and babel-like expressive system.

Naturally, the modern aspect of this linguistic system seemed to someone *like me* to be degrading and aberrant. And it was so objectively – to tell you the truth – precisely because it was so miserable; it announced without reserve or restraint its shameless speculative function. The Yemen is still only a small, even pathetic market for western industries. Thus it is despised and even objectively ridiculed. Its ruin seems natural. The fact that it requires a renunciation by the Yemenis seems quite natural to the German and Italian speculators: the Yemenis need to be completely complicit in their own genocide: cultural and physical, even if it is not necessarily fatal, as in the concentration camps.

My aestheticism is inseparable from my culture. Why should my culture be deprived of one of its elements even if it is an impure or superfluous one? It is part of a totality: and I have no scruples in saying it because in these last few years I have become convinced that poverty and backwardness are not the worst of evils. On this point we were completely mistaken. The modern things introduced by capitalism into the Yemen, besides turning the Yemenis physically into clowns, have made them much more unhappy. The Imam (the exiled king) was awful, but the miserable consumerism that has replaced him is no less miserable.

That gives me the right not be ashamed of my 'sense of the beautiful'. A man of culture, dear Gennariello, can only be either very advanced or very backward (or perhaps, as in my case, both together). Thus it must be listened to: because in its actuality, in its immediacy, that is in its presentness, reality can only be the language of things and it can only be experienced.[4]

Who is Pasolini speaking to? He invents Gennariello, then accuses him, even as he describes the situation in the Yemen, of not being able to hear because Gennariello, and by extension his entire generation, has been taught by the things of capitalism, which they have lived and which has corrupted them. The old values Pasolini sought to hand down to his 'son' Gennariello no longer had any power, or force, or necessity ... at least, to

Gennariello. Gennariello's innocence had been as corrupted and debased by the modern as had Sana'a. The plea to save the city from itself that Pasolini made to UNESCO was equally the plea of 'Gennariello' to all the Gennariellos of Italy. The reason Pasolini addressed Gennariello was equally a reason not to. If he was lost, he could not hear and if he was not lost, there was no reason to address him.

There is not anything Marxist in Pasolini's address to Gennariello, or even anything political. It was instead a poetic statement about the loss of beauty, its useless necessity which is not simply stated by the writing, but mirrored in it, a poetic writing of poetry, a narcissistic reflection. 'Gennariello' is absurd, exasperated, ineffectual, unproductive, an impassioned, hopeless, empty plea for the beautiful. At the end of *Le mura di Sana'a* and accompanying shots which record the sublimity of the city and its miserable ugliness, the film makes its plea to UNESCO:

We appeal to UNESCO – Help Yemen save itself from destruction, begun with the destruction of the walls of Sana'a.

We appeal to UNESCO – Help Yemen to become aware of its identity and of what a precious country it is.

We appeal to UNESCO – Help stop this pitiful speculation in a country where no one denounces it.

We appeal to UNESCO – Find the possibility of giving this nation the awareness of being a common good for humanity which must protect itself so as to remain so.

We appeal to UNESCO – Intervene, while there is still time, to convince an ingenuous ruling class that Yemen's only wealth is its beauty, and that conserving that beauty means possessing an economic resource that costs nothing. Yemen is still in time to avoid the errors of other countries.

We appeal to UNESCO – In the name of the true, unexpressed wishes of the Yemeni people, in the name of the simple men whom poverty has kept pure, in the name of the grace of obscure centuries, in the name of the scandalous, revolutionary force of the past.

Bologna

Bologna has been a Communist Party-governed city almost since 1948. Pasolini was born in Bologna, spent much of his adolescence there, attended the University of Bologna where he studied art history under Roberto Longhi, one of the great Italian art historians of the 30s and 40s. Longhi had a major influence on Pasolini's appreciation of medieval and Renaissance art and Pasolini paid direct homage to him in *Mamma Roma*. Pasolini began a thesis on modern Italian art under Longhi, but in fact completed a thesis on the poet Giovanni Pascoli.

Pasolini has made reference on a number of occasions to his Bologna adolescence when he lived in Via Nosadella where he wrote his first verses. His bourgeois culture first took form in Bologna and Bologna was perhaps also the first home of his political culture. But Bologna in the thirty years since 1945, as Pasolini relates to Gennariello, developed into a unique, indeed anomalous Italian city. It combined a Communist Party administration and one of the most successful urban and regional economies in Italy. It was a model of Communist Party government – 'honest and clean' – and of capitalist progress, a hybrid of revolutionary ideology and capitalist practice.

The link in Bologna between capitalism and communism might have seemed odd, but it was more common than Pasolini made out in his 'lesson' to Gennariello. In fact, in the regions of Tuscany, Reggio Emilia (Bologna is in Reggio Emilia), Umbria, the Marche, communism was very strong. It was not, however, primarily linked to an industrial working class or to a landless peasantry. It had its support instead in small-scale agricultural co-operatives – direct food production and processing – and an industrial base that was linked to small units engaged in artisanal production, often in traditional areas: food production, ceramics, wine making, clothing, shoes. Communism in these areas of production was not anti-capitalist in its economic goals; it simply relied on older forms of social organisation (though not pre-capitalist ones) and an artisanal means of production to achieve these goals. Some of these forms of organisation (and production) were very ancient, but they also stemmed from co-operative 'socialist' efforts in the 19th century. It certainly was not – as has been sometimes suggested and supposed – a Japanese melding of feudal forms and capitalist intentions.

Bernardo Bertolucci's films are perhaps more accurate than the films and writings of Pasolini as reflections of the social situation in the countryside of the north-central regions of Italy – including their apparent contradictions. Bertolucci's *Prima della rivoluzione* (1964), *La strategia del ragno* (1970), *Novecento* (1976) and *La tragedia di un uomo ridicolo* (1981) are particularly acute politically and socially. Bertolucci moves in a different direction from Pasolini's, but like the Tavianis and in part also Visconti, he does personalise and psychologise Italian history within the structures of the family and generational conflicts of sons and fathers.

After 1948 Pasolini lived in Rome, first in Garbatella in the *borgate*, and later, as he succeeded as a writer and film-maker, in the middle-class quarter of Monteverde. He fled to Rome from Casarsa after a homosexual-paedophile scandal and his expulsion from the party. He came to Rome with his mother Susanna. He associated Bologna more or less with his father. Casarsa was associated with his mother, the peasantry, and a poetry of arcadian, primitive, nostalgic longings.

Rome became for Pasolini a displaced Casarsa. In being expelled from Casarsa, he had been expelled from what he represented as Paradise. He replaced it with the Rome *borgate* and its pimps and thugs, later with the slums of Naples and the rural slums of Calabria, and later still with the global slum of the Third World. It was a Paradise ever receding in the face of reality. As he approached it, he found it stained, spoiled in its purity, almost a ruin: no matter how much his sentiments and eroticism were stirred by trips to India, Uganda, Tanganyika or an imagined, remembered Naples which he reinvented in his letters to Gennariello, he was always bound to be disappointed.

A major motif in Pasolini's work is the voyage, and many of his films are road movies in the action of the fiction (such as *Uccellacci e uccellini*) or are set in exotic locations in the operation of the fiction (the *Trilogia della vita*). And many of his films like *Sopralluoghi in Palestina*, *Appunti per un film sull'India*, *Appunti per un'Orestiade africana*, *Le mura di Sana'a* are in search of ideal locations.

The other major motif, one connected to the voyage, is homelessness. Pasolini never finds Paradise in reality. At best he found it in the paradise he invented in the *Trilogia della vita*, but he became disillusioned all the same, as he did with his invented Gennariello. He renounced the *Trilogia* soon after it was completed, responding to it with the bleakness and despair of *Salò*. Home is never anywhere for him. It is the impossible ideal and his voyages to find it inevitably dissatisfied him.

Pasolini was like a gambler who knew he would always lose, but kept on playing nevertheless. The loss encouraged him to continue to play, that is to write, his main subject being the need to write as the only way to reach his lost ideal. Culture and writing, not money and goods, are what enable us to possess the world, he said. His search for an ideal generated a writing which presupposed an ideal fixed in place somewhere and only just out of reach. The certain way to lose Paradise is to arrive there and he devised a writing which did not arrive – nor would it come – but instead expressed the desire for that lost, happy state of things. His letter to Gennariello on Bologna ('Bologna, città consumista e comunista') is about having nowhere to be.

The changes wrought in Bologna since 1945 by economic development caused, he said, a loss of difference. The Communist Party administration, and communism more generally in Italy, seemed to him to be devoted to the administration of Bolognese capitalism, not to a working class or peasantry, still less to communist ideals or revolution. Communism had promoted consumerism and the same, and by so doing it had helped to rob him of his (cultural) home. On the other hand by taking his home from him, he had been given the voice to protest. In his letter to Gennariello, an anthropomorphised Bologna speaks to Gennariello:

> I know that more than anything else what makes you anxious ... is the fact that I pose problems relating to transnational consumerist development linked to a regional communist administration. And in seeking to resolve these problems, accepts them. And accepting these problems ... it also accepts the universe which poses them: that is, the universe of the

second and ultimate bourgeois revolution. What an Italian city has become – for good or bad – is here accepted, assimilated, codified. In the instant that I am, simultaneously, a developed city and a communist city, I am no longer a city where there is an alternative, but a city where, precisely, there is no alterity. I can imagine in this the eventual Italy of the historical compromise: in which in the best instance, that is in the case of an effective communist administration in power, the population will be all petit bourgeois, the workers having been anthropologically eliminated by the bourgeoisie.[5]

The only Pasolini film which depicts Bologna is *Edipo re*. In the framing flashback in the present, at the end of the film, blind Oedipus stumbles into the Piazza Maggiore in front of the main cathedral and is led, playing his pipe, down the Portico della Morte (the Arcade of Death). In the past, Oedipus had killed his father and driven his mother to suicide and now he is all alone with no one left to listen him as he wanders with his daughters, except that Pasolini's Oedipus has only his 'son' Ninetto to take his hand.

Di Gennaro

'Gennariello' is very close to the name 'Di Gennaro'. Pasolini's letters to Gennariello end with one about the magistrate Di Gennaro. It was Di Gennaro who had condemned *La ricotta* 'fascistically' in the early 60s. Di Gennaro had just been seized, along with another magistrate, Sossi, by left-wing terrorists, the Red Brigades, in 1975 when Pasolini wrote to Gennariello:

Now no one is more reactionary, in my memory, than this Di Gennaro. His harangue against my film was counter-reformist and 'sanfedista' to such an extent that, as the many intellectuals and journalists who heard him could tell you, it approached the Grand Guignol and the ridiculous, not to mention the vulgar. It was the verbal masterpiece of the clerical-fascism of the 50s [the trial was in 1963].[6]

What was the connection, Pasolini asked, between this reactionary figure of Di Gennaro of the 50s and early 60s, and the terrorists who kidnapped him?

In the 50s (and earlier), especially during election time, miracles often occurred in churches. A statue of the Madonna might shed tears, and this would strengthen the power and authority of the Church, and thus of the conservative politics of the Christian Democrats whom the Vatican supported. What caused these tears? Either, Pasolini said, a parish priest went to Rome and came to an agreement with powerful figures in the Vatican, etc., or an emissary sent by one of the Christian Democrat leaders, Fanfani or Andreotti, descended on some parish, contacted the local priest and told him what was needed, etc., or the priest arrived at the right conclusion himself without outside prompting. Now, Pasolini said, the Madonna no longer cries. She stopped shedding tears because the social framework in which those tears were effective had ceased to exist.

> We are in the midst of the end of the universe. Millions and millions of peasants and also workers – from the south and from the north – who came from a time certainly longer than the two thousand years of Catholicism, have been destroyed. Their 'quality of life' has radically changed. On the one hand they have emigrated in their masses to bourgeois countries, or, on the other hand, bourgeois civilisation has reached them. Their very nature has been abrogated for the sake of the producers of goods.[7]

The tears of the Madonna, insofar as they supported the Christian Democrats in the 50s, were anti-communist tears. In the 70s, in the epoch of ideological, political and social compromise, it was not the pursuit of ideology that was required, but its debasement, a centrism in which all ideology would be compromised for the sake of and by the means of the instruments of consumer capitalism. Instead of the unambiguous anti-communist tears of the Madonna, what was now required were gestures that were simultaneously anti-communist and anti-fascist. The kidnapping of magistrates was precisely not this kind of gesture. The terrorists were not the enemies of power, but their accomplices. There was no longer a difference between a Di Gennaro and a Gennariello, and on that note the letters to Gennariello end.

Come E Mutato il Linguaggio delle Cose/How the Language of Things Has Changed

> If, at your age (and even somewhat older), I were to be walking in the periphery of a city (Bologna, Rome, Naples …), what that periphery would say to me 'in its Latin' would be: the poor live here and the life they lead is poor. But the poor are workers. And the workers are different from you bourgeois. Thus they want a different future. But the future is slow in coming. Therefore their tomorrow – lived in this periphery by them and regarded by you – is very much like today. It is a today that repeats itself. The sons have been assured of an existence similar to that of their fathers. They are in fact destined to repeat and reincarnate their fathers. The revolution has the laziness of the sun that shines in the bare fields, on the shacks, on the peeling buildings. All this does not wound the past, does not lacerate its values and its models. Urbanism is still peasant. The world of the worker is still physically a peasant world: and its recent anthropological tradition is not transgressive. The countryside can still absorb this new form of life (*bidonvilles*, shacks, slums) because its spirit is identical with that of the villages, the farms. And exactly in this way the worker revolution has this 'spirit'.

If, however, you now walk in this periphery, still 'in its Latin' it will say to you: 'Here the popular spirit is gone.' Peasants and workers are 'elsewhere', even if they naturally enough still live here. The *bidonvilles* (certainly, thank God) have disappeared. Instead the 'centres' of apartment blocks have multiplied. There is no point any longer in speaking of their amalgamation with the old or peasant world. Garbage is like a frightening strange corpse. The rivers and the canals are awful. The right of the poor to a better life has had the final result of degrading life. The future is nigh and apocalyptic. Sons have been stripped of any resemblance to their fathers and have instead been projected towards a tomorrow that, by conserving the problems and the misery of today, can only end by being completely different in its quality. There is no point any longer in speaking about revolution. ... The split from the past and the lack of relation (even ideal and poetic) with the future has become a radical one.[8]

The changes in the world Pasolini saw were changes in the things in the world, of daily reality, including the means by which things were produced and the people who produced them. The changes in things were physically evident to him in the faces and physical gestures of whole classes. Physiognomies had disappeared along with languages and values. It had created a gap which Pasolini felt he could not bridge. The world had become estranged from him and he from it. Between him and the Gennariello he invented, and whom he in vain tried to address, there was a tremendous gap because the past, his past and the past as he understood it, had been erased, the peasant past to which Gennariello might have once belonged and the bourgeois past to which Pasolini still belonged, and from out of which he wrote and sought a connection with the world but found none. The old bourgeoisie were gone. And the other to the bourgeoisie, which had sustained him, and with whom he identified, had, he felt, been eliminated. Without an other he was hardly himself. The end of the past 'implies a separation between what has not divided fathers from sons for centuries and millennia'.[9] It seemed a new epoch of history had been installed.

The new, capitalist world had caused Pasolini to lose his father, insofar as his father identified with that world and Pasolini could not. His father, by conforming to the awful present, had ushered in the present. To save his ideal father (and his ideal world), not the real one (and not the real world) who threatened his ideals, Pasolini had to defend a past against a present, myth against actuality, an ideal father against a real one.

It was in the present that new sons were being born without knowledge of the past. They were not ideal sons, nor by that fact were they real ones. Without the past, there was no reality for Pasolini. The new sons, lacking the dimension of the past or an otherness to attach themselves to, were fake, vulgar, false, ugly sons, the bourgeois sons of bourgeois fathers even though some were workers and even peasants. Economic differences remained, but consciousness and ideology had become one in consumerist values. The universal was not an ideal any longer, but a vulgarity. In the name of the past, and against the sons, Pasolini renounced all sons, for with such sons there could no longer be a future.

Perhaps that was why 'Di Gennaro', the father, became in 'E l'Africa?' the producer Bini and the father of Pasolini who materialised from out of Bini's body. Di Gennaro had rejected *La ricotta* and as a result had made the realisation of *Il padre selvaggio* impossible, thereby vetoing the possibility that the Utopia of Davidson and his teacher might ever even be expressed. Might it have been that Di Gennaro suggested to Pasolini the sweet, unteachable Neapolitan 'Gennariello', who emerged out of similitude of sound, just as the biological ooze of Pasolini's father in 'E l'Africa?' emerged from a physical similitude with Bini, both pricks?

If there was no difference and all had become bourgeois and sons were only the spoiled bourgeois brats of indulgent bourgeois fathers, even if some of these sons challenged the fathers in the student revolts, and if consumerism was everywhere, and all was the same, then Gennariello and the entirety of youth whom Pasolini had him represent – were they not equally oppressors with their fathers?

In 1968 Pasolini wrote 'Il Pci ai giovani' ('The Italian Communist Party to the Young') addressed to the Italian students fresh from the barricades. He taunted them. They were bourgeois brats.

> They lick
> your arse. Not me, friends.
> You have the faces of spoiled brats
> ...
> ...
> they lick your arse. You are their sons,
> their hope, their future. ... [10]

Chapter 6
Writing

The first modern painting perhaps is the painting which finds in itself, and not in some god or value, its infiniteness, its sacredness, its end.
(Yves Bonnefoy)

On 1 March 1968, there was a violent clash between police and students in the Valle Giulia in Rome, near the faculty of architecture at the University of Rome. The students were protesting against the structures of instruction and administration at the University and demanding educational reform. During the clash some students were badly hurt.

Pasolini wrote a poem to the students published in *Nuovi Argomenti*, a literary/political journal of the left, in its issue of April–June 1968. The poem was entitled 'Il Pci ai giovani!', to which was added a parenthetical title: ('Appunti in versi per una poesia in prosa seguiti da una "Apologia" ') ('Notes in verse for a poem in prose followed by an "Apology"').

The poem accused the students of being bourgeois and petit bourgeois, said their protests were those of the children of the bourgeoisie dressed up as radicalism with no class content, hence no revolutionary significance or potential. The poem described the students as belonging to and committed to the system they criticised. The events at the Valle Giulia then had no more importance than a storm in a teacup, a minor family squabble. The students had not outraged society, rather they reassured it. '*Popolo* and *Corriere della Sera*, *Newsweek* and *Monde*/kiss your arse. You are their children,/their hope, their future; if they reproach you/they are certainly not preparing a class conflict/against you! ...' The poem sympathised not with the students who were beaten but with the police who beat them up.

> When yesterday at Valle Giulia you fought
> with policemen,
> I sympathised with the policemen!
> Because policemen are children of the poor.
> They come from the outskirts, be they rustic or urban.
> As for me, I know very well
> the way they were as children and youths,
> the precious dollar, the father still a youth himself,

because of the misery, which doesn't give authority.
The mother, callused like a porter, or tender,
like a bird, because of some illness;
the many brothers; the hovel
among the meadows with the red sage (on the subdivided land
of others); the slums
overlooking the sewers; or the apartments in the big
lower-class tenements, etc., etc.
And then, look at how they dress them: like clowns,
with that rough cloth that stinks of rations,
the orderly room, and people. Worst of all, naturally,
is the psychological state to which they are reduced
(for roughly sixty dollars a month);
with a smile no longer,
with friends in the world no longer,
separated,
excluded (in an exclusion which is without equal);
humiliated by the loss of the qualities of men
for those of policemen (being hated generates hatred).
...
The boy policemen
whom you, out of the sacred hooliganism ...
...
of spoiled children, have beaten up,
belong to the other social class.
At Valle Giulia, yesterday, we have thus had a fragment
of class conflict; and you, my friends (even though on the side
of reason), were the rich,
while the policemen (who were in the
wrong) were poor. A nice victory, then,
yours![1]

The poem provoked some puzzlement and not a little anger. Though the student movement had distanced itself from the Communist Party and intervened politically as an independent force, the communists wanted to approach the students and in direct contrast to Pasolini's position described them as a genuine potential political force, even a revolutionary one. A communist intellectual:

I am speaking about students and young workers: in my opinion and in the light of the co-ordinated attempt to isolate this movement of young people ... against the grouping of forces that seeks to isolate them, the students have lacked the voice of a poet. Now a poetic voice has appeared, but it accuses them of bad faith, of being petit-bourgeois ... but today we are witnessing a revolutionary process, or at least the symptoms of it: though initial steps, they are very clear ones.[2]

Police represent the authority of the state no matter what their class origins. And the students were challenging the authority of the state irrespective of their class origins. Pasolini's poem took the position that the events at the Valle Giulia were not a class conflict, but a civil disturbance within the confines of the class in power and that the matter of class and revolution was the crucial issue, hence the distinctions the poem made between the bourgeois origins of the students and the proletarian and peasant origins of the police.

Pasolini's view was that class conflict implied an otherness, therefore an alternative to the bourgeoisie and its political order. Lacking a class otherness, the student protest lacked a revolutionary dimension. Revolution, he said, was a class revolution. It required an identification within the revolutionary sectors of the bourgeoisie – intellectuals, artists, students – with the revolutionary sectors of the working class and the peasantry. These radical students could not imagine, Pasolini said, anything other than themselves, any history or values but their own bourgeois ones.

The student protests were evidence, therefore, in fact and also imaginatively, of the elimination of class as a social-historical factor, hence an end to revolutionary political ideology and all possibility of real revolution. Pasolini's accusations against the students were a nostalgic lament for what he believed had happened within his own class and therefore what had happened to the possibility for finding an otherness on which his writing and his commitment depended. The student protests were in part then a sign of his increasing isolation and the untenability of his social politics. If the students were truly a radical force, he had no place. And if their radicalism was only apparent, as he claimed, that left him even less of a place.

It was on Pasolini's identification with a pre-bourgeois world that his opposition to the present rested. His position was not negotiable. Like the students, Pasolini was bourgeois but unlike them, he said, he recalled another and counter-universe. His poem was not simply the statement of a lost otherness, but its enactment in language. It *was* that otherness as poetry. The poem worked by a series of paradoxes, substantively and formally: the poem in prose, prose in poetry, an apology which reversed sense. It asserted one thing and negated it. 'Il Pci ai giovani!' is essentially ambiguous, provocative and it contains therefore the complexity of an otherness and the uncertainty of an otherness in its structure.

The gap was enormous between Pasolini's desire for an otherness that he felt had been lost and the bourgeois demands of the students which precluded an otherness. He wanted the ideal, the revolution, the impossible compared to which what the students wanted seemed pragmatic, grey and compromised.

> ... Strange,
> abandoning the revolutionary language
> of the poor, old, official Communist
> Party of Togliatti,

you have adopted a heretical variant of it
but on the basis of the lowest jargon
of sociologists without ideology (or of the bureaucratic
daddies).
So speaking,
you ask for *everything* in words,
while with the facts, you ask for *only that*
to which you have a right (as good bourgeois children):
a series of reforms that can't be put off,
the application of new pedagogical methods,
and the renewal of the state organism.
Good for you! Sacred sentiments!
May the good bourgeois star help you![3]

The poem ends with a parenthesis. In doing so it keeps open a possibility
for a further writing.

(Oh God! must I take into consideration
the eventuality of fighting the Civil War alongside you
putting aside my old idea of Revolution?)

If the student protests did not belong to a class conflict but to a conflict
within the bourgeoisie and was at best only a civil war within a class, and
if civil war was the only radical possibility available since 'there was no
other class but the bourgeoisie and no other history but bourgeois history',
then the past as Pasolini had dreamt it was gone. If the past was gone then
there was no one to speak to because there was no other to what now was,
hence no reason to speak. The future had been obliterated with the obliteration of the past. There was a present for others but not for Pasolini
whose present was this past and from out of it his projected future. Writing
for him presupposed an otherness and exemplified an otherness. Without
the other there was no writing and without writing there was no other,
there was only nothing. Yet Pasolini continued to write, including this
useless poem. As with the letters to Gennariello he began an address which
ended without an interlocutor. It was a writing which erased its addressee
until it stood alone, a pure writing, a testament to writing, in absolute
uselessness.

He ended the poem, cancelled the students out, in order to continue
to write and for that reason he he ended the poem as he did, parenthetically and interrogatively. What was the function of the poem? And perhaps of all his work of which this 'bad' poetry, these 'ugly verses', were
emblematic?

What are 'ugly verses' ... ? ... Ugly verses are those which do not in
themselves say what the author wants to say: that is, in them meanings
are altered by context, and the context obscures the meanings.

... I have written these ugly verses on a number of registers simultaneously: thus they are all 'doubled', that is ironic and self-parodying. Everything is said *within inverted commas*. The fragment on the police is a piece of *ars retorica* ... the inverted commas are therefore intended to be provocative.

For a young person of today ... it is much more difficult to look at the bourgeoisie objectively through the eyes of another social class. Because the bourgeoisie is triumphing, it is transforming both the workers and the ex-colonial peasants into bourgeois. In short, through neo-capitalism the bourgeoisie is becoming the human condition. Those who are born into this entropy cannot in any way, metaphysically, be outside it. It's over. For this reason I provoke the young. They are, presumably, the last generation which sees workers and peasants; the next generation will only see bourgeois entropy around itself.

... Given my 'total' lack of faith in the bourgeoisie, I therefore resist the idea of civil war, which, perhaps through the student explosion, the bourgeoisie would fight against itself. Already the young people of this generation are, I would say physically, much more bourgeois than we. Well? Don't I have the right to provoke them? In what other way should I put myself in rapport with them, if not thus?[4]

If you speak knowing in advance that you won't be heard or won't be understood, how do you speak? How do you speak against the bourgeoisie if there are only bourgeois? Pasolini never kept silent. He wrote, and excessively. It was a paradoxical writing filled with passionate despair, thus split at its centre. Whatever it said it contradicted by the need to continue to speak. It spoke of its own uselessness, made itself useless with passion and desire. It was as if it cancelled itself out in order to avoid being cancelled out by anything so definite as an end or a conclusion or a meaning and thus it could continue to live on its own terms.

What resisted in Pasolini was the ideal which the writing embodied. His struggle with the world and himself was essentially aesthetic and linguistic. He wrote not about this or that but purely. It was a writing which was its own subject, which contained its own otherness and therefore its self-identity. To write in such a way is to write parenthetically in order to delay the end of writing and hence keep the ideal alive in ambiguity, in the provisional, as an eternal potential. 'Ugly verses are those that are not sufficient alone to express what the author wants to express', 'a bad will in good faith'.

Pasolini's writing was formed in the paradox, the citation, the contrary, the denial, the contradiction, the mirror, the imitation, that is always with this other that reflected on it, that was not it, and that went beyond itself as ideal and as ungraspable ideal. It was a writing which seemed to annul itself, cancelling its own traces, often becoming unpalatable, indigestible, difficult, unconsumable, unacceptable, a scandal of writing. The unacceptability of the writing was a sign for him of its ideality, a perfectly ideal writing which communicated nothing but its own forms and sounds, a poetry. It was outside meaning, hence unpossessable and uncompromising, and thus for him, and in these times of function and commodification, it was a revolutionary gesture even though it came close to identifying the revolution with himself and purity as his preserve alone as if he were the last good soul left in hell.

How do you end a book on Pasolini? How can you kill the father? Pasolini bestowed the gift of his writing on his father and also scandalised and condemned him with it. He was the obedient son and the disobedient one. His writing was an offer of love and a provocation. Fathers can help in self-definition, and one place for it is writing, a discourse made up of the symbolic and something else. To take a journey with Pasolini, which was not always pleasant, can help you to find what you are, which is also what you are not yet. The not yet has the potentiality for revolution, or at the very least it bestows on you a derivation of potential, that of potency, and in a paradoxical place: writing.

Chapter 7

Marilyn

Of the world of the past and the world of the future
only beauty had remained, and you,
poor little younger sister,
the one who tags after her older brothers,
laughing and crying with them, to imitate them,
you the smallest younger sister
who wore your beauty with such humility,
and your soul, the daughter of ordinary people,
never knew it,
otherwise it would not have been beauty.
The world taught it to you.
Thus your beauty became the world's.
Of the fearful old world and the fearful new world
only beauty had remained, and you
carried away your beauty.
It disappeared like golden dust.
Of the stupid old world
and the fierce future world
a beauty had remained that was not ashamed
to allude to the little breast of the younger sister,
to the little belly easily exposed.
And for this reason it was beauty, the same
that the sweet girls of your world have ...
the daughters of merchants
winners of beauty-contests in Miami or in London.
It disappeared like a golden dove.
The world taught it to you
and thus your beauty was no longer beauty.
But you went on being a child,
silly like the past, cruel like the future,

and between you and your beauty possessed by Power
was set all the stupidity and cruelty of the present.
You carried it with you like a smile through tears,
shameless in its passivity, indecent in its obedience.
It disappeared like a white golden dove.
Your beauty surviving from the ancient world,
requested by the future world, possessed
by the present world, became a mortal sickness.
Now, finally, the older brothers turn around,
cease for a moment their cursed games,
emerge from their relentless distraction,
and ask one another: 'Is it possible that Marilyn,
little Marilyn, has shown us the way?'
Now it is you,
who counts for nothing, poor little one, with her smile,
you are the first to go beyond the doors of the world
abandoned to your destiny of death.

(From the Marilyn Monroe sequence in *La rabbia*)

Notes

Notes to Chapter 1

1. Pier Paolo Pasolini, *Le belle bandiere* (Rome: Riuniti, 1978), pp. 87–8. Originally published in *Vie Nuove*, vol. 15, no. 30, July 1960.
2. Ferdinando Camon, 'Pier Paolo Pasolini', in *La moglie del tiranno* (Rome: Lerici, 1969), p. 120.
3. André Bazin, 'The Ontology of the Photographic Image' and 'The Evolution of the Language of Cinema', in *What is Cinema?* vol. 1 (Berkeley: University of California Press, 1967), pp. 9–16, 23–40.
4. Requoted in Christian Metz, *Film Language: A Semiotics of Cinema* (New York: Oxford University Press, 1974), p. 36.
5. Baranski commented to me that the heterogeneity and miming of languages in Pasolini's writing belong to a tradition in Italian culture which begins with Dante.
6. Quoted in Virgilio Fantuzzi, 'La visione religioso', in Fernaldo Di Giammatteo (ed.), *Lo scandalo Pasolini*, special edition of *Bianco e Nero*, vol. 37, nos 1–4, January–April 1976.
7. In an interview with Mario Serenellini, 'Un regista "esiliato" dal mondo consumi', *Gazzetta del Popolo*, 9 January 1975. Pasolini made similar remarks in 'Il mio Accattone in Tv dopo il genocidio', in *Lettere luterane* (Turin: Einaudi, 1976), pp. 152–8, originally published in *Corriere della Sera*, 8 October 1975.
8. Umberto Eco, 'Form as Social Commitment', in *The Open Work* (London: Hutchinson Radius, 1989), p. 126.
9. Requoted in Franco Faldini and Goffredo Fofi, *L'avventurosa storia del cinema italiano 1960–1969* (Milan: Feltrinelli, 1980), p. 44.
10. Walter Benjamin, 'Naples', in *One Way Street and Other Writings* (London: New Left Books, 1979).
11. Roland Barthes, 'Si fallisce sempre di parlare di ciò che si ama', in *Carte, Segni* (Milan: Electa 1981), pp. 24–37.
12. Pier Paolo Pasolini, 'La ricotta', in *Ali dagli occhi azzurri* (Milan: Garzanti, 1989), pp. 474–5. In *La ricotta* the poem is quoted from the book containing the screenplay of *Mamma Roma* (Milan: Rizzoli, 1962), p. 162. The poem forms part of an entry by Pasolini to his diary kept while shooting *Mamma Roma*.
13. Quoted in Tommaso Chiaretti, 'Lo stile di Pasolini', *Mondo Nuovo*, vol. 4, no. 18, 14 October 1962.
14. In 'Introduzione' to the script of *Mamma Roma*; part of the statement can also be found in an interview with Carlo Laurenzi, 'Seri e silenziosi i ragazzi di vita', *Corriere della Sera*, 2 September 1962.

15. Benjamin, 'Chinese Curios', in *One Way Street and Other Writings*.
16. Franz Kafka, *The Great Wall of China and Other Short Works* (London: Penguin, 1991), pp. 58–70.
17. Pasolini, *Un paese di temporali e di primule* (Parma: Guanda 1993).
18. Pasolini, 'Introduzione', *Mamma Roma*.
19. Theodor Adorno, 'Commitment', in *Aesthetics and Politics* (London: Verso, 1980), p. 180.

Notes to Chapter 2

1. Pier Paolo Pasolini, 'Sopralluoghi o la ricerca dei luoghi perduti' (1973), in Michele Mancini and Giuseppe Perella, *Pier Paolo Pasolini: corpi e luoghi* (Bologna: Theorema, 1982), p. 25.
2. Pier Paolo Pasolini, *L'odore dell'India* (Parma: Guanda, 1990), pp. 9–11.
3. Elsa Morante, *L'isola di Arturo*, in Elsa Morante, *Opere*, vol. 1 (Milan: Mondadori, 1988), pp. 963–4.
4. Pier Paolo Pasolini, 'Il cinema impopolare' (1970), in *Empirismo eretico* (Milan: Garzanti, 1972), p. 272. See also Jean Duflot (ed.), *Pier Paolo Pasolini: il sogno del centauro* (Rome: Riuniti, 1983), p. 92.
5. Elsa Morante, *Opere,* vol. 1, p. 62, from her diary entry of 20 September 1952.
6. Pasolini, *L'odore dell'India*, p. 110.
7. Jean-André Fieschi, 'Pier Paolo Pasolini, *Edipo Re*' (interview), *Cahiers du cinéma,* no. 195, November 1967, pp. 13–6.
8. Requoted in Virgilio Fantuzzi, 'La "visione religiosa" ', in Fernaldo di Giammatteo (ed.), *Lo scandolo Pasolini*, special edition of *Bianco e Nero,* vol. 37, nos. 1–4, January–April 1976, p. 70.
9. An interview with Mario Serenellini, 'Un regista "esiliato" dal mondo dei consumi', *Gazzetta del Popolo*, 9 January 1975.
10. In an interview with Enzo Golino in Enzo Golino, *Letteratura e classi sociali* (Bari: Laterza, 1976), p. 112.
11. Pasolini, *L'odore dell'India*, p. 30.
12. Gilles Deleuze, *Cinema 2: The Time–Image* (Minneapolis: University of Minnesota Press, 1989), pp. 174–6.
13. Pasolini, 'Il "cinema di poesia" ' (1965), in *Empirismo eretico*, pp. 172ff.
14. Pasolini, 'Sopralluoghi o la ricerca dei luoghi perduti', p. 23.
15. Ibid., p. 24.
16. The first quote is from an interview with Sergio Arecco, 'Ancora il linguaggio della realtà', in *Filmcritica*, no. 214, March 1971, collected in Enrico Magrelli (ed.), *Con Pier Paolo Pasolini* (Rome: Bulzoni, 1977), p. 98. The second quote comes from a television interview in 1974 for RAI's 'Settimo giorno – Attività culturali' with Francesco Savio, 'Al cuore della realtà' (in typescript and on tape at the Fondo Pasolini).
17. Mortante, *L'isola di Arturo,* pp. 1057–59.
18. Pasolini, 'Appunti per un poema sul Terzo Mondo' (1968), in M. Mancini and G. Perella, *Pier Paolo Pasolini*, p. 37.
19. Federico Fellini, *Fare un film* (Turin: Einaudi, 1993), p. 62. Magnani's response was more colourful than I have translated it: 'Ah Federi, ma ti pare che una come me si fa chiudere nel cesso da uno stronzo d'attore?'
20. Pier Paolo Pasolini, 'Storia indiana: *Appunti per un film sull'India*. Soggetto', in Luciano De Giusti (ed.), *Il cinema in forma di poesia* (Pordenone: Cinemazero, 1979), p. 134.
21. In Pier Paolo Pasolini, 'Dal laboratorio (Appunti *en poète* per una linguistica marxista)', in *Empirismo eretico* pp. 67–8. Requoted in Luciano De Giusti, 'Il modello del ricordo nel sogno di un'opera', *Eidos*, 1980, p. 47.
22. Ibid., p. 68, and in the De Giusti, 'Il modello', pp. 47–8.

23. See Pasolini, 'Dialogo 1' (interview with Adriano Apra and Luigi Faccini), *Cinema e Film*, vol. 1, no. 1, 1966–7.
24. Pasolini, 'Il cinema impopolare', in *Empirismo eretico,* pp. 274–5.
25. Duflot, *Pier Paolo Pasolini*, pp. 163–4.
26. Pasolini, 'Il cinema impopolare', in *Empirismo eretico,* p. 270.
27. Jean Narboni and Tom Milne (eds), *Godard on Godard* (London: Secker & Warburg, 1972), p. 141.
28. Helen Van Dongen, 'Robert J. Flaherty: 1884–1951' (1965), in Richard Meran Barsam (ed.), *Nonfiction Film Theory and Criticism* (New York: E. P. Dutton, 1976), p. 222.
29. Requoted in Eric Barnouw, *Documentary: A History of the Non-Fiction Film* (New York: Oxford University Press, 1974), pp. 98–9. See also Paul Rotha, *Documentary Film* (London: Faber & Faber, 1939), pp. 118–9.
30. Pasolini, 'Storia indiana'.
31. Pasolini, *L'odore dell'India,* p. 42.
32. Ibid. These passages were selected at random. There are similar passages throughout the book. I have not taken the trouble to indicate the page numbers for the passages quoted.
33. Duflot, *Pier Paolo Pasolini*, p. 52.
34. Ibid., p. 52.

Notes to Chapter 3

1. Pier Paolo Pasolini, 'Nota per l'ambientazione dell'Orestiade in Africa', *La città futura*, 7 June 1978 (written in 1969).
2. Pier Paolo Pasolini, *Empirismo eretico* (Milan: Garzanti, 1972): 'Essere è naturale', p. 247, and 'Il cinema impopolare', p. 270.
3. Pier Paolo Pasolini, *Il padre selvaggio* (Turin: Einaudi, 1975), p. 19.
4. Ibid., pp. 51–2.
5. Ibid., p. 55.
6. Friedrich Nietzsche, 'The Triple Fate of Oedipus', in Sophocles's *Oedipus Tyrannus*, L. Berkowitz and T. F. Brunner (eds) (New York: W. W. Norton & Co., 1966), p. 136. It was reprinted from Nietzsche's *The Birth of Tragedy*.
7. Jean Duflot (ed.), *Pier Paolo Pasolini: Il sogno del centauro* (Rome: Riuniti, 1983). p. 52.
8. Pasolini, *Il padre selvaggio*, pp. 58–61.
9. See 'Il "cinema di poesia"', pp. 167–87, in Pasolini, *Empirismo eretico*.

Notes to Chapter 4

1. Jean Duflot (ed.), *Pier Paolo Pasolini: il sogno del centauro* (Rome: Riunti, 1983), pp. 22–3.
2. Pier Paolo Pasolini, 'Gennariello', in *Lettere luterane* (Turin: Einaudi, 1976), p. 45.
3. *L'Unità*, 28 October 1949.
4. Pier Paolo Pasolini, *Le belle bandiere: dialoghi 1960–1965* (Rome: Riuniti, 1978), pp. 51–2. From *Vie Nuove*, vol. 15, no. 26, 25 June 1960.
5. Tzvetan Todorov, *Nous et les autres: La réflexion française sur la diversité humaine* (Paris: Editions du Seuil, 1989). A discussion of the relation made by French writers and philosophers since the Enlightenment with the 'other' of the Third World.
6. Quoted in Todorov, ibid., p. 107.
7. Pasolini, 'Giovani infelici', in *Lettere luterane*, p. 7.
8. Umberto Eco, 'The Death of Gruppo '63', in *The Open Work* (London: Hutchinson Radius, 1989), pp. 238–9.

9. Ibid., pp. 248–9.

10. Quoted in Corrado Vivanti, 'Lacerazioni e contrasti', in Ruggero Romano and Corrado Vivanti (eds), *Storia d'Italia: i caratteri originali*, vol. 3 (Turin: Einaudi, 1989), p. 931.

11. Mikhail Bakhtin, *Rabelais and His World* (Bloomington: Indiana University Press, 1984).

12. Carlo Ginzburg, 'Folklore, magia, religione', in Romano and Vivanti , *Storia d'Italia*.

13. Ibid., p. 616.

14. Giulio Carlo Argan and Maurizio Fagiolo, 'Premessa all'arte italiana', in Romano and Vivanti , *Storia d'Italia*, p. 734.

15. Bakhtin,. *Rabelais and His World*, pp. 465–6, 471.

16. Duflot, *Pier Paolo Pasolini*, p. 22.

17. Lino Peroni, 'Incontro con Pier Paolo Pasolini', *Inquadrature*, nos 15–16, Autumn 1968, p. 34.

18. Interview with Gideon Bachmann, 'Ideologia e poetica', in Enrico Magrelli (ed.), *Con Pier Paolo Pasolini* (Rome: Bulzoni, 1977), pp. 101–2.

19. Ginzburg, 'Folklore, magia, religione', pp. 615–16.

20. Quoted in Piero Zanotto, 'La motivazione', *Rivista del Cinematografo*, September–October 1964.

21. From the voice-over narration in *La rabbia*.

22. Pier Paolo Pasolini, 'In Africa tra figli obbedienti e ragazzi moderni' (1970), in Michele Mancini and Giuseppe Perella, *Pier Paolo Pasolini: corpi e luoghi* (Bologna: Theorema, 1981), pp. 45ff.

23. Pier Paolo Pasolini, 'Ciò che è neo-Zdanovismo e ciò che non lo è' (1968), in *Empirismo eretico* (Milan: Garzanti, 1977), p. 164.

Notes to Chapter 5

1. Jean Duflot (ed.), *Pier Paolo Pasolini: il sogno del centauro* (Rome: Riuniti, 1983), p. 23.

2. Pasolini, 'Gennariello', in *Lettere luterane* (Turin: Einaudi, 1976), p. 17.

3. Ibid., pp. 40–1.

4. Ibid., pp. 39–40.

5. Ibid., p. 51.

6. Ibid., p. 66.

7. Ibid., pp. 64–5.

8. Ibid., pp. 45–8.

9. Ibid., p. 44.

10. Pier Paolo Pasolini, 'Il Pci ai giovani! (Appunti in versi per una poesia in prosa seguiti da una "Apologia")', in *Empirismo eretico* (Milan: Garzanti, 1977), p. 151.

Notes to Chapter 6

1. Pier Paolo Pasolini, 'Il Pci ai giovani! (Appunti in versi per una poesia in prosa seguiti da una "Apologia")', in *Empirismo eretico* (Milan: Garzanti, 1977), pp. 151–2. Originally in *Nuovi Argomenti*, no. 10, April–June 1968.

2. Vittorio Foa, *L'Espresso*, vol. 14, no. 24, 16 June 1968. See also *L'Espresso*, no. 25, 23 June 1968, for further discussions of the poem, and Pasolini's reply in *L'Espresso*, no. 26, 30 June 1968. See also Roberto Longo, 'Il movimento studentesco nella lotta anticapitalistica', *Rinascita*, vol. 25, no. 18, 3 May 1968, and Giorgio Amendola, 'Necessità della lotta sui due fronti', *Rinascita*, vol. 25, no. 23, 7 June 1968.

3. 'Il Pci ai giovani!', pp. 154–5.

4. Ibid., p. 158.

Filmography

Films are listed according to their release date, not their production date. Detailed filmographies for Pasolini's films can be found in Michele Mancini and Giuseppe Perrella, *Pier Paolo Pasolini: corpi e luoghi*, Bologna: Theorema, 1981, and in Associazione 'Fondo Pier Paolo Pasolini', *Pier Paolo Pasolini: A Future Life*, Rome, 1989. Unaccountably, the Mancini and Perrella book has no entries for *Appunti per un film sull'India* and *Le mura di Sana'a*, while *Future Life* has no entry for *Dodici dicembre*.

I. Directed by Pasolini

Accattone (1961)
p Alfredo Bini *st/sc* Pier Paolo Pasolini *asst d* Bernardo Bertolucci (first) and Leopoldo Savona (second) *c* Tonino Delli Colli *ad* Flavio Mogherini *ed* Nino Baragli *mus* Johann Sebastian Bach arranged by Carlo Rustichelli.
lp Franco Citti (*Vittorio Cataldi/Accattone*), Franca Pasut (*Stella*), Silvana Corsini (*Maddalena*), Paola Guidi (*Ascenza*), Adriana Asti (*Amore*), Adele Cambria (*Nannina*), Silvio Citti (*Sabino*), Sergio Citti (*a waiter*), Elsa Morante (*Lina*), Umberto Bevilacqua (*Salvatore*), Franco Bevilacqua (*Franco*), Amerigo Bevilacqua (*Amerigo*). 120 mins.

Mamma Roma (1962)
p Alfredo Bini *st/sc* Pier Paolo Pasolini *asst d* Carlo di Carlo (first) and Gianfranceso Salina (second) *c* Tonino Delli Colli *ad* Flavio Mogherini *ed* Nino Baragli *mus* Antonio Vivaldi's *Concert in C Major*, Cherubini-Bixio's *Violino Tzigano* sung by Joselito (arranged by Carlo Rustichelli).
lp Anna Magnani (*Mamma Roma*), Ettore Garofalo (*Ettore*), Franco Citti (*Carmine*), Silvana Corsini (*Bruna*), Luisa Orioli (*Biancofiore*), Paolo Volpone (*the Priest*), Santino Citti (*father of the bride*), Maria Bernardini (*the bride*). 114 mins.

La ricotta (1963)
Episode of **RoGoPaG**
p Alfredo Bini *st/sc* Pier Paolo Pasolini *asst d* Sergio Citti and Carlo di Carlo *c* Tonino Delli Colli *ad* Flavio Mogherini *ed* Nino Baragli *mus* Carlo Rustichelli.

lp Mario Cipriani (*Stracci*), Orson Welles (*the film director*), Laura Betti (*the 'star'*), Vittorio La Paglia (*the journalist*), Maria Bernardini, Ettore Garofalo, Tomas Milian, Franca Pasut (*cast extras*), Elsa De Giorgi, Enzo Siciliano (*invited guests*). 35 mins.

La rabbia (part one) (1963)
p Gastone Ferranti *commentary* Pier Paolo Pasolini (voices of Giorgio Bassani and Renato Guttuso) *asst d* Carlo di Carlo *ed* Nino Baragli *mus* Songs of the Cuban Revolution (The Barbudos), songs of the Algerian Revolution, *Non c'è altro che Dio, I sogni muoiono all'alba* (Simoni, A. F. Lavagnino), *Lo Shimmy* (A. F. Lavagnino), *Concerto disperato* (Simoni), *Tiger Twist* (A. Sciascia). 53 mins.

Comizi d'amore (1964)
p Alfredo Bini *interviewer/commentary* Pier Paolo Pasolini *asst d* Vincenzo Cerami *c* Mario Bernardo, Tonino Delli Colli *ed* Nino Baragli.
lp Adele Cambria, Camilla Cederna, Graziella Chiarcossi, Oriana Fallaci, Graziella Granada, Antonella Lualdi, Alberto Moravia, Cesare L. Musatti, Giuseppe Ungaretti. 92 mins.

Sopralluoghi in Palestina (1964)
p Alfredo Bini *interviewer/commentary* Pier Paolo Pasolini. *c* Aldo Pennelli, Otello Martelli, Domenico Cantatore *ed* Pier Paolo Pasolini.
lp Pier Paolo Pasolini, Don Andrea Carraro. 52 mins.

Il Vangelo secondo Matteo (1964)
p Alfredo Bini *st/sc* Pier Paolo Pasolini from *The Gospel According to St Matthew asst d* Maurizio Lucidi, Paolo Schneider *c* Tonino Delli Colli. *ad* Luigi Scaccianoce *ed* Nino Baragli *mus* Johann Sebastian Bach, Wolfgang Amadeus Mozart, Sergei Prokofiev, Anton Webern, the '*Missa Luba*', spirituals, Russian revolutionary songs (arranged by Carlo Rustichelli, Luis E. Bacalov).
lp Enrique Irazoqui (*Christ, dubbed by Enrico Maria Salerno*), Margherita Caruso (*the young Mary*), Susanna Pasolini (*the old Mary*), Marcello Morante (*Joseph*), Mario Socrate (*John the Baptist*), Settimio Di Porto (*Peter*), Otello Sestili (*Judas Iscariot*), Ferruccio Nuzzo (*Matthew*), Giacomo Morante (*John*), Alfonso Gatto (*Andrew*), Enzo Siciliano (*Simon*), Giorgio Agamben (*Philip*), Guido Cerretani (*Bartholomew*), Luigi Barbini (*James, son of Alfeo*), Marcello Galdini (*James, son of Zebediah*), Elio Spaziani (*Thaddeus*), Rosario Migale (*Thomas*), Amerigo Bevilacqua (*Herod I*), Francesco Leonetti (*Herod II*), Natalia Ginzburg (*Mary of Bethany*). 137 mins.

Uccellacci e uccellini (1966)
p Alfredo Bini *st/sc* Pier Paolo Pasolini *asst d* Sergio Citti, Carlo Morandi, Vincenzo Cerami *c* Tonino Delli Colli, Mario Bernardo *ad* Luigi Scaccianoce *ed* Nino Baragli *mus* Ennio Morricone (the lyrics for the credits song written by Pier Paolo Pasolini and sung by Domenico Modugno, *Carme, Carme* written and sung by Totò).
lp Totò (*the father, Innocenti Totò/Brother Ciccillo*), Ninetto Davoli (*the son, Innocenti Ninetto/Brother Ninetto*). 86 mins.

La terra vista dalla luna (1966)
Third episode of **Le streghe**
p Dino De Laurentiis *st/sc* Pier Paolo Pasolini *asst. d* Sergio Citti, Vincenzo Cerami *c* Giuseppe Rotunno *ad* Mario Garbuglia, Piero Poletto *ed* Nino Baragli *mus* Piero Picconi.
lp Totò (*Ciancicato Miao*), Ninetto Davoli (*Basciu Miao*), Silvana Mangano (*Assurdina Cai*), Laura Betti (*the tourist's wife*). 31 mins.

Edipo re (1967)
p Alfredo Bini *sc* Pier Paolo Pasolini based on Sophocles' *Oedipus Rex* and *Oedipus at Colonus* *asst d* Jean-Claude Biette *c* Giuseppe Ruzzolini *ad* Luigi Scaccianoce *ed* Nino Baragli *mus* Wolfgang Amadeus Mozart's *Quartet in C Major K 475*, Romanian folk songs, ancient Japanese music (coordinated by Pier Paolo Pasolini).
lp Silvana Mangano (*Jocasta*), Franco Citti (*Oedipus*), Alida Valli (*Merope*), Carmelo Bene (*Creon*), Julian Beck (*Tiresias*), Pier Paolo Pasolini (*the High Priest*). 104 mins.

Appunti per un film sull'india (1968)
p Gianni Barcelloni *st* Pier Paolo Pasolini *commentary* written and narrated by Pier Paolo Pasolini *c* Federico Zanni, Roberto Nappa *ed* Jenner Menghi. 34 mins.

Che cosa sono le nuvole? (1968)
Third episode of **Capriccio all'italiana**.
p Dino De Laurentiis *st/sc* Pier Paolo Pasolini *asst d* Sergio Citti *c* Tonino Delli Colli *ad* Jurgen Henze *ed* Nino Baragli *mus* Domenico Modugno.
lp Totò (*Jago*), Ninetto Davoli (*Otello*), Laura Betti (*Desdemona*), Franco Franchi (*Cassius*), Ciccio Ingrassia (*Roderigo*), Adriana Asti (*Bianca*), Francesco Leonetti (*puppeteer*), Domenico Modugno (*garbage collector*). 22 mins.

Teorema (1968)
p Franco Rossellini, Manolo Bolognini *st/sc* Pier Paolo Pasolini *asst d* Sergio Citti *c* Giuseppe Ruzzolini *ad* Luciano Puccini *ed* Nino Baragli *mus* Wolfgang Amadeus Mozart's *Requiem*, Ennio Morricone.
lp Silvana Mangano (*Lucia, the mother*), Terence Stamp (*the visitor*), Massimo Girotti (*Paolo, the father*), Anne Wiazemsky (*Odetta, the daughter*), Laura Betti (*Emilia, the maid*), Andres Jose Cruz Soublette (*Pietro, the son*). 98 mins.

La sequenza del fiore di carta (1969)
Third episode of **Amore e rabbia**
p Carlo Lizzani *st* from an idea by Puccio Pucci and Piero Badalassi *sc* Pier Paolo Pasolini *asst d* Maurizio Ponai, Franco Brocani *c* Giuseppe Ruzzolini *ed* Nino Baragli *mus* Giovanni Fusco.
lp Ninetto Davoli (*Riccetto*), Bernardo Bertolucci, Graziella Chiarcossi, Pier Paolo Pasolini, Aldo Puglisi (*voices of God*). 10 mins.

Porcile (1969)
p Gian Vittorio Baldi *st/sc* Pier Paolo Pasolini *asst d* Sergio Citti, Fabio Garriba, Sergio Elia *c* Tonino Delli Colli *ed* Nino Baragli *mus* Benedetto Ghiglia.
lp Pierre Clementi (*first cannibal*), Franco Citti (*secondo cannibal*), Jean-Pierre Léaud (*Julian*), Alberto Lionello (*Klotz*), Anne Wiazemsky (*Ida*), Margherita Lozano (*Madame Klotz*, dubbed by Laura Betti), Ugo Tognazzi (*Herdhitze*), Marco Ferreri (*Hans Gunther*). 98 mins.

Medea (1969)
p Franco Rossellini, Marina Cicogna *sc* Pier Paolo Pasolini based on Euripides's *Medea* *asst d* Carlo Carunchio *c* Ennio Guarnieri *ad* Dante Ferretti *ed* Nino Baragli *mus* Pier Paolo Pasolini, Elsa Morante.
lp Maria Callas (*Medea*), Laurent Terzieff (*the Centaur*), Massimo Girotti (*Creon*), Giuseppe Gentile (*Jason*). 110 mins.

Appunti per un'Orestiade africana (1970)
sc/commentary Pier Paolo Pasolini *c* Pier Paolo Pasolini, Giorgio Pelloni, Mario Bagnato, Emore Galeassi *ed* Cleofe Conversi *mus* Gato Barbieri. 63 mins.

Il Decameron (1971)
p Franco Rossellini *sc* Pier Paolo Pasolini based on Boccaccio's *Il decamerone asst d* Umberto Angelucci, Sergio Citti, Paolo Andrea Mettel *c* Tonino Delli Colli *ad* Dante Ferretti *ed* Nino Baragli, Tatiana Casini Morigi *mus* Pier Paolo Pasolini, Ennio Morricone.
lp Franco Citti (*Master Cepparello/Saint Ciappelletto*), Ninetto Davoli (*Andreuccio*), Pier Paolo Pasolini (*Giotto*), Giuseppe Zigaina (*a friar*), Silvana Mangano (*Madonna*). 110 mins.

Dodici Dicembre (1972)
d Giovanni Bonfanti (Pasolini was involved in directing at least half of the film; Maurizio Ponzi was also involved in the direction) *p* Lotta Continua *st* Giovanni Bonfanti, Goffredo Fofi *asst d* Fabio Pellarin, Umberto Angelucci *c* Giuseppe Pinori, Dimitri Nicolau *ed* Giovanni Bonfanti, Maurizio Ponzi *mus* Pino Masi. 104 mins.

I racconti di Canterbury (1972)
p Alberto Grimaldi *sc* Pier Paolo Pasolini fom Geoffrey Chaucer's *The Canterbury Tales asst d* Sergio Citti, Umberto Angelucci, Peter Shepherd *c* Tonino Delli Colli *ad* Dante Ferretti *ed* Nino Baragli *mus* Pier Paolo Pasolini, Ennio Morricone.
lp Hugh Griffith (*Sir January*), Laura Betti (*the Wife of Bath*), Ninetto Davoli (*Perkin*), Franco Citti (*the Devil*), Josephine Chaplin (*May*), Pier Paolo Pasolini (*Chaucer*). 110 mins.

Le mura di Sana'a (1974; made in 1971, but released with *Il fiore delle Mille e una notte*)
p Franco Rossellini *sc/commentary* Pier Paolo Pasolini *c* Tonino Delli Colli *ed* Tatiana Casini. 13 mins.

Il fiore delle Mille e una Notte (1974)
p Alberto Grimaldi *sc* Pier Paolo Pasolini with Dacia Maraini from *The 1001 Arabian Nights asst d* Umberto Angelucci, Peter Shepherd *c* Giuseppe Ruzzolini *ad* Dante Ferretti *ed* Nino Baragli, Tatiana Casini Morigi *mus* Ennio Morricone.
lp Ninetto Davoli (*Azia*), Franco Citti (*genie*), Ines Pellegrini (*Zumurrud*). 129 mins.

Salò o Le 120 giornate di Sodoma (1975)
p Alberto Grimaldi *sc* Pier Paolo Pasolini from the novel by the Marquis de Sade *asst d* Umberto Angelucci, Fiorella Infascelli *c* Tonino Delli Colli *ad* Dante Ferretti *ed* Nino Baragli, Tatiana Casini Morigi *mus* Ennio Morricone (advisor).
lp Paolo Bonacelli (*Duke: Blangis*), Giorgio Cataldi (*Bishop*), Umberto Paolo Quintavalle (*Curval, the President of the Court of Appeal*), Aldo Valletti (*President Durcet*, dubbed by Marco Bellocchio), Caterina Boratto (*Signora Castelli*), Elsa De Giorgio (*Signora Maggi*), Helene Surgere (*Signora Vaccari*, dubbed by Laura Betti). 116 mins.

II. Scripts and stories for other directors

La donna del fiume (1954) *d* Mario Soldati *sc* Antonio Altoviti, Giorgio Bassani, Basilio Franchina, Pier Paolo Pasolini, Florestano Vancini.
Il prigioniero della montagna (1955) *d* Luis Trenker *sc* Giorgio Bassani, Pier Paolo Pasolini, Luis Trenker.
Le notti di Cabiria (1957) *d* Federico Fellini. Pasolini was the dialogue consultant for Roman slang.

Marisa la Civetta (1957) *d* Mauro Bolognini *sc* Mauro Bolognini, Titina Demby, Pier Paolo Pasolini.

Giovani mariti (1958) *d* Mauro Bolognini *sc* Mauro Bolognini, Ezio Cureli, Luciano Martino, Pier Paolo Pasolini.

Grigio (1959) *d* Ermanno Olmi. Pasolini wrote the commentary.

Morte di un amico (1959) *d* Franco Rossi *st* Giuseppe Berto, Oreste Biancoli, Pier Paolo Pasolini, Franco Riganti.

La notte brava (1959) *d* Mauro Bolognini *st/sc* Pier Paolo Pasolini.

Il bell'Antonio (1960) *d* Mauro Bolognini *sc* Mauro Bolognini, Pier Paolo Pasolini, Gino Visentini.

La giornata balorda (1960) *d* Mauro Bolognini *sc* Alberto Moravia, Pier Paolo Pasolini, Marco Visconti.

Il carro armato dell'8 settembre (1960) *d* Gianni Puccini *sc* Bruno Baratti, Elio Bartolini, Goffredo Parise, Pier Paolo Pasolini, Giulio Questi.

La lunga notte del '43 (1960) *d* Florestano Vancini *sc* Ennio De Concini, Pier Paolo Pasolini, Florestano Vancini.

La canta delle marane (1960) *d* Cecilia Mangini *commentary* Pier Paolo Pasolini.

La ragazza in vetrina (1961) *d* Luciano Emmer *sc* Luciano Emmer, Vinicio Marinucci, Luciano Martino, Pier Paolo Pasolini.

La commare secca (1962) *d* Bernardo Bertolucci *st* Pier Paolo Pasolini *sc* Bernardo Bertolucci, Sergio Citti, Pier Paolo Pasolini.

Ostia (1970) *d* Sergio Citti *sc* Sergio Citti, Pier Paolo Pasolini.

Storie scellerate (1973) *d* Sergio Citti *st/sc* Sergio Citti, Pier Paolo Pasolini.

III. Unrealised scripts and stories (with date of publication)

Il padre selvaggio (Turin: Einaudi, 1975), short film.

San Paolo (Turin: Einaudi, 1977).

Porno-Teo-Kolossal (*Cinecritica*, vol. 11, no. 13, April/June 1989).

Bibliography

This bibliography of writings by and about Pasolini is not exhaustive. Nevertheless, it includes most of Pasolini's works and the material listed on Pasolini is extensive. The works listed as having been written by Pasolini include his literary and critical works. The works listed about Pasolini relate, on the whole, only to his cinema. All the material included in the bibliography has been consulted and found useful in some manner.

The works I found most stimulating about Pasolini were Rinaldo Rinaldi's *Pier Paolo Pasolini*, Milan: Mursia, 1982; Michele Mancini and Giuseppe Perella, *Pier Paolo Pasolini: corpi e luoghi*, Bologna: Theorema edizioni, 1981; Jean Duflot, *Il sogno del centauro*, Rome: Riuniti, 1983, originally published in 1981 in French as *Les Dernières paroles d'un impie*; and the remarks by Deleuze in his *Cinema 2* book published by the University of Minneapolis. The Rinaldi book contains the most comprehensive bibliography of works written by Pasolini and the Mancini and Perella contains a comprehensive bibliography of Pasolini's writings.

Duflot's work is a book-length interview with Pasolini. It is rich, eloquent and illuminating. Rinaldi's study of Pasolini's writings and films is unrivalled though written nearly fifteen years ago. The Mancini and Perella book is a model of what writing on the cinema should be. It includes previously unavailable material written by Pasolini in relation to his projected Third World film. Two articles listed by Geoffrey Nowell-Smith, one in English and the other in French, are especially fine.

The Associazione Fondo Pier Paolo Pasolini in Rome is the best source for material on Pasolini. It has a comprehensive collection of books, articles, press clippings, original screenplays, interviews and a videotape library.

Writings by Pasolini
1942 *Poesie a Casarsa,* Bologna: Libreria Antiquaria Landi
1945 *Diarii,* Casarsa: Pubblicazione dell'Accademia
     Poesie, S. Vito di Tagliamento: Primon

1946 *I pianti*, Casarsa: Ed. dell'Academiuta
       Paolo Weiss, Rome: Piccola Galleria
1949 *Dov'è la mia patria?*, Casarsa: Ed. dell'Accademiuta
1950 *Roma 1950 'diario'*, Milan: All'insegna del pesce d'oro
1952 *Poesia dialettale del '900*, eds P. P. Pasolini and M. dell'Arco, Parma:
       Guanda
1953 *Tal cour di un frut*, Trecesimo: Ed. in Lingua Friulana
1954 *Il canto popolare*, Milan: Della Meridiana
       Dal diario, Caltanisetta: Sciascia
       La meglia gioventù, Florence: Sansoni
1955 *Ragazzi di vita*, Milan: Garzanti (*The Ragazzi*, New York: Grove Press,
       1968)
       Canzoniere italiano, P. P. Pasolini (ed.), Parma: Guanda
1956 'Il neo-sperimentalismo', *Officina*, no. 5, February
       'Arte e divulgazione', *Il Punto*, vol. 1, no. 28
1958 *L'usignolo della chiesa cattolica*, Milan: Longanesi
1959 *Una vita violenta*, Milan: Garzanti (*A Violent Life*, London: Jonathan Cape,
       1985)
       '9 domande sul romanzo', *Nuovi Argomenti*, nos 38–9, May–August
       'Una lettera di P. P. Pasolini', *Filmcritica*, no. 92, November–December
       '*La notte brava*', *Filmcritica*, nos 91–2, November–December
1960 *Donne di Roma*, Rome: Il Saggiatore
       Passione e ideologia (1948–1958), Milan: Garzanti
       Sonetto primaverile, Milan: All'insegna del pesce d'oro
       Giro a vuoto, Milan: All'insegna del pesce d'oro
       La poesia popolare italiana, P. P. Pasolini (ed.), Milan: Garzanti
1961 *Accattone*, Rome: Edizione FM
       'Intellectualism … and the Teds', *Films and Filming*, January
       'Il ministro dell'oscuramento', *Nuovo Generazione*, 10 November
       'Pasolini a Helfer: non moralista ma un qualunquista morale', *Nuovo
       Generazione*, 10 November
       'Le opinioni di Pier Pasolini su …', *Sirena*, December
1962 *L'odore dell'India* Milan: Longanesi (*The Scent of India*, London: Olive
       Press, 1984)
       Mamma Roma, Milan: Rizzoli
       Il sogno di una cosa, Milan: Garzanti
       'Cinematic and Literary Stylistic Figures', *Film Culture*, no. 24, March
1963 *Il vantone*, Milan: Garzanti
1964 *Il Vangelo secondo Matteo*, Milan: Garzanti
       'To a Pope', *Film Comment*, Autumn
       'Confessioni tecniche', *Paese Sera*, 27 September (reprinted in *Cineforum*,
       no. 40, December)
       'Dopo il film sul Vangelo', *Cineforum*, no. 40, December
       'Marxismo e Cristianesimo', Brescia, 13 December 1964, in *L'Eco di
       Brescia*, supplement no. 43, 18 December 1964; republished in *Marxismo e
       Cristianesimo*, Brescia: Fondazione Calzari Trebeschi 1985
1965 *Ali dagli occhi azzurri*, Milan: Garzanti
       'La commare secca', *Filmcritica*, no. 161, October
1966 *Uccellacci e uccellini* (script), Milan: Garzanti
       Uccellacci e uccellini (theoretical and technical writings), Milan: Garzanti
       'In calce al "cinema di poesia"', *Filmcritica*, vol. 27, no. 163, January
       'Una tavola rotonda su *Un uomo a meta* (debate with M. Argentieri, P. P.
       Pasolini, G. Draghi), *Cinema Sessanta*, June
       'L'America di Pasolini', *Paese Sera*, 18 November (reprinted the same year in
       Nuovi Argomenti, nos 3–4, July–December)
1967 'La parola è a Pier Paolo Pasolini', in R. May (ed.), 'Atti ufficiali della
       III settimana cinematografica dei cattolici italiani', *Cinema e Libertà*,
       18–24 September

'Ora tutto è chiaro, voluto, non imposto dal destino', *Cineforum*, no. 68, October

Edipo re, Milan: Garzanti (*Oedipus Rex*, London: Lorrimer, 1971)

1968 *Teorema*, Milan: Garzanti

1969 '*Che cosa sono le nuvole?*', *Cinema e Film*, vol. 8, nos 7–8

'Io non cerco lo scandalo', *Cineforum*, vol. 9, no. 85

'La parola orale meravigliosa possibilità del cinema', *Cinema Nuovo*, vol. 18, no. 201

'Nota per l'ambientazione dell'*Orestiade* in Africa', *La Città Futura*, 7 June 1978

1970 *Medea*, Milan: Garzanti

(with S. Citti), *Ostia*, Milan: Garzanti

Poesie, Milan: Garzanti

'Ho ricominciato proprio ieri 19 marzo a dipingere …', in A. B. Oliva and G. Zigaina, *Disegni e pitture di Pier Paolo Pasolini*, Basle: Balance Rief S. A., 1984

'In Africa tra figli obbedienti e ragazzi moderni', in M. Mancini and G. Perella, *Pier Paolo Pasolini: corpi e luoghi*, Rome: Theorema, 1981

'The Beautiful Flags', *Invisible City*, June 1970

'Il sentimento della storia', *Cinema Nuovo*, no. 205, 1970

1971 'Prayer on Commission', *Invisible City*, no. 3, November 1971

1972 *Empirismo eretico*, Milan: Garzanti (*Heretical Empiricism*, L. K. Barnett (ed.), Bloomington: Indiana University Press, 1988)

'Tetis' (December), in V. Boarini (ed.), *Erotismo, eversione, merce*, Cappelli, 1974

1973 'L'inutile sforzo di Moravia di dimostrare l'inesistenza della realtà', *Il Tempo Illustrato*, 10 October

1974 'La Peccaminose *Mille e una notte* di Pasolini', *Tempo Illustrato*, 31 May

'Pasolini racconta con rabbia l'assurda rovina d'una città', *Corriere della Sera*, 20 June

1975 *Scritti corsari*, Milan: Garzanti

Le Poesie, Milan: Garzanti (includes *Le ceneri di Gramsci* (1957), *La religione del mio tempo* (1961), *Poesia in forma di rosa* (1964), *Transumanar e organizzar* (1971), all published separately on these dates by Garzanti. Important poems by Pasolini from his various books have been translated in *Pier Paolo Pasolini, Poems*, trans. N. MacAfee, New York: Vintage, 1982)

Il padre selvaggio, Turin: Einaudi

Trilogia della vita, Bologna: Capelli

La nuova gioventù, Turin: Einaudi

La divina mimesis, Turin: Einaudi

'Stylistic Reaction', *Invisible City*, February

'Il sesso come metafora del potere' (self-interview), *Corriere della Sera*, 25 March

'Sade 1944: Momenti della conferenza-stampa sul set di *Salò o Le 120 giornate di Sodoma*, il giorno prima della fine delle riprese', in L. De Giusti (ed.), *Pier Paolo Pasolini: Il cinema in forma di poesia*, Edizioni Cinemazero, 1979

Salò o Le centoventi giornate della città di Sodoma (in typescript at the Fondo Pasolini, Rome)

'The Ambiguous Forms of Narrative Rituality', *Framework*, no. 2 (originally published in *Cinema Nuovo*, October 1974)

'La droga: una vera tragedia italiana', *Corriere della Sera*, 24 July

'Il mio *Accattone* in TV dopo il genocidio', *Corriere della Sera*, 8 October

'Figli di papa e ragazzi di borgata', *Corriere della Sera*, 8 October

'*Salò*: L'"intolleranza" dello spettatore per cogliere l'anarchia del fascismo e del potere', *Roma Giovani*, October–November

'Sur *Salò*', *Ecran*, no. 42, 15 December

'Pier Paolo Pasolini sul suo film', *Vacanze Turismo Caravanning*, vol. I, no. 10, December

1976 *Lettere luterane*, Turin: Einaudi
Lettere agli amici, Milan: Guanda
'Per una censura democratica contro la permissività di Stato', *Cinema Nuovo*, no. 239, January–February

1977 *San Paolo*, Turin: Einaudi

1978 *Le belle bandiere: Dialoghi 1960–65*, Rome: Riuniti
Caos, Rome: Riuniti

1979 *Descrizioni di descrizioni*, Turin: Einaudi
'L'ambiguità', in A. Bertini, *Teoria e tecnica del film in Pasolini*, Rome: Bulzoni
'To Allen Ginsberg 1968', *Lumen Avenue A*, vol. 1, no. 1

1982 *Amado mio*, Milan: Garzanti

1984 'Verso Pordenone e il mondo' (nd) in A. B. Oliva and G. Zigaina, *Disegni e pitture di Pier Paolo Pasolini*, Basle: Balance Rief S. A.

1985 '*La ricotta*: osservazioni di Pasolini sulle scene incriminate' (nd), *La Cosa*, no. 2
'L'accelerato Venezia–Udine', *The Italianist*
'Domenica al collina volpi', *The Italianist*

1986 *Lettere 1940–1954*, N. Naldini (ed.), Turin: Einaudi
Roman Nights and Other Stories, Marlboro, Vermont: The Marlboro Press (there are five stories in the collection taken from *Ali dagli occhi azzurri*, Milan: Garzanti 1965)

1987 'Film Music (nd), *Filmviews* 134; *Ecrits sur le cinéma*, ed. H. Joubert-Laurencin, Lyon: Presses Universitaires

1988 *Il portico della morte*, ed. C. Segre, Rome: Associazione 'Fondo Pier Paolo Pasolini'
Teatro, Milan: Garzanti; includes *Calderon* (1973), *Affabulazione*, *Pilade* (1977), *Porcile*, *Orgia*, *Bestia da stile* (1979)
Lettere 1955–1975, ed. N. Naldini, Turin: Einaudi

1989 *Sant'Infame* and *Porno-Teo-Kolossal* (with S. Citti) (probably 1963–4), *Cinecritica*, vol. 11, no. 13 (ns), April–June

1992 *Petrolio*, Turin: Einaudi
The Letters of Pier Paolo Pasolini: 1940–54, ed. N. Naldini, trans. Stuart Hood, London: Quartet Books, 1992

1993 *Un paese di temporali e di primule*, Parma: Ugo Guanda

Interviews

'*Accattone*: Cinque domande a P. P. Pasolini', *Nuova Generazione*, 30 April 1961.

Apra, A., 'Intervista con Pier Paolo Pasolini', *La Cosa*, no. 2, 1985.

Apra, A., and Faccini, L., 'Dialogo 1', *Cinema e Film*, vol. 1, no. 1, Winter 1966–7, pp. 4–8.

Arecco, S., 'Ancora il linguaggio della realtà', *Filmcritica*, no. 214, March 1971, in E. Magrelli, *Con Pier Paolo Pasolini*, Rome: Bulzoni 1977.

Argento, D., 'Pasolini ci parla del suo secondo film', *Paese Sera*, 1–2 September 1962.

Argento, D., 'Pasolini e Moravia girano un film contro i tabù del sesso', *Paese Sera*, 3 July 1963.

Ascanio, S., 'Pasolini si parla del suo nuovo film', *Il Gazzettino*, 21 August 1962.

Ascanio, S., 'P. P. Pasolini promette di rispettare il Vangelo', *Il Gazzettino*, 25 February 1964.

Ascanio, S., 'Con *Edipo* Pasolini continua un viaggio in cerca di sè stesso', *Il Gazzettino*, 13 August 1967.

Bachmann, G., 'Ideologia e poetica: conversazione con Pier Paolo Pasolini', *Filmcritica*, vol. 24, no. 232, March 1973.

Bachmann, G., 'Pasolini's Dice with Politics and Death', *Rolling Stone*, 26 August 1976 (also published as 'Pasolini on De Sade', *Film Quarterly*, vol. 29, no. 2, Winter 1975–6).

Bachmann, G., 'Bachmann on Pasolini', *Filmnews,* July 1976.

Bachmann, G., 'La perdita della realtà e il cinema inintegrabile' (13 September 1974) in L. De Giusti (ed.), *Pier Paolo Pasolini: Il cinema in forma di poesia,* Pordenone: Cinemazero, 1979.

Bachmann, G., 'Pier Paolo Pasolini', *Invisible City,* February 1975.

Bachmann, G., 'De Sade e l'universo dei consumi' (2 May 1975) in L. De Giusti (ed.), *Pier Paolo Pasolini: Il cinema in forma di poesia,* Pordenone: Cinemazero, 1979.

Bachmann, G., and Gallo, D., 'Conversazione con Pier Paolo Pasolini', *Filmcritica,* vol. 26, no. 256, August 1975.

Bachmann, G., 'Il potere e la morte' (31 October 1975) in L. De Giusti (ed.), *Pier Paolo Pasolini: Il cinema in forma di poesia,* Pordenone: Cinemazero, 1979.

Bellezza, D., 'Io e Boccaccio', *L'Espresso Colore,* vol. 16, no. 47, 22 November 1970.

Blaser, M., 'Colloquio: intervista con Pier Paolo Pasolini', 1969 (for Radio Televisione Svizzera Italiana in typescript at the Fondo Pasolini, Rome).

Blue, J., 'Pier Paolo Pasolini: An Interview with James Blue', *Film Comment,* vol. 8, no. 4, 1965.

Boglietti, L., Cabutti, L., Colombo, G., Dodero, C., and Paci, A., 'Le opinioni di Pier Paolo Pasolini', *Sirena,* December 1961.

Bouvard, P., 'Ultima intervista', 31 October 1975 (in typescript at the Fondo Pasolini, Rome, and also on videotape; the interview was transmitted on 'Antenne 2', in France on 8 November 1975; reprinted as 'Scandalizzare e scandalizzarsi', in L. De Giusti (ed.), *Pier Paolo Pasolini: Il cinema in forma di poesia,* Pordenone: Cinemazero, 1979).

Bragin, J., 'Pasolini – A Conversation in Rome, June 1966', *Film Culture,* no. 42, June 1966.

Braucourt, G., '*Theorème*: La démonstration', *Cinéma 69,* no. 136 May 1969.

Brunatto, P., 'La forma della città', 1974 (in typescript at the Fondo Pasolini, Rome).

Brunetta, G. P., 'Entretien avec Pier Paolo Pasolini', *Cahiers du Cinéma,* March 1969.

Bruskin, S. J., Reiner, P., Swaback, D., Walker, J., and Weiskopf, K., 'Film Directors on Film', *Arts in Society,* vol. 4, no. 1, Winter 1966–7.

Camon, F., 'Pier Paolo Pasolini', in *La moglie del tiranno,* Milan: Lerici, 1969.

Camon, F., 'Pier Paolo Pasolini', in *Il mestiere di poeta,* Milan: Garzanti, 1982.

Capelle, A., 'Pasolini sur *Theorème*', *La Quinzaine Littéraire,* no. 68, 1–5 March 1969.

Castaldini, P., 'Razionalità e metafora in P. P. Pasolini', *Filmcritica,* vol. 18, no. 174, January–February 1967.

Ceratto, P., 'Pasolini: anche il consumismo è un lager', *Avanti!,* 9 November 1975.

'Cerco il Cristo fra i poeti', *Italia–Notizie,* 20 November 1963.

Chiaretti, T., and Morini, M., 'Pier Paolo Pasolini: ecco il mio Totò' (1974), *La Repubblica,* 3 August 1976.

Chiesa, A., 'Come Pasolini concilia cinema e letteratura', *Paese Sera,* 20–1 September 1961.

Ciattaglia, C., 'Incontro con Pier Paolo Pasolini, scrittore, regista', in *Voce d'oggi sul Vangelo,* Edizioni cinque lune 1974 (interview: 19 June 1971).

Clerici, M., 'Ci dica Pasolini: È con noi o contro di noi?', *Amica,* 18 August 1974.

Cluny, C.-M., 'Pasolini: c'est *Le Décameron* qui m'a choisi', *La Galerie,* December 1971.

Cluny, C.-M., 'Rencontre avec Pasolini', *Cinéma* (Paris), no. 164, 1972.

Colombo, F., 'Siamo tutti in pericolo', *Tuttolibri,* vol. 1, no. 2, November 1975.

Comolli, J.-L., and Bertolucci, B., 'Entretien avec Pier Paolo Pasolini', *Cahiers du Cinéma,* August 1965 (in English in *Cahiers du Cinéma in English,* no. 6, 1969).

'Conferenza stampa di PPP su *Porcile*', August 1969 (in typescript at the Fondo Pasolini, Rome).

Cornand, A., and Maillet, D., 'Entretien avec Pier Paolo Pasolini', *La Revue du Cinéma,* no. 267, January 1973.

di Carlo, C., 'Pier Paolo Pasolini – cultura e società', 1967 (in typescript at the Fondo Pasolini, Rome).

Duflot, J., *Entretiens avec Pier Paolo Pasolini*, Paris: Pierre Belfond, 1970.

Duflot, J., *Pier Paolo Pasolini: il sogno del centauro*, Rome: Riuniti, 1983 (originally published in 1981 by Pierre Belfond as *Les dernières paroles d'un impie*).

'Ed ora Pasolini?', *Jet*, May 1969.

Faccini, L., and Ponzi, M., 'Intervista con Pier Paolo Pasolini', *Filmcritica*, nos 156–7, April–May 1965.

Ferrero, N., 'Intervista', *Filmcritica*, no. 116, January 1962, in E. Magrelli, *Con Pier Paolo Pasolini*, Rome: Bulzoni, 1977.

Fieschi, J.-A., 'Pier Paolo Pasolini: *Edipo re*', *Cahiers du Cinéma*, no. 195, November 1967.

Fieschi, J.-A., 'Pasolini l'enragé', in A. Bergala and J. Narboni, *Pasolini Cinéaste*, Cahiers du Cinéma Editions de l'Etoile, 1981 (interview: July 1966).

Fini, M., 'Eros e cultura', *Europeo*, 19 September 1974.

Gennari, A., 'Conversazione con Pier Paolo Pasolini', *Filmcritica*, vol. 25, no. 247, August–September 1974.

Giovannini, M., 'Pasolini mille e uno', *Panorama*, 30 May 1974.

Golino, E., 'Pier Paolo Pasolini', *Letteratura e classi sociali*, Bari: Laterza, 1976.

Guido, G., 'Quattro mesi di reclusione a Pasolini responsabile di vilipendio alla religione', *Il Tempo*, 8 March 1963.

Hennebelle, G., 'A Paris Pasolini déclare: "La porcherie symbolise pour moi la société bourgeoise" ', *Revue du Cinéma International*, April 1969.

' "Il piacere di raccontare": Conferenza–stampa di Pier Paolo Pasolini al Festival di Berlino, 1972', in L. De Giusti, *Il cinema in forma di poesia*, Pordenone: Cinemazero, 1979 (also in *Jeune Cinéma*, no. 68, February 1973).

'Incontro con Pier Paolo Pasolini', *Note Schedario*, Centro dello spettacolo e della comunicazione sociale, 28 April 1969 (meeting of 27 February 1969 between Pasolini, A. Bernardini, university and high school students).

'Intervista a Totò e Pasolini', 1966 (in typescript and video at the Fondo Pasolini).

'Intervista al sig. Pasolini per la rivista, *Film*', 1970 (in typescript at the Fondo Pasolini, Rome).

Kezich, T., 'Il suo cinema, un mito', *Panorama*, 13 November 1975.

Langlois, G., 'Un drôle d'uccello pour Pasolini', *Les Lettres Françaises*, 1 March 1972.

'*Le Mille e una notte*, Conferenza–stampa: Cannes, May 1974', in L. De Giusti (ed.), *Pier Paolo Pasolini: Il cinema in forma di poesia*, Pordenone: Cinemazero, 1979.

Mahaini, N. R., '*Decameron*: Intervista con P. P. Pasolini', *Cinema 60*, January 1972.

Maingois, M., 'Pier Paolo Pasolini', *Zoom*, October 1974.

Mariani, D., 'Interview with Pasolini', *Interview*, vol. 1, no. 4, 1969.

Mariani, D., 'E tu chi eri?', *Vogue* (Italy), May 1971.

Mariani, D., 'Ma la donna e una slot-machine', *L'Espresso*, 22 October 1972.

Martini, D., 'L'*Accattone* di Pier Paolo Pasolini', *Cinema Nuovo*, no. 158, March–April 1961.

Maurin, F., 'L'un des chefs de file du jeune cinéma italien en visite à L'*Humanité-Dimanche*', *L'Humanité-Dimanche*, 1 April 1962.

Narboni, J., 'Rencontre avec Pier Paolo Pasolini', *Cahiers du Cinéma*, no. 192, July–August 1967.

Paolozzi, L., 'Pasolini: "Adesso vi parlo di Pasolini"', *Vie Nuove*, 23 December 1970.

Paolozzi, L., 'La verità continua a essere nuda', *Vie Nuove*, 19 July 1972.

'Pasolini: theoreme', *Jeune Cinéma*, no. 33, October 1968.

'Pasolini TV difende *Medea*', *Paese Sera*, 29 January 1970.

'Pasolini come Giotto', *Epoca*, 18 October 1970.

'Pasolini: 'Conosco di più gli arabi che i milanesi", *Stampa Sera*, 24 August 1974.

Peroni, L., 'Incontro con Pier Paolo Pasolini', *Inquadrature,* nos 15–6, Autumn 1968.

'Razionalità e metafora' (with P. Castaldini), *Filmcritica,* no. 174, February 1967, in E. Magrelli, *Con Pier Paolo Pasolini,* Rome: Bulzoni, 1977.

Rondi, G. L., 'Pasolini: per esorcizzare un futuro di intolleranza', *Il Tempo,* 28 April 1974.

Rondi, G. L., 'Pasolini: L'Italia una fossa dei serpenti', *Il Tempo,* 24 August 1975.

Rusconi, M., '4 registi al magnetofono: Pier Paolo Pasolini: un uomo mistico-epico-lirico', *Sipario,* no. 222, October 1964.

Rusconi, M., 'Pier Paolo Pasolini e l'autobiografia', *Sipario,* vol. 22, no. 258, October 1967.

'Sade 1944: Momenti della conferenza–stampa sul set di *Salò o le 120 giornate di Sodoma,* il giorno prima della fine delle riprese', in L. De Giusti (ed.), *Pier Paolo Pasolini: Il cinema in forma di poesia,* Pordenone: Cinemazero, 1979.

Sanavio, P., '*Porcile* o no tiriamo le somme', *Il Dramma,* no. 12, September 1969, pp. 83–94.

Sarris, A., 'Pier Paolo Pasolini', in *Interviews with Film Directors,* Bobbs-Merrill Co., 1967.

Savio, F., 'Al cuore della realtà', 1974 (in typescript at the Fondo Pasolini, Rome).

Serenellini, M., 'Un regista "esiliato", dal mondo dei consumi', *Gazzetta del Popolo,* 9 January 1975.

Stabile, V. P., 'Intervista con Pasolini', *La Rassegna,* vol. 4, no. 1, January 1970.

Stack, O. (Jon Halliday), *Pasolini on Pasolini,* London: Secker & Warburg, 1969.

Stucchi, G., 'Una lucida passione: Intervista a Pier Paolo Pasolini', *Settegiorni,* no. 11, 27 August 1967.

'Sul doppiaggio' (with E. Chaluja, J. Fillion, G. Mingrone, S. Schadhauser), *Filmcritica,* no. 208, July–August 1970, in E. Magrelli, *Con Pier Paolo Pasolini,* Rome: Bulzoni, 1977.

Tournes, A., and Rougette, R., 'Entretien avec Pasolini', *Jeune Cinéma,* March 1970.

'Una visione del mondo epico-religioso', *Bianco e Nero,* vol. 25, no. 6, June 1964.

Wolfowicz, E., 'Pier Paolo Pasolini: Cinema and Literature', *Antaeus,* December 1976 (interview: June 1975).

General Bibliography

Abruzzese, A., '*Uccellacci e uccellini* ovvero le ceneri di Togliatti', *Cinema Sessanta,* vol. 7, no. 58, April 1966, pp. 14–23.

Abruzzese, A., 'Pasolini e l'industria culturale', in L. Lucignani and C. Molfese (eds), *Per conoscere Pasolini,* Rome: Bulzoni and Teatro Tenda, 1978.

Acconciamessa, M., 'Pasolini da due giovani in pasto alle bestie', *L'Unità,* 9 February 1969.

Adorno, T., 'Commitment', in *Aesthetics and Politics,* London: Verso, 1980.

Aeschylus, *The Oresteian Trilogy,* London: Penguin, 1956.

Alemanno, R., '*Il fiore delle Mille e una notte*', *Il Manifesto,* 25 August 1974.

Alessandrini, L., 'La crisi del film d'arte', *Osservatore Romano,* 13 September 1961.

Amendola, G., 'I comunisti e il movimento studentesco: necessità della lotta sui due fronti', *Rinascità,* 7 June 1968.

Andrews, R., 'Italo Calvino', in M. Caesar and P. Hainsworth (eds), *Writers and Society in Contemporary Italy,* New York: St Martin's Press, 1984.

Anon., 'Pasolini: un film africano', *Il Paese,* 5 January 1962.

Anon., 'Guareschi–Pasolini battibecco al vertice', *ABC,* vol. 4, no. 14, 7 April 1963.

Anon., 'Pasolini non firma più *La rabbia*', *L'Unità,* 14 April 1963.

Anon., 'I dodici apostoli al premio Strega', *L'Espresso,* 21 June 1964.

Anon., 'Pasolini: Vangelo alla lettera', *Panorama,* July 1964.

Anon., 'Diario di Pasolini', *Paese Sera,* 13 July 1965.

Anon., 'Pasolini TV bocciato della RAI', *Paese Sera,* 18 April 1970.

Anon., 'Pier Paolo Pasolini', in *Jeune Cinéma,* no. 68, February 1973.

Anon., 'La condanna di *Salò* nella sentenza del tribunale', *Cinema Nuovo*, no. 244, November–December 1976.

Anon., '*Accattone*', in A. Panicali and S. Sestini (eds), *Pier Paolo Pasolini. Testimonianze,* Florence: Nuovo Salani, 1982.

Anon., '*Mamma Roma*', in A. Panicali and S. Sestini (eds), *Pier Paolo Pasolini, Testimonianze,* Florence: Nuovo Salani, 1982.

Anon., 'Il gran picconatore', *Panorama,* 19 January 1992.

Annartone, C., 'Il deprimento della storia nell'egotismo di Pasolini', *Cinema Nuovo,* vol. 30, no. 270, April 1981.

Apra, A., '*Comizi d'amore*', *Cahiers du Cinéma,* August 1965.

Apra, A., 'Il film testimonianza', *Filmcritica,* vol. 16, no. 161, October 1965.

Arbasino, A., 'A che serve sul Petrolio versato', *L'Espresso,* 22 November 1992.

Arecco, S., '*Porcile* di Pier Paolo Pasolini', *Filmcritica,* vol. 20, no. 200, September 1969.

Arecco, S., *Pier Paolo Pasolini,* Rome: Partisan, 1972.

Argan, G. C., 'Prefazione', in G. Zigaina (ed.), *Pier Paolo Pasolini: I disegni 1941/ 1975,* Milan: Edizioni di Vanni Scheiwiller 1978.

Argan, G. C. and Fagiolo, M., 'Premessa all'arte italiana', in R. Romano and C. Vivanti (eds), *Storia d'Italia: I caratteri originali,* vol. 2, Turin: Einaudi, 1989.

Argentieri, M., '*Accattone* senza lieto fine', *Vie Nuove,* 12 November 1960.

Argentieri, M., 'Nella periferia romana nasce il film di Pier Paolo Pasolini', *L'Unità,* 7 April 1961.

Argentieri, M., 'Cinque giovani registi alla ribalta', *Cinema Sessanta,* nos 13–4, July–August 1961.

Argentieri, M., '*Accattone* bloccato in censura', *L'Unità,* 14 October 1961.

Argentieri, M., 'Tre film al Festival di Venezia', *Il Contemporaneo,* October 1964.

Argentieri, M., 'Poesia e sincerità di Pasolini', *Rinascità,* no. 21, 21 May 1966.

Argentieri, M., 'La Cina e Venezia', *Rinascità,* 8 September 1967.

Argentieri, M., '*Salò o le 120 giornate di Sodoma* di Pier Paolo Pasolini', *Cinema Sessanta,* nos 114–15, May–June 1975.

Aristarco, G., '*Porcile*', *Cinema Nuovo,* vol. 28, no. 201, September–October 1969.

Arosio, M., 'La morte del corvo', *Discussione,* 5 June 1966.

Associazione 'Fondo Pier Paolo Pasolini', *Pier Paolo Pasolini: un cinema di poesia,* Rome, 1988.

Associazione 'Fondo Pier Paolo Pasolini', *Pier Paolo Pasolini: A Future Life,* Rome, 1989.

Bacconnier, F., '*Médée*', *Téléciné,* no. 160, March 1970.

Bachmann, G., 'Pasolini in Persia: The Shooting of 1001 Nights', *Film Quarterly,* vol. 27, no. 2, Winter 1973–4.

Bachmann, G., 'Pier Paolo Pasolini's *Salò*: No rationales, no alibis', *Take One,* September–October 1974.

Bachmann, G., 'The 220 Days of *Salò*', *Film Comment,* March–April 1976.

Bakhtin, M., *Rabelais and His World,* Bloomington: Indiana University Press, 1984.

Baldelli, P., 'Natura e storia nel film *Accattone* di Pasolini', *Mondo Operaio,* vol. 16, nos 10–11, October–November 1961.

Baldelli, P., 'Pasolini e lo "scandalo della contraddizione"', *Giovane Critica,* no. 6, December–January 1964–5.

Baldelli, P., 'Il "caso" Pasolini e l'uso della morte', in G. De Santi, M. Lenti and R. Rossini (eds), *Perchè Pasolini,* Florence: Guaraldi, 1978.

Banti, A., 'Gli errori di un poeta', *L'Approdo Letterario,* vol. 18, nos 59–60, September 1972.

Baranski, A. G., 'The Texts of *Il Vangelo secondo Matteo*', *The Italianist,* 1985.

Barthes, R., 'The Two Criticisms' (1963), in *Critical Essays,* Evanston: Northwestern University Press, 1972.

Barthes, R., *Sade, Fourier, Loyola,* New York: Hill and Wang, 1976.

Barthes, R., 'Pasolini's *Salò*: Sade to the Letter', in P. Willemen (ed.), *Pier Paolo Pasolini,* London: British Film Institute, 1977.

Baudrillard, J., 'The Ecstasy of Communication', in H. Foster (ed.), *The Anti-Aesthetic: Essays on Postmodern Culture*, Port Townsend, Washington: Bay Press, 1983.

Bellezza, D., 'Pasolini fa ancora paura', *Paese Sera*, 8 January 1978.

Bergala, A., and Narboni, J., 'Pasolini cinéaste', *Cahiers du Cinéma* (hors série), Paris: Editions de l'Etoile, 1981.

Bernardini, A., 'Religiosità e sacralità nel *Teorema* di Pasolini', *Cineforum*, no. 85, May 1969.

Bersani, L., and Dutoit, U., 'Merde alors', *October*, no. 13, Summer 1980, pp. 23–35.

Bertetto, P., and Volpi, G., 'Un teorema sulla borghesia', *Ombre Rosse*, no. 6, January 1969.

Bertini, A., '*Rogopag*', *Nuova Generazione*, 10 March 1963.

Bertini, A., *Teoria e tecnica del film in Pasolini*, Rome: Bulzoni, 1979.

Bertolucci, B., 'Borgata romana', in F. Faldini and G. Fofi, *L'avventurosa storia del cinema italiano*, Milan: Feltrinelli, 1981.

Betti, L., *Cronaca giudiziaria, persecuzione, morte*, Milan: Garzanti, 1977.

Betti, L., and Vecchio, S. (eds.), *Pier Paolo Pasolini: Une vie future*, Rome: Fondo P. P. Pasolini, 1987.

Bevan, D. G., 'Pasolini and Baccaccio, *Literature/Film Quarterly*, vol. 5, no. 1, Winter 1977.

Beylie, C., '*Oedipe Roi, Theorème*: Le mythe. C'est l'homme même', *Cinéma 69*, no. 136, May 1969.

Beylie, C., 'Pasolini l'exorciseur', in M. Gervais, *Pier Paolo Pasolini*, Paris: Seghers, 1973.

Beylot, P., 'Pasolini, du réalisme au mythe', *CinémAction* (special issue: *Le néoréalisme italien*), no. 70, January–March 1994.

Biamonte, L., 'S'intitola *Il padre selvaggio* il film africano di P. P. Pasolini', *Paese Sera*, 25 February 1962.

Bianchi, P., 'Resnais e Pasolini a Venezia', *L'Illustrazione Italiana*, October 1961.

Bianchi, P., 'Hanno composto un film ambizioso', *Il Giorno*, 22 February 1963.

Bini, L., 'Pier Paolo Pasolini poeta del sottoproletariato', *Letture*, no. 1, 1975.

Bini, L., 'La parabola della rivoluzione nel cinema di Pasolini', *Letture*, no. 3, 1975.

Bini, L., '*Salò o le 120 giornate di Sodoma*', *Rivista del Cinematografo*, vol. 49, no. 5, May 1976.

Bini, L., 'Pier Paolo Pasolini verso "l'inaccettabile degradazione" ', *Letture*, April 1977.

Biondi, D., 'Pasolini a Colono', *Il Resto del Carlino*, 4 September 1967.

Biraghi, G., 'Curiosa ma chiara parabola di Pasolini', *Il Messaggero*, 14 May 1966.

Bo, C., 'Pasolini: il mio San Paolo', *Corriere della Sera*, 6 November 1977.

Bondi, C., '*Medea*: il cinema e le parole', *Mondo Operaio*, August 1970.

Bongioanni, M., '*Il Vangelo secondo Matteo* di Pier Paolo Pasolini', *Il Teatro dei Giovani*, 1965.

Bontemps, J., '*Uccellacci e uccellini* de Pier Paolo Pasolini, Italie', *Cahiers du Cinéma*, no. 170, June 1966.

Borgna, G., 'Pasolini e il cinema (o della corporeita)', in G. De Santi, M. Lenti, R. Rossini (eds), *Perchè Pasolini*, Guaraldi, 1978.

Bottai, B., 'Bottai risponde a Painai e Giussani', *Il Telegrafo*, 24 June 1966.

Branzoli, E., 'Sarà presentato a Venezia il film di Pier Paolo Pasolini', *Paese Sera*, 19 July 1961.

Braucourt, G., 'Dernier Tango à Salò', *Ecran*, no. 42, 15 December 1975.

Briganti, G., *Italian Mannerism*, London: Thames & Hudson, 1962.

Briganti, L., 'Three New Italian Film-Makers', *Film Culture*, no. 24, March 1962.

Brunetta, G. P., 'Gli scritti cinematografici di Pier Paolo Pasolini', *La Battana*, vol. 11, no. 32, March 1974.

Brunetta, G. P., 'Temi della visione di Pier Paolo Pasolini', *Italian Quarterly*, vols 21–2, nos 82–3, Fall 1980–Winter 1981.

Bruno, E., 'I film, dentro e fuori', *Filmcritica*, vol. 12, nos 112–13, August–September 1961.

Bruno, E., 'Cinema contemporaneo e no: *Mamma Roma*', *Filmcritica*, vol. 13, no. 126, October 1962.

Bruno, E., '*Sopralluoghi in Palestina*', *Cahiers du Cinéma*, August 1965.

Bruno, E., 'Ideologia e simbolo in Pasolini', *Filmcritica*, vol. 17, no. 167, May–June 1966.

Bruno, E., 'La sacralità erotica del *Decameron* di Pasolini', *Filmcritica*, vol. 12, no. 217, August 1971.

Bruno, E. and Tomasino, R., '*Salò*: due ipotesi', *Filmcritica*, vol. 26, no. 257, September 1975.

Bruno, E., 'Pier Paolo e la Nebbiosa', *Panorama*, 15 November 1992.

Bruno, G., 'Heresies: The Body of Pasolini's Semiotics', *Cinema Journal*, Spring 1991.

Butler, M., '*The Canterbury Tales*', *Lumière*, no. 32, March 1974.

Buttafava, G., '*Salò* o il cinema in forma di rosa', in F. Di Giammatteo, *Lo scandalo Pasolini/Bianco e Nero* (special issue), vol. 1, no. 4, January–April 1976.

Buzzonetti, R., '*Uccellacci e uccellini*', *Rivista del Cinematografo*, no. 7, July 1966

Caesar, M., 'Elsa Morante', in M. Caesar and P. Hainsworth (eds), *Writers and Society in Contemporary Italy*, New York: St Martin's Press, 1984.

Caesar, M., and Hainsworth, P., 'The Transformation of Post-War Italy', in *Writers and Society in Contemporary Italy*, New York: St. Martin's Press, 1984.

Calvino, I., 'Delitto in Europa', *Corriere della Sera*, 8 October 1975.

Calvino, I., 'Sade è dentro di noi', in *Corriere della Sera*, 30 November 1975 (reprinted as 'Sade est en nous', *Cahiers du Cinéma*, July–August 1989).

Calvino, I., 'Les Romans de Pasolini', in M. A. Macciocchi, *Pasolini: Séminaire dirigé par Maria Antonietta Macciocchi*, Paris: Bernard Grasset, 1980.

Cambria, A., 'Non ho cambiato una parola del testo sacro, dice lo scrittore', *La Stampa*, 5 September 1964.

Camon, F., 'Studio introduttivo', *La moglie del tiranno*, Lerici, 1969.

Canziani, A., 'Dopo i leoni, le oselle d'oro', *Il Mulino*, November 1969.

Capdenac, M., '*Mamma Roma*', *Ecran*, no. 44, 15 February 1976.

Capitta, G., 'In forma di donna', *Il Manifesto*, 26 January 1992.

Cappabianca, A., 'Prodigi e incidenti sulle vie del cinema italiano', *Filmcritica* vol. 25, no. 224, April 1974.

Carravetta, P., 'Lines of Canonical Protest: Pasolini's Unfinished Revolution', *Art & Text*, no. 33, Winter 1989.

Casi, S., *Desiderio di Pasolini*, Turin: La Sonda 1990.

Casiraghi, U., 'Un lacrimoso melodramma americano e la cruda "opera prima" di Pasolini', *L'Unità*, 1 September 1961.

Casiraghi, U., 'La parabola antica in volti e paesi del Sud', *L'Unità*, 5 September 1964.

Castellani, L., '*Il Vangelo secondo Matteo*', *Rivista del Cinematografo*, nos 9–10, September–October 1964.

Cecchini, G., '*La ricotta*: ovvero il "dies irae" di Stracci', in A. Panicali and S. Sestini (eds), *Pier Paolo Pasolini. Testimonianze*, Florence: Nuovo Salani, 1982.

Cecere, M., 'Pasolini: "sono morali *I racconti di Canterbury*"', *L'Unità*, 20 June 1973.

Centro Studi sul Cinema e sulle Communicazioni di Massa, *Le giovani generazioni e il cinema di Pier Paolo Pasolini*, supplement to nos 1–2, *La scena e lo schermo*, December 1989.

Ceretto, A., 'Il *Decameron* di Pasolini', *Corriere della Sera*, 11 July 1970.

Chapier, H., 'L'Érotisme selon Pasolini', *Cinéma d'Aujourd'hui*, no. 4, Winter 1975–6.

Chiaretti, T., 'Lo stile di Pasolini', *Mondo Nuovo*, vol. 4, no. 18, 14 October 1962.

Chiaretti, T., 'Autobiografia minima', *Giovane Critica*, no. 8, April–May 1965.

Chiarini, L., '*Accattone* è soprattutto l'espressione di un'inconscia volontà suicida', *Cineforum*, vol. 1, no. 10, December 1961.

Cluny, C. M., '*Mamma Roma*: Le rire comme le désespoir', *Cinéma* (Paris), no. 206, February 1976.
Collet, J., 'A ciascuno la sua verità', *Cineforum*, vol. 9, no. 85, May 1969.
Comolli, J.-L., '*Mamma Roma*', *Cahiers du Cinéma,* August 1965.
'La condanna di *Salò* nella sentenza del tribunale', *Cinema Nuovo,* November–December 1976.
Conrad, R., '*Accattone*', *Film Quarterly,* no. 2, Winter 1966–7.
Cordelli, F., 'Per "Sade-Salò"', *Nuovi Argomenti* (ns), no. 49, January–March 1976.
Cornand, A., '*Salò ou les 120 journées de Sodome*', *Image et Son,* no. 302, January 1976.
Costa, A., 'Pasolini: il fiore dell'ossessione', *Cinema e Cinema,* vol. 2, no. 2, January–March 1975.
Costa, A., 'The Semiological Heresy of Pier Paolo Pasolini', in P. Willemen (ed.), *Pier Paolo Pasolini,* London: British Film Institute, 1977 (extracted from Costa, A., *Teorie e metodi di analisi del linguaggio cinematografico,* Milan, 1974).
Daney, S., 'Note sur *Salò*', *Cahiers du Cinéma,* nos 268–9, July–August 1976.
De Fornari, O., 'Le mutazioni divertenti', *Cinema e Film,* June 1969.
De Giorgi, E., 'Il successo di *Accattone*', *Il Punto,* 16 September 1961.
De Giusti, L., 'Il modello del ricordo nel sogno di un'opera', *Eidos,* no. 2, 1980.
De Giusti, L., *I film di Pier Paolo Pasolini,* Rome: Gremese, 1990.
De Lauretis, T., 'Language, Representation, Practice: Re-reading Pasolini's Essays on Cinema', *Italian Quarterly,* vols 21–2, nos 82–3, Fall 1980–Winter 1981.
De Lauretis, T., 'Imaging', in *Alice Doesn't,* London: Macmillan, 1984.
Del Bosco, P., '*La terra vista dalla luna*', *Cinema e Film,* vol. 1, no. 2, March 1967.
Del Buono, O., 'Pasolini', *L'Europeo,* 17 April 1975.
Deleuze, G., *Cinema 1: The Movement–Image,* Minneapolis: University of Minnesota Press, 1986.
Deleuze, G., *Cinema 2: The Time–Image,* Minneapolis: University of Minnesota Press, 1989.
De Melis, F., 'Le mie carrellate sul sole e sul fango', *Il Manifesto,* 26 January 1992.
De Paoli, E., 'Dalla metodologia marxista alla visione classica', *Cinema Nuovo,* vol. 21, no. 216, March–April 1972.
De Santi, G., 'Pier Paolo Pasolini: cinema come immagine della memoria e del sogno', in G. De Santi (ed.), *Pesaro cinema 1978,* Comune di Pesaro, 1978.
De Santi, G., '*Appunti per un'Orestiade africana*', *Cineforum,* no. 222, March 1983.
De Santi, P. M., 'Pasolini fra cinema e pittura', *Bianco e Nero,* no. 3, 1985.
Di Carlo, C., 'Carnet di *Mamma Roma*', *Europa Letteraria,* October 1962.
Di Giammatteo, F., 'Pasolini la quotidiana eresia', in '*Lo scandalo Pasolini*', special issue of *Bianco e Nero,* vol. 37, nos 1–4, January–April 1976.
Dorigo, F., '*Il Vangelo secondo Matteo* – guida al film', *Il Piccolo,* October–November 1964.
Dorigo, F., '*Edipo re*', *Cineforum,* vol. 7, no. 68, October 1967.
Eco, U., *The Open Work,* London: Hutchinson Radius, 1989.
Escobar, R., '*Salò o le 120 giornate di Sodoma*', *Cineforum,* vol. 16, no. 4, April 1976.
Escobar, R., 'Pasolini: progetto per un film su San Paolo', *Cinema Sessanta,* no. 121, May–June 1978.
Estève, M. (ed.), *Pier Paolo Pasolini: le mythe et le sacré. Études cinématographique,* nos 109–11, Paris: Minard, 1976.
Faccini, L., 'Dialettica come necessità', *Filmcritica,* vol. 16, no. 161, October 1965.
Fantuzzi, V., 'La visione religiosa, in F. Di Giammatteo (ed.), '*Lo scandalo Pasolini*', special issue *Bianco e Nero,* vol. 37, nos 1–4, January–April 1976.
Fantuzzi, V., 'La morte di un poeta', *Rivista del Cinematografo,* vol. 49, no. 5, May 1976 (also in *Cinema e Cinema,* vol. 3, nos 7–8, April–September 1976).

Fantuzzi, V., 'La religiosità nel cinema di Pasolini', in L. Lucignani and C. Molfese (eds), *Per conoscere Pasolini*, Rome: Bulzoni and Teatro Tenda, 1978.

Ferrata, G, Spinazzola, V. and Pelizzari, L., 'Interventi: Sopralluoghi in Terrasanta di Pier Paolo Pasolini', *Il Barcone Documenti*, no. 1, 1967.

Ferrero, A., '*Uccellacci e uccellini*', *Mondo Nuovo*, 6 June 1966.

Ferrero, A., 'Il giallo di Petri e le favole di Pasolini', *Mondo Nuovo*, no. 2, April 1967.

Ferrero, A., 'Pier Paolo Pasolini', *Inquadrature*, nos. 15–16, Autumn 1968.

Ferrero, A., 'Una metafora autobiografica', *Mondo Nuovo*, no. 6, October 1968.

Ferrero, A., '*Salò*: metafore della morte borghese', *Cinema e Cinema*, vol. 3, nos 7–8, April–September 1976.

Ferrero, A., *Il cinema di Pier Paolo Pasolini*, Venice: Marsilio, 1977.

Ferrero, N., '*Mamma Roma* ovvero dalla responsabilità individuale alla responsabilità collettiva: conversazione con Pier Paolo Pasolini', *Filmcritica*, no. 125, September 1962.

Ferretti, G. C., *Pasolini: l'universo orrendo*, Rome: Riuniti, 1976.

Ferretti, G. C., 'Il Gruppo '63 tra industria e letteratura', *Il mercato delle lettere*, Turin: Einaudi, 1979.

Ferrucci, F., 'Il j'accuse di Pasolini', *Italian Quarterly*, nos 82–3, Fall 1980–Winter 1981.

Fieschi, J.-A., '*Edipo re* de Pier Paolo Pasolini', *Cahiers du Cinéma*, no. 195, November 1967.

Fillippini, E., 'Il corsaro ossessionato', *La verità del gatto*, Turin: Einaudi, 1990.

Finetti, U., 'Nella struttura di Salò la dialettica erotismo-potere', *Cinema Nuovo*, no. 244, November–December 1976.

Fink, G., 'Prosa e crisi dell'ideologia nell'ultimo film di Pier Paolo Pasolini', *Cinema Nuovo*, November 1966.

Fofi, G., 'Antonioni e Pasolini', *Quaderni Piacentini*, vol. 3, nos 17–18, July–September 1964.

Forgacs, D., 'Franco Fortini', in M. Caesar and P. Hainsworth (eds), *Writers and Society in Contemporary Italy*, New York: St Martin's Press, 1984.

Fortes, M., 'Oedipus and Job', in *Oedipus and Job in West African Religion*, Cambridge: Cambridge University Press, 1959.

Fortini, F ,'Fortini: nelle poesie il meglio di Pasolini', in 'Processo a Pasolini', *Avanti!*, 17 November 1976.

Fortini, F., 'Le poesie italiane di questi anni: Pasolini', *Il Menabo*, no. 2, 1960.

Foucault, M., *The History of Sexuality*, London: Penguin, 1976.

Foucault, M., 'Les matins gris de la tolérance', *Le Monde*, 23 March 1977 (in English as 'Grey Mornings of Tolerance', *Stanford Italian Review*, vol. 2, no. 2, Fall 1982).

Fowlie, W., 'Rimbaud's Desert as Seen by Pasolini', *Evergreen Review*, January 1970.

Freud, S., 'The Oedipus Complex', in *The Interpretation of Dreams* (J. Strachey ed.), New York and London: Basic Books, 1955.

Fusini, N., 'Pasolini nel grande occhio di Medea-Callas', *Il Manifesto*, 26 January 1992.

G., M., '*Accattone* di Pier Paolo Pasolini', *Avanti!*, 23 November 1961.

Gambetti, G., '*La rabbia*', *Bianco e Nero*, vol. 24, no. 5, May 1963, pp. 75–6.

Gambetti, G., 'Sopralluogo in Terra Santa', and 'Da un incontro con Pasolini', in P. P. Pasolini, *Il Vangelo secondo Matteo*, Milan: Garzanti, 1964.

Gambetti, G., 'Un traguardo d'arrivo e una base di partenza', *Cineforum*, no. 40, December 1964.

Gambetti, G., 'Per una trilogia popolare, libera, erotica', *Cineforum*, vol. 13, no. 121, March 1973.

Garroni, E., '*Teorema*: osceno no, velleitario sì', *Paese Sera*, 5 October 1968.

Gatt-Rutter, J., 'Pier Paolo Pasolini', in M. Caesar and P. Hainsworth (eds), *Writers and Society in Contemporary Italy*, New York: St Martin's Press, 1984.

Gatta, G., 'Signor Pasolini, ma è proprio sicuro di essere ancora comunista?', *Oggi*, 22 October 1964.

Gérard, F. S., *Pasolini ou le mythe de la barbarie*, Brussels: Université de Bruxelles, 1981.

Gérard, F. S., 'Ricordi figurativi di Pasolini', *Prospettiva,* no. 32, January 1982.

Gervais, G., '*Oréstie africaine*', *Jeune Cinéma,* July–August 1976.

Gervais, M., *Pier Paolo Pasolini,* Paris: Seghers, 1973.

Gervais, M., 'Pier Paolo Pasolini: Le dernier cri d'un cinéaste au bord de l'abîme', *Cinéma Québec,* no. 43, 1975.

Gili, J. A., 'Mort d'un cinéaste', *Ecran,* no. 42, 15 December 1975.

Gili, J. A., 'D'*Accattone* aux fascistes de Salò et autres lieux', *Ecran,* no. 42, 15 December 1975.

Ginsborg, P., *Storia d'Italia dal dopoguerra a oggi,* Turin: Einaudi, 1989.

Ginzburg, C., 'Folklore, magia, religione', in R. Romano and C. Vivanti (eds), *Storia d'Italia: I caratteri originali,* vol. 2, Turin: Einaudi, 1989.

Ginzburg, N., 'In *Salò* la vita è assente', *Mondo,* 4 December 1975.

Giuliani, A., 'Disperato pedagogo', *Il Messaggero,* 3 November 1975.

Golino, E., 'L'esperienza di "Officina"', in *Letteratura e classi sociali,* Bari: Laterza, 1976.

Golino, E., 'Pasolini, politico esistenziale', *Italian Quarterly,* nos 82–3, Fall 1980–Winter 1981.

Golino, E., 'Pasolini, l'eresia pedagogica', Papers: NYU Conference: Pasolini: The Aesthetics of Transgression, 11–12 May 1990 (in typescript at the Fondo Pasolini, Rome).

Gramsci, A., 'Arte e cultura', in *Antologia degli scritti,* Rome: Riuniti, 1963.

Grassi, G., 'Il *Decamerone* dei guaglioni', *Domenica del Corriere,* vol. 72, no. 47, 24 November 1970.

Green, M., 'The Dialectic of Adaptation: *The Canterbury Tales* of Pier Paolo Pasolini', *Film and Literature Quarterly,* vol. 4, no. 1, Winter 1976.

Greene, N., *Pier Paolo Pasolini: Cinema as Heresy,* Princeton, NJ: Princeton University Press, 1990.

Guiguet, J.-C., '*Les Contes de Canterbury*', *Image et Son,* no. 268, February 1973.

Habermas, J., 'Modernity – An Incomplete Project', in H. Foster (ed.), *The Anti-Aesthetic: Essays on Postmodern Culture,* Port Townsend, Washington: Bay Press, 1983.

Jameson, F., 'Postmodernism and Consumer Society', in H. Foster (ed.), *The Anti-Aesthetic: Essays on Postmodern Culture,* Port Townsend, Washington: Bay Press, 1983.

Jatterelli, E., '*Il Decameron*', *Il Tempo,* 19 September 1971.

Lacqua, P. A., '*Medea* di Pasolini dal mito all'autobiografia', *Cineforum,* nos 37–8, November–December 1970.

Laurenzi, C., 'Seri e silenziosi i ragazzi di vita', *Corriere della Sera,* 2 September 1962.

Lawton, B., 'The Evolving Rejection of Homosexuality, the Sub-Proletariat, and the Third World in the Films of Pier Paolo Pasolini', *Italian Quarterly,* vol. 21–2, nos 82–3, Fall 1980–Winter 1981.

Legrand, G., '*Mamma Roma*', *Positif,* no. 179, March 1976.

Levi, C., 'Le parole della rabbia', *La Stampa,* 31 August 1961.

Levi, C., 'La condanna di *Accattone*', *La Stampa,* 22 May 1962.

Liverani, M., '*Mamma Roma*: una prostituta che aspira al decoro borghese', *Paese Sera,* 1–2 September 1962.

Liverani, M., 'Pier Paolo Pasolini ritira la firma dal film *La rabbia*', *Paese Sera,* 14 April 1963.

Liverani, M., 'Pasolini e Guareschi: c'è rabbia e rabbia', *Paese Sera,* 14 April 1963.

Lodato, N., '*Le streghe*', *Filmcritica,* vol. 18, no. 176, April 1967.

Longo, L., 'Il movimento studentesco nella lotta anticapitalistica', *Rinascità,* 3 May 1968.

Macciocchi, M. A., 'Cristo e il marxismo', *L'Unità,* 22 December 1964.

Macciocchi, M. A., *Letters From Inside the Italian Communist Party to Louis Althusser,* London: New Left Books, 1969.

Macciocchi, M. A., 'Esquisse pour une biographie de Pasolini', in M. A. Macciocchi, *Pasolini: Séminaire dirigé par Maria Antonietta Macciocchi*, Paris: Bernard Grasset, 1980.

Magny, J., 'La Seconde Mort de Pier Paolo Pasolini', *Téléciné*, no. 209, June 1976.

Magrelli, E., '*Salò* e l'immaginario silenzioso', *Filmcritica*, vol. 27, no. 261, January–February 1976.

Mamprini, L., 'Il Patriarca di Venezia rileva i limiti del film di Pasolini', *Giornale del Mattino*, 6 September 1964.

Manacorda, G., 'Speranza e disperazione', in L. Lucignani and C. Molfese (eds), *Per conoscere Pasolini*, Rome: Bulzoni and Teatro Tenda, 1978.

Mancini, M., and Perella, G., *Pier Paolo Pasolini: corpi e luoghi*, Rome: Theorema, 1981.

Manzi, C., 'Le frontiere dell'impegno', *Nuova Generazione*, vol. 12, no. 1, 15 October 1967.

Maraini, D., 'Ricordo d'una amicizia', in L. Lucignani and C. Molfese (eds), *Per conoscere Pasolini*, Rome: Bulzoni and Teatro Tenda, 1978.

Marcus, M., 'The *Decameron*: Pasolini as a Reader of Boccaccio', *Italian Quarterly*, vols 21–2, nos 82–3, Fall 1980/Winter 1981.

Marini, V., 'E scoppiata la guerra fredda tra Pasolini e la gente del cinema', *La Settimana*, 23 April 1961.

Maupin, F., '*Mamma Roma*', *Image et Son*, no. 304, March 1976.

Mele, R., 'Dada o le 120 giornate di Sodoma', *Filmcritica*, vol. 19, no. 281, January 1978.

Meneghelli, L., 'Perchè scrivono', *Mondo Nuovo*, 17 March 1963.

Micciche, L., 'De Seta, Olmi, Pasolini: tre strade per il cinema italiano', *Avanti!*, 30 December 1961.

Micciche, L., 'Solitudine di Cristo nel *Vangelo secondo Matteo*', *Avanti!*, 3 October 1964.

Micciche, L., 'Edipo secondo Pasolini e Mao "le fou" di Godard', *Avanti!*, 5 September 1967.

Micciche, L., 'Simboli pasoliniani e "machetes" cubani', *Avanti!*, 31 August 1969.

Micciche, L., 'Una *Medea* tra il mito e la realta', *Avanti!*, 9 January 1970.

Micciche, L., 'L'ideologia di *Canterbury*', *Avanti!*, 23 September 1972.

Micciche, L., '*Il fiore delle Mille e una notte* di Pasolini. Il regista ha realizzato uno dei suoi film migliori', *Avanti!*, 23 August 1974.

Micciche, L., 'In *Salò* Pasolini celebra la distruzione della ragione', *Avanti!*, 23 November 1975.

Micciche, L., 'Pasolini: la morte e la storia', *Cinema Sessanta*, no. 121, May–June 1978.

Micciche, L., 'Contestazione e controcontestazione', in L. Lucignani and C. Molfese (eds), *Per conoscere Pasolini*, Rome: Bulzoni and Teatro Tenda, 1978.

Micciche, L., 'L'ideologia della morte nell'ultimo Pasolini', in *Storia del cinema: autori e tendenze negli anni cinquanta e sessanta*, Venice: Marsilio, 1978.

Micciche, L., De Vincenti, G., Fantuzzi, V., Ward, D., Giordana, M. T., Samona, G. P., and Donolo, C., 'Pier Paolo Pasolini: intellettuale senza frontiere – tavola rotonda', *Fai la cosa giusta*, no. 0, 1993.

Micheli, S., 'Perpetuazione e sublimazione del "nudo" nei film di P. P. Pasolini', *Salvo Imprevisti*, January 1976.

Morandini, M., 'Da Sofocle a Camus', *L'Osservatore Politico Letterario*, vol. 14, no. 3, March 1968.

Morante, E., '9 domande sul romanzo', *Nuovi Argomenti*, nos 38–9, May–August 1959.

Moravia, A., 'Censura politica dietro il sesso', *L'Espresso*, 27 November 1960.

Moravia, A., 'Immagini al posto d'onore', *L'Espresso*, 1 October 1961.

Moravia, A., *Un'idea dell'India*, Milan: Bompiani, 1962.

Moravia, A., 'L'uomo medio sotto il bisturi', *L'Espresso*, 3 March 1963.

Moravia, A., 'Il predicatore iconoclasta', *L'Espresso*, 4 October 1964.

Moravia, A., 'Un corvo che ha letto Marx', *L'Espresso*, 15 May 1966.

Moravia, A., 'Un Edipo che viene dalle borgate', *L'Espresso*, 17 September 1967.

Moravia, A., 'Si spogliano fra le ciminiere', *L'Espresso*, 15 September 1968.

Moravia, A., 'L'antropofago fa un comizio', *L'Espresso*, 28 September 1969.

Moravia, A., 'Oreste a 30 all'ombra', *L'Espresso*, 14 February 1971.

Moravia, A., 'Eros parla in dialetto', *L'Espresso*, 11 July 1971.

Moravia, A., 'I foruncoli di Canterbury', *L'Espresso*, 1 October 1972.

Moravia, A., 'Ma perchè tanta passione per l'Oriente', *L'Espresso*, vol. 10, no. 38, 22 September 1974.

Moravia, A., 'Sade per Pasolini: un sasso contro la società', *Corriere Della Sera*, 6 December 1975 (reprinted as 'Sade pour Pasolini: Une pierre contre la société', *Cahiers du Cinéma*, July–August 1989).

Moravia, A., 'L'ideologia di Pasolini', in P. P. Pasolini, *Ragazzi di vita*, Milan: Garzanti, 1976.

Moravia, A., 'Il dovere di morire', in *Pasolini: Cronaca giudiziaria, persecuzione, morte*, ed. Laura Betti, Milan: Garzanti, 1977.

Moravia, A., 'Pasolini poeta civile', *Italian Quarterly*, nos 82–3, Fall 1980–Winter 1981.

Moravia, A., and Paris, R., 'L'esperienza dell'India', in P. P. Pasolini, *L'odore dell'India*, Parma: Guanda, 1990 (first published by Longanesi in 1962).

Moscati, I., 'Una passione sublime e dissacrante', Papers: NYU Conference: Pasolini: The Aesthetics of Transgression, 11–12 May 1990.

Mughini, G., 'Macchia di Petrolio', *Panorama*, 8 November 1992.

Musatti, C., 'Il *Salò* di Pasolini regno della perversione', *Cinema Nuovo*, no. 239, January–February 1976.

Naldini, N., *Pasolini, una vita*, Turin: Einaudi, 1989.

Neupert, R., 'A Cannibal's Text: Alternation and Embedding in Pasolini's *Pigsty*', *Film Criticism*, vol. 12, no. 3, Spring 1988.

Nietzsche, F., 'The Triple Fate of Oedipus', in *The Birth of Tragedy*, New York, 1956.

Nowell-Smith, G., 'Pasolini's Originality', in P. Willemen (ed.), *Pier Paolo Pasolini*, London: British Film Institute, 1977.

Nowell-Smith, G., 'Pasolini dans le cinéma: sur la façon dont on peut être auteur d'un film', in M. A. Macciocchi, *Pasolini: Séminaire dirigé par Maria Antonietta Macciocchi*, Paris: Bernard Grasset, 1980.

Oliva, A. B., 'Pier Paolo Pasolini e la tradizione del manierismo italiano', in A. B. Oliva and G. Zigaina, *Disegni e pitture di Pier Paolo Pasolini*, Basle: Balance Rief S. A., 1984.

Panzeri, F., *Guida alla lettura di Pasolini*, Milan: Mondadori, 1988.

Passi, M., 'Pasolini a Grado spiega *Porcile*', *L'Unità*, 31 August 1969.

Petrignani, S., 'La sera si andava a Petrolio', 1 November 1992.

Petrignani, S., 'Petrolio brucia', *Panorama*, 15 November 1992.

Pini, M., 'Il Pci dal compromesso storico all'austerità', *Mondo Operaio*, January 1990.

Piovene, G., 'Fino in fondo nel sangue nel buio', *La Fiera Letteraria*, 14 September 1967.

Pleyent, M., 'Le tombeau de Pasolini', *Art Press International*, no. 22, January–February 1976, p. 32.

Ponzi, M., '*Comizi d'amore*', *Filmcritica*, June 1965.

Ponzi, M., '*La ricotta*', *Cahiers du Cinéma*, August 1965.

Ponzi, M., 'La religione tradita', *Filmcritica*, vol. 16, no. 161, October 1965.

Ponzi, M., 'Il cinema di Pasolini', in L. Lucignani and C. Molfese (eds), *Per conoscere Pasolini*, Rome: Bulzoni and Teatro Tenda, 1978.

Ponzi, M., and Rispoli, C., 'Esterno giorno P. P. madre', *Cinema e Film*, vol. 1, no. 4, September 1967.

Prédal, R., 'L'inspiration mythique chez Pasolini', *Cinéma* (Paris), nos. 190–91, September–October 1974.

Prédal, R., 'Pier Paolo Pasolini 1922–1975', *L'Avant-Scène*, no. 176, 15 November 1976.

Procaccini, A., 'Pasolini, the Truant Realist', *Italian Quarterly,* nos 82–3, Fall 1980–Winter 1981.

Prono, F., 'La religione del suo tempo in Pier Paolo Pasolini', *Cinema Nuovo,* no. 215, January–February 1972.

Pullini, G., '*Teorema*: punto di convergenza emblematico dei "volti" di Pasolini', in *L'opera e il suo tempo*, Padua: Cleup, 1983.

Purdon, N., '1001 Nights and 120 Days: The Erotic Cinema of Pier Paolo Pasolini', *Cinema Papers,* July–August 1975.

Quinzio, S., '*Il Vangelo* secondo Pasolini', *Tempo Presente,* vol. 9, nos 9–10, September–October 1964.

Ranieri, T., '*Teorema*', *Bianco e Nero,* May 1969.

Ranvaud, D., '*Salò* or 120 Ways of Remaining Heretical', *Monthly Film Bulletin,* no. 548, 1979.

Renaud, T., '*Les Contes de Canterbury*: pour le plaisir', *Cinéma '73* (Paris), January 1972.

Rinaldi, R. *Pier Paolo Pasolini,* Milan: Mursia, 1982.

Robey, D , 'Umberto Eco', in M. Caesar and P. Hainsworth (eds), *Writers and Society in Contemporary Italy,* New York: St Martin's Press, 1984.

Rohdie, S., 'Afterword to Film Music', *Filmviews,* no. 134, 1987.

Rohdie, S., 'La messa in scena di Pasolini', *Fai la cosa giusta,* no. 0, 1993.

Rohdie, S., 'Pasolini, le populisme et le réalisme', *CinémAction,* no. 70, January–March 1994.

Roncaglia, A., 'Parola poetica e discorso vitale', in L. Lucignani and C. Molfese (eds), *Per conoscere Pasolini,* Rome: Bulzoni and Teatro Tenda, 1978.

Rondi, G. L., 'Pasolini e Padellaro', *Concretezza,* vol. 10, no. 20, 16 October 1964.

Rondolini, G., 'San Paolo è ucciso come Luther King', *La Stampa,* 10 February 1978.

Rosa, A. A., 'Le viscere delle classe', *Il Contemporaneo,* no. 33, February 1961.

Rosa, A. A., *Scrittori e popolo,* Turin: Einaudi, 1988 (originally published in 1968 by Samona e Savelli).

Rossetti, E., 'In Oriente c'è una borgata', *L'Espresso,* 1 September 1974.

Roversi, R., 'La tenerezza vitale di Pasolini', in L. Lucignani and C. Molfese (eds), *Per conoscere Pasolini,* Rome: Bulzoni and Teatro Tenda, 1978.

Rusconi, M., 'I dipinti di un grande artista: tutti i colori di Pier Paolo', *L'Espresso,* 8 November 1992.

Saltini, V., 'Ali Baba è nato in città', *L'Espresso,* vol. 20, no. 38, 22 September 1974.

Santuari, A., 'Il viaggio di Pasolini nell'inferno di *Salò*', *Paese Sera*, 9 February 1975.

Sanvitale, F., 'San Paolo, lo scandalo inattuale della verità', Papers: NYU Conference: Pasolini: The Aesthetics of Transgression, 11–12 May 1990 (in typescript at the Fondo Pasolini, Rome).

Sartre, J.-P., 'Non fate il processo a Pasolini!', *Corriere della Sera,* 4 March 1976.

Scalia, G., 'Pasolini corsaro', in L. Lucignani and C. Molfese (eds), *Per conoscere Pasolini,* Rome: Bulzoni and Teatro Tenda, 1978.

Schwartz, B. D., *Pasolini: Requiem*, New York: Pantheon Books, 1992.

Sciascia, L., 'God Behind Sade', *Stanford Italian Review,* vol. 2, no. 2, Fall 1982 (originally published in *Rinascità*, no. 49, 12 December 1975).

Scola, E., 'Un discorso "contro" i giovani', in L. Lucignani and C. Molfese (eds), *Per conoscere Pasolini,* Rome: Bulzoni and Teatro Tenda, 1978.

Sehrawy, M., 'The Suffering Text. *Poesie a Casarsa* and the Agony of Writing', *The Italianist,* no. 5, 1985.

Semolue, J., 'Après *Le Décameron* et *Les Contes de Canterbury*: réflexions sur le récit chez Pasolini', *Etudes Cinématographiques,* nos 112–14, 1974.

Semprini, E., '*Uccellacci e uccellini*', *Ritz–Cinema d'essai programma,* no. 131, May 1966.

Serenellini, M., 'Pasolini e gli anni '60', *Gazetta del Popolo,* 9 January 1975.

Sesti, M., 'Con Pier Paolo a Sarajevo', *L'Espresso*, 14 February 1993.

Siciliano, E., 'Una vocazione originaria', in L. Lucignani and C. Molfese (eds), *Per conoscere Pasolini*, Rome: Bulzoni and Teatro Tenda, 1978.

Siciliano, E., *La vita di Pasolini*, Milan: Rizzoli, 1978; in English, *Pasolini*, New York: Random House, 1982.

Siciliano, E., 'Lo scandalo e la maledizione di essere un poeta', *Corriere della Sera*, 3 November 1991.

Siciliano, E., Scola, E., Moravia, A., and Mariaini, D., 'Pier Paolo Pasolini: Témoignages', *Cahiers du Cinéma*, nos 268–9, July–August 1976.

Sillanpoa, W. P., 'Pasolini's Gramsci', *Yale Studies*, 1981.

Soncini, I., 'Il regista dissidente tra la mamma e la Callas', *La Stampa*, 31 August 1969.

Snyder, S., *Pier Paolo Pasolini*, Boston: Twaine, 1980.

Szabo, G., 'L'Evangile selon Saint-Matthieu', *Jeune Cinéma*, no. 6, March–April 1965.

Tassoni, A., 'Riandando a *Teorema* dopo *Porcile*', *Bianco e Nero*, November 1969.

Taviani, F., 'Uccellacci e uccellini', *Civitas*, June 1966.

Taviani, P., and Taviani, V., 'Souvenir de Pasolini', *Positif*, no. 400, June 1994, pp. 140–1.

Tinazzi, G., 'Un rapporto complesso', in G. Tinazzi and M. Zancan (eds), *Cinema e letteratura del neorealismo*, Venice: Marsilio, 1990.

Todorov, T., *Nous et les autres: La réflexion française sur la diversité humaine*, Paris: Eds du Seuil, 1989.

Tomasino, R., 'Il vuoto della traccia', *Filmcritica*, vol. 26, no. 257, September 1975.

Tornabuoni, L., 'Venezia, i registi al palo', *La Stampa*, 4 September 1973.

Trombadori, A., 'Passione e ragione secondo Matteo', *Vie Nuove*, vol. 19, no. 37, 10 September 1964.

Turigliatto, R., 'La tecnica e il mito', in F. Di Giammatteo (ed.), 'Lo scandalo Pasolini', special edition of *Bianco e Nero*, vol. 37, nos 1–4, 1976.

Turigliatto, R., 'Letteratura e cinema in Pasolini', in L. Lucignani and C. Molfese (eds), *Per conoscere Pasolini*, Rome: Bulzoni and Teatro Tenda, 1978.

T., C., 'I racconti di Canterbury', *Rivista del Cinematografo*, nos. 3–4, March–April 1974.

Ulmer, G. L., 'The Object of Post-Criticism', in H. Foster (ed.), *The Anti-Aesthetic: Essays on Postmodern Culture*, Port Townsend, Washington: Bay Press, 1983.

Valentini, C., 'Scandaloso Pier Paolo', *L'Espresso*, 1 November 1992.

Vallora, M., 'Pier Paolo Pasolini tra manierismo e metaletteratura', in L. Lucignani and C. Molfese (eds.), *Per conoscere Pasolini*, Rome: Bulzoni and Teatro Tenda, 1978.

Valmarana, P., 'Un commosso film sul primo Vangelo', *Il Popolo*, 5 September 1964.

Valobra, F., 'Campane e guance', *Mondo Nuovo*, 8 November 1964.

Vellacott, P., 'Introduction', in Aeschylus, *The Oresteian Trilogy*, London: Penguin, 1959.

Ventura, G., 'Pasolini difende *Teorema* dalle accuse di oscenità', *Il Gazzettino*, 10 November 1968.

Verdone, M., 'Il Vangelo secondo Matteo', *Bianco e Nero*, vol. 25, nos 8–9, August–September 1964.

Verdone, M., 'Teorema', *Bianco e Nero*, September–October 1968.

Villari, Lucio, 'La società italiana e Pasolini', *Italian Quarterly*, nos. 82–3, Fall 1980–Winter 1981.

Vivanti, C., 'Lacerazioni e contrasti', in R. Romano and C. Vivanti (eds), *Storia d'Italia: I caratteri originali*, vol. 2, Turin: Einaudi, 1989.

Wagstaff, C., 'The Neo-avantgarde', in M. Caesar and P. Hainsworth (eds), *Writers and Society in Contemporary Italy*, New York: St Martin's Press, 1984.

Wagstaff, C., 'Reality into Poetry: Pasolini's Film Theory', *The Italianist*, 1985.

Wahl, F., 'Le discours de la perversion', in M. A. Macciocchi (ed.), *Pasolini: Séminaire dirigé par Maria Antonietta Macciocchi,* Paris: Bernard Grasset, 1980.

Ward, D., 'Una geniale mente analizzatrice: *Empirismo eretico* di Pier Paolo Pasolini', *Fai la cosa giusta,* no. 0, 1993.

White, R. J., 'Myth and Mise en Scène: Pasolini's *Edipo Re*', *Film and Literature Quarterly,* vol. 5, no. 1, Winter 1977.

Willemen, P. (ed.), *Pasolini,* London: British Film Institute, 1977.

Zanarini, R., 'Pasolini adatta il mondo di Sade al suo pessimismo', *L'Unità,* 25 April 1975.

Zanotto, P., 'La motivazione', *Rivista del Cinematografo,* September–October 1964.

Zigaini, G., 'Pasolini pittore', in L. Lucignani and C. Molfese (eds), *Per conoscere Pasolini,* Rome: Bulzoni and Teatro Tenda, 1978.

Zigaini, G., *Pasolini e la morte,* Venice: Marsilio, 1987.

Index